P9-CQE-470

# Why Do You Need This New Edition?

If you're wondering why you should own this new edition of *A Short Guide to College Writing*, here are five good reasons!

As in previous editions of this book, we have emphasized the link between critical thinking and strong writing, stressed the reader's role in the writing process, and offered practical advice on revising and editing. In this edition, we've built on these strengths with several important new features:

* a **plagiarism self-test** that we know students will find useful and engaging;

* an enlarged discussion of **assumptions and implications**;

* an annotated essay by Steven Pinker on **new media**;

* a new pair of essays, pro and con, on **laptops in the classroom**;

* a new essay in which a student **analyzes a visual text**, a recent advertisement for Dolce & Gabbana;

* a new chapter on **summarizing, paraphrasing, and quoting**. Students new to working with texts in college can find in this chapter the answers to their questions about when, why, and how to use the ideas and words of others—and how, exactly, to punctuate those words once they've got them on the page.

PEARSON

# ADVANCE PRAISE FOR
# A SHORT GUIDE TO
# COLLEGE WRITING

"Students respond well to it, and more importantly, they *learn* from it. I see noticeable improvement in student work as a result of assigning parts of this text."

—Devon Fisher,
Lenoir-Rhyne University

"My students actually read *A Short Guide to College Writing* because it gets to the heart of the matter on any topic quickly. The checklists and highlighted segments titled "A Rule for Writers" are appealing in their brevity and practical wisdom."

—Dr. Alison Russell,
Xavier University

"I like its straightforward information, no-nonsense formatting, and the fact that it includes a good handbook."

—Angelia M. Northrip-Rivera,
Missouri State University

PENGUIN ACADEMICS

# A SHORT GUIDE TO COLLEGE WRITING

## FIFTH EDITION

### Sylvan Barnet
Tufts University

### Pat Bellanca
Harvard University

### Marcia Stubbs
Wellesley College

**PEARSON**

Boston  Columbus  Indianapolis  New York  San Francisco  Upper Saddle River
Amsterdam  Cape Town  Dubai  London  Madrid  Milan  Munich  Paris  Montréal  Toronto
Delhi  Mexico City  São Paulo  Sydney  Hong Kong  Seoul  Singapore  Taipei  Tokyo

**Senior Acquisitions Editor:** Katharine Glynn
**Assistant Editor:** Rebecca Gilpin
**Senior Marketing Manager:** Sandra McGuire
**Production Manager:** S. S. Kulig
**Project Coordination, Text Design, and Electronic Page Makeup:** Integra
**Cover Design Manager:** John Callahan

**Cover Art:** Bridgeman-Giraudon / Art Resource, NY; © Artists Right Society (ARS), New York
**Senior Manufacturing Buyer:** Dennis Para
**Printer/Binder:** Edwards Brothers
**Cover Printer:** Lehigh-Phoenix Color Corporation

For more information about the Penguin Academics series, please contact us by mail at Pearson Education, attn. Marketing Department, 51 Madison Avenue, 28th Floor, New York, NY 10010, or visit us online at www.pearsonhighered .com/english.

Credits and acknowledgments borrowed from other sources and reproduced, with permission, in this textbook appear on the appropriate page within text or on page 336.

**Library of Congress Cataloging-in-Publication Data**

Barnet, Sylvan.
    A short guide to college writing / Sylvan Barnet, Pat Bellanca, Marcia Stubbs.—5th ed.
        p. cm.—(Penguin academics)
    Includes index.
    ISBN-13: 978-0-205-23861-3
    ISBN-10: 0-205-23861-0
        1. English language—Rhetoric—Handbooks, manuals, etc. 2. Report writing—Handbooks, manuals, etc. I. Bellanca, Pat. II. Stubbs, Marcia. III. Title. IV. Series: Penguin academics.
    PE1408.B4315 2011
    808'.042—dc23

                           2011033850

Copyright © 2013, 2010, 2008, 2005 by Pearson Education, Inc.
All rights reserved. Manufactured in the United States of America. This publication is protected by Copyright, and permission should be obtained from the publisher prior to any prohibited reproduction, storage in a retrieval system, or transmission in any form or by any means, electronic, mechanical, photocopying, recording, or likewise. To obtain permission(s) to use material from this work, please submit a written request to Pearson Education, Inc., Permissions Department, One Lake Street, Upper Saddle River, New Jersey 07458, or you may fax your request to 201-236-3290.

10 9 8 7 6 5 4 3 2—EB—14 13 12

**PEARSON**

www.pearsonhighered.com

ISBN 10:    0-205-23861-0
ISBN 13: 978-0-205-23861-3

# contents

CHAPTER 3   Shaping Paragraphs 31

CHAPTER 4   Revising for Conciseness 57

## MLA FORMAT 295

# preface

*A Short Guide to College Writing*, Fifth Edition, offers students practical advice on writing successful college essays from the beginning of the process to the end. Students can turn to this book for advice about matters large and small—about choosing a topic, developing a thesis, constructing a paragraph, documenting a source, and using a semicolon. The instructor can suggest chapters or passages that the student should consult in generating ideas, revising a draft, editing a revision, or preparing final copy. As in earlier editions of this book, we emphasize critical thinking, which is to say that we emphasize analysis, argument, and research, because skill in these matters is central to college writing—whether the student is writing a brief essay for a required first-year composition course, a longer essay for an art history course, or even a term paper for a political science seminar.

When students write essays, most of what they write sets forth a thesis and its support, which is to say that their writing advances a point of view, explains ideas, and lets readers see how the writers arrived at them.

Because writers want to be believed, they must present their ideas and evidence persuasively, and they must cite and document their sources accurately.

As in previous editions of this book, we have emphasized the link between critical thinking and strong writing, and we have stressed the reader's role as a collaborator in the writing process. Because our own readers have told us that they need more material on using sources, we have developed a new chapter on summarizing, paraphrasing, and quoting that also contains a plagiarism self-test that we know students will find useful and engaging. Students new to working with texts in college can find in this chapter the answers to their questions about when, why, and how to use the ideas and words of others—and how, exactly, to punctuate those words once they've got them on the page. We've developed our discussion of implications and assumptions in Chapter 9 ("Persuading Readers"). We've also added new essays, including a piece by Steven Pinker on new media; a pair of essays, pro and con, on laptops in the classroom; and a sample essay on a recent advertisement for Dolce and Gabbana that we reprint in Chapter 8.

A *Short Guide to College Writing*, Fifth Edition, offers practical and accessible advice on all matters that concern student writers. This text will be useful not only to students in first-year composition courses but also to those in writing-intensive and writing-across-the-curriculum courses—courses that focus on a particular academic topic. We therefore omit writing assignments and extended readings. Where there is too much, the saying goes, something is missing. This book, we hope, offers just enough.

# Acknowledgments

We thank Cynthia K. Marshall, author of "The Pearson Guide to the 2008 *MLA Style Manual* Updates," for material from the guide that we have incorporated into our chapter on documentation.

We thank the following reviewers for valuable suggestions that we have incorporated into this revision of the book: Devon Fisher, Lenoir-Rhyne University; Edwina Jordan, Illinois Central College; Kirk Lockwood, Illinois Valley Community College; Angelia M. Northrip-Rivera, Missouri State University; and Alison Russell, Xavier University.

We thank the following reviewers of the first, second, and third editions for their suggestions: Alan Baragona, Virginia Military Institute; Karin Becker, Fort Lewis College; Kerry L. Ceszyk, University of Wyoming; Bruce Closser, Andrews University; Dr. Linda Cullum, Kutztown University; Dr. Lynnell Edwards, University of Louisville; Shawn Fullmer, Fort Lewis College; Gloria Gitlin, Baylor University; Catherine A. Henze, University of Wisconsin–Green Bay; Lisa Justine Hernandez, St. Edwards University; Cheryl Hindrichs, The Ohio State University; Arden Jensen, Lee University; J. Paul Johnson, Winona State University; Mary M. Juzwik, University of Wisconsin–Madison; Erika Kreger, San Jose State University; Joan Livingstone-Weber, Western Illinois University; Kari Miller, Georgia Perimeter College; Craig N. Owens, Indiana University; Amy Pawl, Washington University;

Chere L. Peguesse, Valdosta State University; Roxanne Pisiak, SUNY–Morrisville; Rachana Sachdev, Susquehanna University; Mary Sauer, IUPUI-Indianapolis; Julianne Seenan, Bellevue Community College; Von Underwood, Cameron University; and Arnold Wood, Jr., Florida Community College at Jacksonville, South.

We are grateful to our colleagues at Pearson Longman—senior sponsoring editor Katharine Glynn, assistant editor Rebecca Gilpin, and senior marketing manager Sandra McGuire. We are also grateful to project manager Jessica Werley at Integra-Chicago for all of her careful attention to our book throughout the production process. Julie Kennedy proofread the manuscript for this edition with a fine eye for the details; we thank her, too.

Finally, we thank the following friends and colleagues for their advice and support: Marilyn Brown, Patricia A. Cahill, Jody Clineff, Michael Curley, Nancy Sommers, Kerry Walk, and Wini Wood.

Sylvan Barnet
Pat Bellanca
Marcia Stubbs

SYLVAN BARNET was born in Brooklyn, New York, and educated at Erasmus Hall High School, New York University (BA), and Harvard University (MA, PhD). For a while he was a semiprofessional magician, but when he found that he could fool all of the people all of the time the work became boring, and so he became a college professor. He taught composition and English literature at Tufts University for thirty years, published scholarly articles on Shakespeare, and is the author and coauthor of several books about the art of writing.

PAT BELLANCA was born in East Hanover, New Jersey; she holds degrees in English from Wellesley College (BA) and Rutgers University (MA, PhD). She teaches in the Harvard College Writing Program and is Director of Writing Programs at the Harvard Extension School, the university's open-enrollment evening division. Her research interests include composition studies and Gothic fiction, fields that are not unrelated.

MARCIA STUBBS was born in Newark, New Jersey, where she was drum majorette of Weequahic High School's band, and she was educated at Stanford University and the University of Michigan. She has taught at Tufts University, Harvard University, and Wellesley College, where she has directed the Writing Program. In addition to annotations on students' compositions, she has written poems and verse translations, and she is the coauthor of several books on writing.

# PART ONE

# The Writing Process

**The Balloon of the Mind**
Hands, do what you're bid:
Bring the balloon of the mind
That bellies and drags in the wind
Into its narrow shed.

—William Butler Yeats

**CHAPTER**

# Developing Ideas

All there is to writing is having ideas. To learn to write is to learn to have ideas.

—Robert Frost

## Starting

### *How to Write: Writing as a Physical Act*

"One takes a piece of paper," William Carlos Williams wrote, "anything, the flat of a shingle, slate, cardboard and with anything handy to the purpose begins to put down the words after the desired expression in mind." Good advice, from a writer who produced novels, plays, articles, book reviews, an autobiography, a voluminous correspondence, and more than twenty-five books of poetry, while raising a family, enjoying a wide circle of friends, and practicing medicine in Rutherford, New Jersey. Not the last word on writing (we have approximately 30,000 of our own to add), but where we would like to begin: "One takes a piece of paper . . . and . . . begins to put down the words. . . ."

### *Some Ideas About Ideas: Strategies for Invention*

When asked to write an essay for a college course, students often have one of two complaints: "I have nothing to say," or "I have the ideas but I don't know how to express them." When we face a blank page, words and ideas may elude us. We must actively seek them out. Since classical times the term "invention," from the Latin *invenere* ("to come upon," or "to find"), has been used to describe the active search for ideas. Invention includes such activities as asking and answering questions, listing, scratch outlining, clustering, and freewriting. In the following pages we'll briefly describe several invention strategies. All of these strategies have one step in common: starting to write by writing.

## Asking Questions and Answering Them

One of the first things journalists learn to do in getting a story is to ask six questions:

- Who?
- What?
- When?
- Where?
- Why?
- How?

The questions journalists ask are appropriate to their task: to report who did what to whom, and so on. Learning to write academic essays is largely learning to ask—and to answer—questions appropriate to academic disciplines.

Asking questions can be a useful strategy early in the writing process, especially for students who feel they don't have much to say about the material they've been asked to write about. That material, most often, will be a text of some kind: a written text (perhaps a treaty, or a judicial opinion, or a speech, or a poem), or some other object of interpretation (a film, painting, music video, even food on a plate). The first step in developing ideas about a text is to look closely at it. Asking questions and answering them is one way to focus your attention; it's also a way to begin finding things to say. Unexpected answers often emerge as soon as you raise a question.

In analyzing a visual text, for example, an art history student might ask and answer certain basic questions:

- When, where, and by whom was the work made?
- Where would the work originally have been seen? (Almost certainly not in a museum.)
- What purpose did the work serve?
- In what condition has the work survived?
- For whom was the work made?
- From what materials was it made?

Dorothea Lange, *Migrant Mother, Nipomo, California,* 1936. Gelatin silver print.

Then, depending on the work, the student might pose more detailed questions. If, say, the work is a photograph (for example, Dorothea Lange's *Migrant Mother*), the following questions might be appropriate:

- What is the focus of the composition?
- What is the apparent distance between the viewer and the subjects?
- What is the mother's facial expression?
- How are the figures arranged?
- What's surprising or strange about the image?
- How might the subject have felt about being photographed?

A student in a sociology seminar writing a review of research on a topic would ask other kinds of questions about each study under review:

- What major question is posed in this study?
- What is its chief method of investigation?
- What mode of observation was employed, and is the mode limited in some way?
- How is the sample of observations defined, and is the sample representative?

A student in a literature class writing an analysis or exposition of a poem (for example, the Yeats poem on p. 1) would ask yet other kinds of questions:

- What is the poem about?
- What does the balloon represent?
- What is the speaker's tone?

- What does his tone reveal about his attitude toward the poem's subject?
- What makes this attitude complicated, tricky to pin down?

Students in all disciplines—art history, social science, and literature are given here only as examples—learn what questions matter by listening to lectures, participating in class discussions, and reading assigned books and articles. The questions differ from discipline to discipline, but the process of asking and answering the questions that matter is common to all of them.

## Listing

Like asking questions and answering them, **listing** is a way to generate ideas; it can also help you pin down ideas that seem formless or vague. Listing is an especially useful strategy when you are making a comparison—of two figures in a photograph, for example, or two characters in a story, or two positions on an issue. Start writing by listing the similarities, and then list the differences. Or, start writing both lists at once, making brief entries as they occur to you, in parallel columns.

Listing can help you generate and develop ideas; it can also help you to find a **topic** to write about. For instance, if you are writing an essay on whether torture is ever acceptable for a course in ethics—using an example such as getting information that will prevent a bomb from destroying a building and killing hundreds of persons—you might find yourself drawing up lists of pros and cons in which you in effect argue with yourself.

Jot down a point, and then play the devil's advocate by jotting down the best arguments that can be made against it. You may then see the need to find better arguments for your position, or you may even come to shift sides.

Here are the first points one student listed in preparation for writing an essay about the use of torture.

| Pro | Con |
|---|---|
| 1. Given a ticking bomb, surely everyone would agree that to save thousands of lives—to prevent another 9/11, for example—it would be acceptable to torture a person who knew of the plan and could | 1. But *would* everyone agree? Someone might argue that there are things we do not do, under any circumstances, and one of them is torture. Torture is something we expect |

reveal it in time to
avert disaster.

2. The circumstances would
have to be *extreme*,
and the procedure
would have to be au-
thorized at a high
level, by high-ranking
judges or cabinet
officers. Certain peo-
ple would have to be
held responsible; they
couldn't just say "cir-
cumstances required" or
"we were only obeying
orders." Because they
would know that they
would be held account-
able, we can assume
(a) they would authorize
torture infrequently
and (b) it would be
as a last resort.

3. The issue—specifi-
cally, whether tor-
ture is an acceptable
response to terror-
ism—is immensely
important, and, given
the disaster of 9/11,
suicide bombings in
Iraq, and bombings
in Madrid and London—
it is not merely
hypothetical; it
is very real.

4. Wouldn't anyone today
think it would have

in dictatorships, NOT
in a democracy.

2. Well, how extreme is
extreme? Suppose only
one life might be
taken—a politician's,
for example? Would
it be OK to torture
the person who—in our
view—had the neces-
sary information? And
would Supreme Court
judges, or cabinet
members, accept re-
sponsibility for au-
thorizing torture?
Maybe this whole busi-
ness about a ticking
bomb is a fantasy. Are
there any cases when
a person was appre-
hended with informa-
tion that would have
saved lives?

3. The "ticking bomb"
isn't relevant here. In
these cases no one was
apprehended before the
incident. And there are
plenty of false reports
about imminent danger.
(After all, certain of-
ficials believed that
Iraq possessed weapons
of mass destruction,
but that wasn't true.)
What if the authorities
mistakenly tortured
an innocent person?
Is this how things are
done in the land of
freedom?

4. The business about
Hitler is off the

been perfectly accept-
able to have assassi-
nated Hitler in order
to save countless lives
that he later took?

point. We are talking
about using torture to
prevent future deaths,
not about killing a
guilty man.

In this case, the list provides more than a topic; the student who wrote the list is now several steps closer to a draft of an essay she may actually be able to write.

## Scratch Outlining

Some instructors recommend (or require) that students submit a formal outline of an essay before they begin to write it; others ask students to write a paragraph outline *after* they've completed a draft, to check for gaps or contradictions in the discussion. (We'll have advice on these matters later in the book. See pages 202–03 for a discussion of rough outlines and 204–05 for an example of a paragraph outline.) **Scratch outlining** is the least formal version of outlining, and for some writers it can be an effective way to generate and categorize ideas. The process is a little like making a shopping list. You write down "bread" and remember that you're almost out of chocolate, too. One idea leads to another. Ideas can be added, crossed out, and rearranged until something like a logical progression emerges.

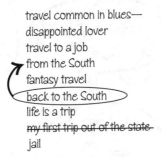

travel common in blues—
disappointed lover
travel to a job
from the South
fantasy travel
back to the South
life is a trip
~~my first trip out of the state~~
jail

## Clustering

Although it takes a different visual form, **clustering** is similar to listing. Sometimes ideas don't seem to line up vertically one after another. Instead, they seem to form a cluster, with one idea or word or phrase related to a group of several others. It may be useful then to start by putting a key phrase or statement (usually a tentative thesis) in a circle in the center of the page, and then to jot down other phrases and sentences as they occur.

The example shown here concerns the issue of whether states ought to support gambling by sponsoring lotteries. It was sent to us, with the

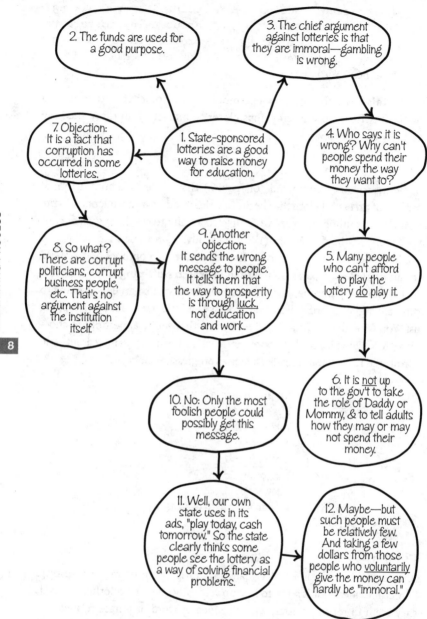

permission of the student, by a professor who teaches in Maryland, where the state has authorized a lottery. (The student has numbered the sequence of thoughts, and has drawn arrows, which are helpful to us as readers but which normally are not part of the procedure.)

If you start writing by putting down phrases that occur to you in a map or cluster, it may help you to visualize the relationship between ideas. The visualization may also prompt still other ideas and connections between them.

## Freewriting

One reason students have trouble getting words down on paper is that they mistakenly believe they must draft, revise, and edit their work simultaneously. In fact, however, these processes are separate, and the attempt to do them all at once can be paralyzing. **Freewriting** can help students who feel that they have ideas, but don't know how to get them on paper, because the strategy enables them to forget the rules for a while and just start writing.

To begin the process of freewriting, all you need to do is put your hands on a keyboard or pick up a pen or pencil and *start writing*. Forget about crafting the perfect introductory paragraph; don't worry about grammar or spelling or punctuation. If you can't think of the right word, write something close to it, or leave a blank space and move on. If you find yourself going in a direction you hadn't anticipated, keep writing anyway. Maybe there's something worth thinking about down the road—you won't know until you get there. If, for example, you're writing about why you disagree with one argument in the passage, a point on which you agree with the author may occur to you. Fine. Write it down now while you're thinking of it. You can organize your points of agreement and disagreement later. Even if what you're thinking is something along the lines of "I hate this poem" (or photograph or whatever), put the thought down on paper and keep going. Why do you hate the poem? Is it confusing? Why? Does it appear to say two different things? What are they? Even an apparently unpromising line of thought can produce ideas. But if you reach what appears to be a dead end, simply move on, or start again someplace else. You are writing to discover what you think, and it's a good idea to work as quickly as you can. (Take Satchel Paige's advice: Don't look back; something might be gaining on you.)

# Focusing

## *Critical Thinking: Subject, Topic, Thesis*

So far, we've discussed several strategies for discovering and generating ideas. But to write a successful college essay, it's not enough simply to choose a **subject** and to generate ideas about it; you must also give those ideas focus, narrowing your area of interest to a **topic** within the subject, a process you may already have begun as you followed one or more of the above invention strategies. And you must state your idea about that topic in the form of a **thesis**, an argument, a *point*.

To do all this, you must think critically about the ideas you have generated. You probably have already begun to refine your ideas as you followed one or more of the invention strategies above. Note, for example, that as our student listed reasons for torturing suspects, she was able also to generate an opposing list of arguments against torture.

### Finding a Topic

Any assignment requires you to narrow the subject so that you can treat it thoroughly in the allotted space and time. Therefore, you write not on political primaries (a subject), but on a specific proposal to abolish them (a topic); not on penguins (a subject), but on the male penguin's role in hatching (a topic). A good general rule in finding a topic is to follow your inclinations: Focus on something about the subject that interests you.

Suppose that for a religion course, your assignment is to read the Book of Ruth in the Hebrew Bible and to write an essay of 500 to 1000 words on it. If you start with a topic like "The Book of Ruth: A Charming Tale," you're in trouble. The topic is much too vague. In writing about it you'll find yourself hopping around from one place in the book to another, and in desperation saying things like "The Book of Ruth is probably one of the most charming tales in all literature," when you haven't read all literature, and couldn't define *charm* precisely if your life depended on it.

What to do? Focus on something that interested you, or surprised you, or confused you about the book. (If you read the book with pencil in hand, taking some notes, underlining some passages, putting question marks at others, you'll have some good clues to start with.) The book is named after Ruth, but perhaps you find Naomi the more interesting character. If so, you might jot down: "Although the Book of Ruth is named after Ruth, I find the character of Naomi more interesting."

Stuck again? Ask yourself questions; **think critically**. *Why* do you find her more interesting? To answer that question, reread the book, focusing your attention on all the passages in which Naomi acts or speaks or is spoken of by others. Ruth's actions, you may find, are always clearly motivated by her love for Naomi. But Naomi's actions are more complex, more puzzling. If you're puzzled, trust your feeling—*there is something puzzling there*. *What* motivated Naomi? Convert your question to "Naomi's Motivation" and you have a *topic*.

"Naomi's Motivation" is a topic in literary criticism, but if your special interest is, for example, economics, or sociology, or law, your topic might be one of these:

Economic Motivation in the Book of Ruth
Attitudes Toward Intermarriage in the Book of Ruth
The Status of Women in the Book of Ruth

Any one of these topics might be managed in 500 to 1000 words. But remember, you were assigned to write on the Book of Ruth. Suppress the impulse to put everything you know about economics or intermarriage or the-status-of-women-through-the-ages in between two thin slices, an opening sentence and a concluding sentence, on the Book of Ruth.

Let's take another example. Suppose that in a course on modern revolutionary movements you're assigned a research essay on any subject covered by the readings or lectures. You're interested in Mexican history, and after a preliminary search you decide to focus on the Revolution of 1910 or some events leading up to it. Depending on what is available in your library, or what you find in an Internet search, you might narrow your topic to one of these:

Mexican Bandits: The First Twentieth-Century Revolutionists
The Exploits of Joaquin Murieta and Tiburcio Vasquez: Romantic
    Legend and Fact

In short, it is not enough to have a subject (the Book of Ruth, revolutions); you must concentrate your vision on a topic, a significant part of the field, just as a landscape painter or photographer selects a portion of the landscape and then focuses on it. Your interests are your most trustworthy guides to the portion of the landscape on which to focus. Thinking critically about your focus will enable you to refine it as you develop your **thesis** about it—as you make your topic your *own*.

### Developing a Thesis

As you think about your topic and information relating to it, try to formulate a **tentative thesis**. This *tentative* thesis is a working hypothesis, a proposition to be proved, disproved, or revised in light of information you discover.

## A RULE FOR WRITERS

A thesis ought to be a statement about which intelligent people might disagree.

Readers won't bother to finish reading an essay if its thesis is an obvious truth, such as:

George Washington owned slaves.
More men than women attend major league baseball games.

There's no particular reason to argue a point that everyone would agree on. The two theses just specified can of course be supported with evidence: the number of slaves Washington owned, or the number of men and women who attend major league games. Nevertheless, the theses themselves remain unarguable and uninteresting. Upon reading either of them, a reader would be likely to say "so what?" The theses need to be developed, most likely after additional reading and thinking, into more debatable statements:

Although Washington owned slaves, some evidence indicates that he believed slavery was an evil institution.
The number of women who attend major league games has in the past decade slightly increased, probably because . . .

Your "working thesis," which usually can be stated in a sentence or two, will help you to maintain your focus, to keep in mind the points that you must support with evidence: quotations, facts, statistics, reasons, descriptions, and illustrative anecdotes. But be prepared to modify your working thesis, perhaps more than once, and perhaps substantially. Your first draft might, for example, contain this tentative thesis:

```
Naomi's character is more interesting than Ruth's
because her behavior is more complicated.
```

That tentative thesis might be revised at a later stage:

```
Although Naomi's actions suggest her concern for her
daughter-in-law, they also reveal self-interest.
```

Note that both the working thesis and the revised thesis are *arguable*. One can imagine a reader *disagreeing* with either statement. "No," such a reader might say, "Naomi's behavior is *not* more complicated than Ruth's." Or: "I disagree—Naomi *is* concerned about her daughter-in-law; she's not self-interested at all." Once you begin amassing evidence to support your arguments, you may find to your surprise that the evidence supports a different thesis. Your best ideas on your topic may turn out to be radically different from the ideas with which you began. As we pointed out earlier, writing is not simply a way to express ideas you already have; it is also a way to discover new ones.

Although essays based on substantial analysis or research almost always include an explicit thesis sentence in the finished essay, short essays based on personal experience often do not. An essay recounting a writer's experience of racism, for example, or conveying the particular atmosphere of a neighborhood, is likely to have a central idea or focus, a **thesis idea**, rather than a **thesis sentence**. But whether stated or implied, the thesis idea must be developed (explained, supported, or proved) by evidence presented in the body of the essay. The kind of evidence will vary, of course, not only with your topic but also with your audience and purpose.

## CHECKLIST for a Thesis Sentence

☐ Does the sentence make a claim rather than merely offering a description or a generalization?

☐ Is the claim arguable rather than self-evident, universally accepted, and of little interest?

☐ Does it say something that the reader is likely to find compelling, or surprising, or interesting? (Would a reader be likely to say "so what?" in response to it?)

☐ Can evidence be adduced to support the claim?

☐ Is the claim narrow enough to be convincingly supported within the allotted time and in an essay of the assigned length?

# Developing Ideas

What constitutes evidence, and where does it come from? Writers explain, support, and develop their ideas with material derived from the reading, thinking, note-taking, questioning, and remembering that are part of the writing process from beginning to end. Materials for developing an essay on Naomi's motivation will be passages from the Book of Ruth, quotations that the writer introduces and explains. Materials for developing an essay on Dorothea Lange's photograph will include a detailed description of the figures, a discussion of their relation to each other, and perhaps some information about the photographer herself. In all of these instances, in fact, imagining a reader helps a writer develop ideas.

## Thinking About Audience and Purpose: The Reader as Collaborator

Thinking about your audience, about what you want your readers to understand and believe, is central to the revision process, which we discuss in Chapter 2. But thinking about audience and purpose can be helpful at earlier stages of writing too, when you are trying to develop an idea and to work up evidence to support it. If you are uncertain how to begin, or if, on the other hand, you are overwhelmed by the materials you have unearthed and don't know how to sort them out, try asking yourself these questions:

- Who are my readers?
- What do they need to know?
- What do I want them to believe?
- Why should they care about what I have to say?

When you ask, "Who is my reader?" the obvious answer—the teacher who assigned the essay—is, paradoxically, the least helpful. To learn to write well, you'll have to force that fact out of your mind, pretend it isn't true, or you're likely to feel defeated from the beginning. Write instead for an interested intelligent person who understands your material less well than you: a classmate, a roommate.

### A RULE FOR WRITERS

When you write, you are the teacher. It's probably easier to assume the role of the teacher if you imagine your reader to be someone in your class—that is, someone intelligent and reasonably well informed who shares some of your interests but who does not happen to be you, and who therefore does not see the material in precisely the same way you do. That reader can't know your thoughts unless you organize them and explain them clearly and thoroughly.

Writing academic essays usually requires examining and evaluating texts and other evidence beyond your personal experience or previous knowledge. Nevertheless, you still must trust your own ideas. Trusting your own ideas does not, of course, mean being satisfied with the first thought that pops into your head. Rather, it means respecting your ideas enough to examine them thoughtfully; it means testing, refining, and sometimes changing them. But it is always your reading of a text, your conduct of an experiment, your understanding of an issue that your essay attempts to communicate. If it does so, your reader will care—because you've brought new ideas, new insights, to the topic at hand.

## Writing the Draft

If you have used one or more of the invention strategies we discuss above, and if you've begun to develop a focus on a topic within your larger subject, you should at this point have some sense of what your essay will be about. Now is the time to start writing the draft. How to begin?

1. **Sit down and start writing.** If you have the ideas but don't know how to express them, start writing anyway. Resist the temptation to check your e-mail, to make a cup of soup, to call your mother. Now is *not* the time to do your laundry or to make your bed. Sit down and start putting one word after another.

2. **Start with something easy.** Start anywhere. Start with what comes to mind first. For example, you might start by summarizing the passage you're responding to or by sketching any one of your ideas about it. *Don't think you must start with an introductory paragraph;* you can write an introduction later, when your ideas have become better defined. It doesn't matter where you begin, only that you do begin. Start anywhere, and keep going.

3. **Try freewriting.** Just write. Pick up a pen, grab a pencil, or put your hands on the keyboard; think about the material you've chosen to write about, and write what you're thinking. Don't worry about spelling or punctuation or grammar; don't censor yourself. No one but you will see what you've written. Your goal here is simply to put words on paper; you can evaluate them later.

4. **Plan to stop writing.** Give yourself a time limit. If you tend to procrastinate, try keeping your first sessions short. Promise yourself that you'll stop working after, say, twenty minutes, and *keep that promise.* If at the start you limit your writing sessions, you accomplish two things. You reduce anxiety: The thought of working at your desk for twenty minutes is not nearly as daunting as the thought of writing four or five pages.

And after twenty minutes you'll have *something* down on paper. You can gradually increase the length of the sessions—to an hour, or three, or whatever is reasonable, given the assignment and your schedule.

5. **Revise later.** After a few false starts and probably more than one session, your ideas will begin to take form on the page. But at this early stage, don't expect them to appear in final form, beautifully organized and in polished sentences. Ideas rarely exist that way in one's mind. In fact, until we put them into words, ideas are usually only rough impressions or images, not clear thoughts at all. (As E. M. Forster wrote, "How do I know what I think until I see what I say?") Once you do get some ideas down on paper, you can begin to see which ones must be developed or deleted, where connections need to be made, where examples need to be added. At this stage, you may be close to having a first draft. Whether or not you like what you've written, take a rest from it. Do something else. Make your bed or, if you like, just climb into it.

# CHAPTER 2

# Drafting and Revising

> I have never thought of myself as a good writer. Anyone who wants reassurance of that should read one of my first drafts. But I'm one of the world's great revisers.
>
> —James Michener

## Reading Drafts

In Chapter 1, we focused on how to have ideas and how to get them down on paper. From the start of a project, the writer is almost simultaneously both inventing ideas and refining them. But we also advised that, particularly at the start, it's best to suspend critical judgment until you have begun to capture your thoughts, however roughly expressed, on paper. In this chapter, we will focus on ways to improve and refine rough drafts. We want to begin by making what may seem like an obvious point: To improve the draft you have written, *you must first read it*. Moreover, you must try to read it objectively and critically.

### Imagining Your Audience and Asking Questions

To read your draft objectively, to make sure that you have said what you intended to say, put it aside for a day, or at least for a couple of hours. Then read it through, as if you were not the writer, but someone reading it for the first time.

---

**A RULE FOR WRITERS**

Try to read at least one hard copy draft of your essay; don't plan to do all of your revising on the computer screen. The change in form can give you a fresh perspective on what you have written.

---

As you read, try to imagine the questions such a reader might ask you about what you have written. Then, read your draft again, asking yourself the following questions:

- Does the draft present an idea? Does it have a focus or make a unified point?
- Is the idea or are the ideas clearly supported? Is there convincing evidence? Are there sufficient specific details?
- Is the material effectively organized?

There are many other questions you might ask as you think critically about what you've written, and we'll suggest some before we're done. But let's start with these.

1. **Does the draft present an idea? Does it have a focus or make a unified point?** Let's first consider the rare case: If on reading your draft objectively, you find that it doesn't present an idea, a point to develop, then there's probably no reason to tinker with it. It may be better to start again, using the invention techniques we discussed in Chapter 1. (Rereading the assignment is probably a good idea, too.)

Almost surely, however, you will find some interesting material in your draft, but you won't yet be sure what it adds up to. The chances are that some extraneous material is getting in your way—some false starts, needless repetition, or interesting but irrelevant information. Some pruning is probably in order.

Picasso said that in painting a picture he advanced by a series of destructions. A story about a sculptor makes a similar point. When asked how he had made such a lifelike image of an elephant from a block of wood, the sculptor answered, "Well, I just knocked off everything that didn't look like elephant." Often, revising a draft begins with similar "destructions." Having identified your main point, don't be afraid to hack away competing material until you can see that point clearly in its bold outline. Of course, you must have a lot of stuff on paper to begin with. (At the start, nothing succeeds like excess.) But often you must remove some of it before you can see that you have in fact roughly formulated the main point you want to make, and even produced some evidence to support it.

2. **Is the idea or are the ideas clearly supported? Is there convincing evidence? Are there sufficient specific details?** Writers are always reluctant to delete. Students with an assignment to write 500 or 1000 words by a deadline are, understandably, among the most reluctant. But, almost certainly, when you have settled on the focus of your essay,

you will be adding material as well as deleting it. It isn't enough simply to state a point; you must also prove or demonstrate it.

If you argue, for example, that smoking should be banned in all public places, including parks and outdoor cafes, you must offer reasons for your position and also meet possible objections with counterarguments. If you are arguing that in Plato's *Apology*, Socrates's definition of truth goes beyond mere correspondence to fact, you will need to summarize relevant passages of the *Apology* and introduce quotations illuminating Socrates's definition. Almost all drafts need the addition of specific details and examples to support and clarify generalizations.

3. **Is the material effectively organized?** As you prune away the irrelevancies and add the specific details and examples that will clarify and strengthen your point, as your draft begins more and more to "look like an elephant," ask yourself if the parts of your draft are arranged in the best order.

- If you have given two examples, or stated three reasons, with which one is it best to begin?
- Are paragraphs presented in a reasonable sequence?
- Will the relationship of one point to the next be clear to your reader?
- Does the evidence in each paragraph support the point of that paragraph? (The same evidence may be more appropriate to a different paragraph.)
- Does your opening paragraph provide the reader with a focus? Or, if the paragraph performs some other important function, such as getting the reader's attention, does the essay provide the reader with a focus soon enough?

In general, when working on the organization of drafts, follow two rules:

- Put together what belongs together.
- Put yourself in the position of your reader; make it as easy as possible for the reader to follow you.

## A RULE FOR WRITERS

Whether or not you write an outline before drafting your essay, you should consider outlining your final draft to see (1) if it is organized, and (2) if the organization will be evident to the reader.

# Peer Review: The Benefits of Having a Real Audience

Occasionally a writing assignment will specify the reader you should address. More often, your reader must be imagined. As we note in Chapter 1, you should imagine an intelligent reader who knows the material less well than you do, someone who has not thought about your topic or considered the specific evidence you intend to examine.

In many writing classes, students routinely break into small groups to read and discuss each other's work. **Peer review**, as this practice is commonly called, is useful in several ways.

Peer review gives the writer a real audience, readers who can point to what puzzles or pleases them, who ask questions and make suggestions, who may often disagree (with the writer or with each other), and who frequently, though not willfully, misread. Although writers don't necessarily like everything they hear, reading and discussing their work with others almost always gives them a fresh perspective on their work. (Having your intentions misread, because your writing isn't clear enough, can be particularly stimulating.)

Moreover, when students write drafts that will be commented on, they are doing what professional writers do. Like journalists, scholars, engineers, lawyers—anyone whose work is ordinarily reviewed many times, by friends and spouses, by colleagues, and by editors, before the work is published—students who write drafts for peer review know they will have a chance to discuss their writing with their colleagues (other students) before submitting a final version for evaluation. Writers accustomed to writing for a real audience are able, to some extent, to internalize the demands of a real audience. Even as they work on early drafts, they are sensitive to what needs to be added, or deleted, or clarified. Students who discuss their work with other students derive similar benefits. They are likely to write and revise with more confidence and more energy.

The writer whose work is being reviewed is not the sole beneficiary. When students regularly serve as readers for each other, they become better readers of their own work, and consequently better revisers. *Learning to write is in large measure learning to read.*

Peer review in the classroom takes many forms; we'll look in a moment at an example as we trace a student's essay that is revised largely as a result of peer review. But even if peer review is not part of your writing class, you may want to work with a friend or another student in the class, reading each other's drafts.

When you work on your essay with your classmates or your friends, good manners and academic practice require that you thank them for their help, that you **document** their contributions. You can offer a sentence or two of general thanks at the end of the essay—something like this:

> I'd like to thank the members of my peer revision group, Rebecca Sharp and Isabella Thorpe, for helping me to clarify the main idea of my essay and for suggesting ways to edit my sentences.

Or you can thank your peer reviewers for their specific contributions by inserting a footnote or endnote at the end of the sentence that contains an idea or words you wish to acknowledge, and then writing a sentence like this:

> Kevin Doughten drew my attention to the narrator's play on words here; I wish to thank him for helping me develop this point.

**A RULE FOR WRITERS**

Be sure to document the contributions of your peer readers and editors.

## From Assignment to Essay: A Case History

On September 12, Suki Hudson was given the following assignment:

> Write an essay (roughly 500 words) defining racism or narrating an experience in which you were either the victim or the perpetrator of a racist incident. Your essay should offer a thesis supported by evidence from your experience. Bring a first draft with two copies to class on September 16 for peer review. Revised essay due September 26.

Suki kept no record of her first thoughts and jottings on the topic, but what follows is an early attempt to get something down on paper. Because it was far from the finished essay she would write, not yet even a first draft, we label it a Zero Draft:

Zero Draft. Sept. 13

It was a warm sunny day in the playground.
My three-year-old brother and other children
were playing gaily until one of the boys'
mothers interrupted. She called her son, whispered something, and when he went back to the
playground he excluded my brother from playing
together. I didn't know what to call the incident, but my heart ached as I watched my little
brother enviously looked at the other kids. I
immediately left the playground with him, and the
playground has never been the same since that day.

At that point, having reached the end of the anecdote, Suki stopped. What she had written was not yet an essay, and it was far short of the suggested 500 words, but it was a start, which is all she had hoped to accomplish on this first try.

Later she read what she had written, and asked a friend to read it and see if he had any suggestions. It was a frustrating conversation. The friend didn't understand why Suki thought this was a "racist incident." Why did Suki leave the playground? Why hadn't she just asked the boy's mother for an explanation? The questions took her by surprise; she felt annoyed, then miserable. So she changed the subject.

But "the subject" didn't go away. Still later, she wrote the following account of the conversation in her journal:

Sept. 13

I asked J to read my paper and he thought
I was being paranoid. Why didn't I just ask the
boy's mother what was the matter? But I could
not have even thought of going up to the woman to
question her motives. It was beyond my control if
she wanted to be ignorant and cruel to a different
race. (Or was it really my ignorance to walk away
from a simple explanation?)

The following day, looking over what she had written, it occurred to her to try adding the journal entry to the anecdote. Maybe in a concluding paragraph she could explain why what happened in the playground was obviously a racist incident.

Here is the conclusion:

Sept. 14

> Most people in modern society don't recog-
> nize the more subtle cases of racism. People feel
> if they are not assaulting physically they are not
> violating the law, and as long as they are liv-
> ing according to the law, racism is not committed.
> However, the law or the constitution does not pro-
> tect the human heart from getting hurt, and with-
> out a doubt the most critical racist action could
> be committed by close friends or their loved ones.

But having written that last line Suki was struck by something odd about it. The woman in the playground was not a loved one, nor was she a close friend. Still, it was true that racist acts can be committed by friends, and even if the acts are not dramatic, they should be recognized as racist acts. At this point, she thought that she had a thesis for her essay, but she also realized that she had begun to recall a different experience. Starting again, she wrote the following account:

> In Korea, I had a very close friend whose
> father was Chinese. Although her mother was a
> Korean woman, they were treated as foreign people
> in town, and they were singled out on many oc-
> casions. Her father died when she was little but
> everyone in town knew she was a half Chinese. Her
> mother ran a Chinese restaurant, and they lived
> very quietly. My family knew her mother well and
> I was close friends with the girl and for many
> years I was the only friend she ever had. However,
> as I entered junior high school my new group of
> friends didn't approve of her background, and
> I drifted away from her. She was a very quiet, shy
> person and although I stopped calling or visiting
> her, she always remembered me on holidays to send
> presents. After graduating from junior high school
> she went to Taiwan to live with her grandparents,
> whom she had never met. I gathered she could not
> stand the isolation any longer at her age. Many
> years later I realized how cruel I have been to
> her, and I tried to locate her without success.

The following day Suki combined the two drafts (hoping to come closer to the 500 words), added a new concluding paragraph, and (rather disgusted with the whole assignment) typed up her first draft to hand in the next day. She photocopied it, as instructed, for peer review in class.

Peer review in the classroom takes many forms. Ordinarily, the instructor distributes some questions to be answered by both the writer and the readers. Typically the writer is asked to speak first, explaining how far along he or she is in writing the essay, and what help readers might give. The writer might also be asked, "What are you most pleased with in your writing so far?"

## CHECKLIST for Peer Review

☐ What is the essay's topic? Is it one of the assigned topics, or a variation from it? Does the draft show promise of fulfilling the assignment?

☐ Does the opening sentence of the essay say something interesting? Does the opening paragraph raise a question or make a point that makes you want to keep reading?

☐ Is the thesis stated or implied? If stated, where is it? If implied, can you say it in your own words?

☐ Does each paragraph make one main point? Does each paragraph relate to the main point of the essay and to the paragraph that precedes it?

☐ Is each sentence within a paragraph clearly related to the previous sentence?

☐ Is each paragraph adequately developed? Are there sufficient details or examples?

☐ Is the conclusion clear? Is the last sentence satisfying?

☐ Is the title interesting and informative?

☐ What is the greatest strength of the essay? What is its main weakness?

☐ What is the most important piece of advice you would offer on this essay?

Readers are then asked to respond. Instructions may vary, depending on the particular assignment, but the questions in our checklist are fairly typical.

## First Draft

What follows is first the draft Suki gave the two members of her group, and then a summary of the group's discussion. Before reading her draft aloud (the procedure the instructor recommended for this session), Suki explained how she had happened to narrate two experiences and asked which narrative she should keep, or if she could keep both.

```
First Draft
S. Hudson
Sept. 16
```

1        It was a warm sunny day in the playground.
My three-year-old brother and other children
were playing gaily until one of the boys' mothers
interrupted. She called her son to whisper something and when he went back to the playground he
excluded my brother from playing together. I didn't
know what to call the incident, but my heart ached
as I watched my little brother enviously looked at
other kids. I immediately left the playground with
him, and the playground has never been the same
since that day.

2        A friend of mine said I was being paranoid.
It would have been appropriate to ask the boy's
mother what was the matter, or if she had anything
to do with the kids excluding my brother from playing. But I could not have even thought of going up
to the woman to question her motives. It was beyond
my control if she wanted to be ignorant and cruel
to a different race, or perhaps my ignorance to
walk away from a simple explanation.

3        Most people in modern society recognize only
the dramatic instances of racism, and on a daily
basis people don't recognize the more subtle cases
of racism. People feel if they are not assault-
ing physically they are not violating the law, and
as long as they are living according to the law,
racism is not committed. However, the law or the
constitution does not protect the human heart from
getting hurt, and without a doubt the most critical racist action could be committed by close
friends or their loved ones.

4        In Korea, I had a very close friend whose
father was Chinese. Although her mother was a
Korean woman they were treated as foreign people
in town, and they were singled out on many occasions. Her father died when she was little, but
everyone in town knew she was a half Chinese. Her

mother ran a Chinese restaurant, and they lived very quietly. My family knew her mother well and I was close friends with the girl and for many years I was the only friend she ever had. However, as I entered junior high school my new group of friends didn't approve of her background and I drifted away from her. She was a very quiet, shy person, and although I stopped calling or visiting her, she always remembered me on holidays to send presents. After graduating from junior high school she went to Taiwan to live with her grandparents whom she had never met. I gathered she could not stand the isolation any longer at her age. Many years later, I realized how cruel I have been to her, and I tried to locate her without success.

5    She was a victim in a homogeneous society, and had to experience the pain she did not deserve. It is part of human nature to resent the unknown, and sometimes people become racist to cover their fears or ignorance.

## Summary of Peer Group Discussion

1. The group immediately understood why the friend (in the second paragraph) had difficulty understanding that the first incident was racist. It might well have been racist, but, they pointed out, Suki had said nothing about the racial mix at the playground. It does become clear by the fourth paragraph that the writer and her brother are Korean, but we don't get this information early enough, and we know nothing of the race of the woman who whispers to her son. Suki had neglected to say—because it was so perfectly obvious to her—that she and her brother were Korean; the mother, the other child, in fact all others in the playground, were Caucasian.

### A RULE FOR WRITERS
Keep your readers in mind as you revise.

2. Suki's readers confirmed her uneasiness about the third paragraph. They found it confusing for several reasons:

- Suki had written "people don't recognize the more subtle cases of racism." Did she mean that the mother didn't recognize her action as racist, or that Suki didn't?

- In the first paragraph Suki had written "I didn't know what to call the incident." But then the second paragraph is contradictory. There she seems to accuse the mother of being "cruel to a different race."
- And the last sentence of the third paragraph, they agreed, in which Suki writes of racist acts "committed by close friends," did not tie in at all with the first part of the essay, although it did serve to introduce the second anecdote.

3. Her group was enthusiastic, though, about Suki's telling of the two stories and advised her to keep both. Both were accounts of more or less subtle acts of racism. One student thought that they should appear in chronological order: first the Korean story and then the more recent story, set in the playground. But both readers were sure that she could find some way to put them together.

4. They were less sure what the essay's thesis was, or whether it even had one. One student proposed this:

```
Subtle racist acts can be as destructive as
dramatic instances (implied in paragraph 3).
```

The other proposed combining two points:

```
It is part of human nature to resent the unknown
```

and

```
...sometimes people become racist to cover their
fears or ignorance (from the final paragraph).
```

All three members of Suki's group (Suki included) thought that the ideas in the essay were supported by the narratives. But the draft didn't yet hang together: Suki would have to work on the way the separate parts connected.

5. One member of the group then pointed out that the second paragraph could be deleted. The friend mentioned in it (who called Suki "paranoid") had been important to Suki's thinking about her first draft, but served no useful purpose in the draft they were looking at, and other details in that paragraph were murky.

6. On the other hand, the first paragraph probably needed additional details about the setting, the people involved, what each did. How does a three-year-old know he's been excluded from a play group? What

happened? What did the other children do? What did he do? And, as the group had seen at once, some details were needed to establish the racist nature of the incident. They also reminded Suki that her essay needed a title.

7. Finally, some small details of grammar. Suki's English is excellent, although English is her second language. But the other two in her group, being native speakers of English, were able to catch the slightly odd syntax in

```
she always remembered me on holidays to send
presents
```

and the error in

```
my heart ached as I watched my little brother
enviously looked at other kids.
```

Suki asked if the past tense was right in

```
I realized how cruel I have been to her
```

and the others supplied

```
I realized how cruel I had been to her
```

(though they could not explain the difference).

### Final Version

Several days later, Suki consulted her notes and resumed work on her draft, and by September 25, the night before it was due, she was able to print the final version, which follows here.

```
Suki Hudson
Ms. Cahill
Writing 125R
September 26, 2011


                Two Sides of a Story

1        It was a warm sunny day in the playground.
    My three-year-old brother and two other small boys
    were playing together in the sandbox. My brother
    was very happy, digging in the sand with a shovel
    one of the other boys had brought, when one of the
```

mothers sitting on a bench across from me called to her son. She bent over and whispered something to him, and he went right over to my brother and pulled the shovel out of his hand. He pushed my brother aside and moved to the other side of the sandbox. The other boy followed him, and they continued to play. My heart ached as I watched my little brother enviously looking at the other kids. I didn't fully understand what had happened. I looked across at the mother, but she turned her head away. Then I picked up my brother and immediately left the playground with him.

2    I thought the woman was extremely rude and cruel, but I didn't think then that she was behaving in a racist way. We had only recently come here from Korea, and although I had been told that there was much racism in America, I thought that meant that it was hard for some people, like blacks, to find jobs or go to good schools. In some places there were street gangs and violence. But I didn't understand that there could be subtle acts of racism too. I was aware, though, in the playground that my brother and I were the only Koreans, the only nonwhites. When the woman turned her face away from me it felt like a sharp slap, but I was ignorant about her motives. I only guessed that she told her child not to play with my brother, and I knew that the playground was never the same since that day.

3    That incident was several months ago. When I started to think about it again recently, I thought also of another time when I was ignorant of racism.

4    In Korea, I had a very close friend whose father was Chinese. Although her mother was a Korean woman they were treated as foreign people in town, and they were singled out on many occasions. Her father died when she was little, but everyone in town knew she was half Chinese. Her mother ran a Chinese restaurant, and they lived very quietly. My family knew her mother well and I was close friends with the girl, and for many years I was the only friend she ever had. However, as I entered junior high school my new group of

friends didn't approve of her background and I drifted away from her. She was a very quiet, shy person, and although I stopped calling or visiting her, she always remembered to send me presents on holidays. After graduating from junior high school, she went to Taiwan to live with her grandparents, whom she had never met. I gathered she could not stand the isolation any longer at her age. Many years later, I realized how cruel I had been to her, and I tried to locate her without success.

5      She was a victim in a homogeneous society, and had to experience pain she did not deserve. There was no law to protect her from that, just as there was no law to protect my little brother. Perhaps the woman in the playground did not realize how cruel she was being. She probably didn't think of herself as a racist, and maybe she acted the way I did in Korea, without thinking why. It isn't only the dramatic acts that are racist, and maybe it isn't only cruel people who commit racist acts. It is part of human nature to fear the unknown, and sometimes people become racist to cover their fears, or ignorance.

---

### Acknowledgments

I would like to thank Ann Weston and Tory Chang for helping me to develop my main point and to organize and edit my essay.

---

## CHECKLIST for Drafting and Revising

- ☐ Have I reread my draft? (See pp. 17–19.)
- ☐ Have I imagined my audience? (See pp. 17–19.)
- ☐ What is my main idea? (See p. 18.)
- ☐ Is it a good one? (See p. 18.)
- ☐ How and where is the idea supported? (See pp. 18–19.)
- ☐ Do I offer specific details? (See pp. 18–19.)
- ☐ How is the material organized? (See p. 19.)
- ☐ Is the organization effective? (See p. 19.)
- ☐ Has the essay been read by peers or friends? (See pp. 20–21.)
- ☐ Have I acknowledged help from my readers? (See p. 21.)

# CHAPTER 3

# Shaping Paragraphs

## Paragraph Form and Substance

It is commonly said that a good paragraph is

- *unified* (it makes one point, or it indicates where one unit of a topic begins and ends);
- *organized* (the point or unit is developed according to some pattern); and
- *coherent* (the pattern of development, sentence by sentence, is clear to the reader).

In this chapter, we will say these things too. But first we feel obliged to issue this warning: You can learn to write a unified, organized, coherent paragraph that no one in his or her right mind would choose to read. Here is an example:

> Charles Darwin's great accomplishments in the field of natural science resulted from many factors. While innate qualities and characteristics played a large part in leading him to his discoveries, various environmental circumstances and events were decisive factors as well. Darwin himself considered his voyage on the *Beagle* the most decisive event of his life, precisely because this was to him an educational experience similar to if not more valuable than that of college, in that it determined his whole career and taught him of the world as well.

Notice that the paragraph is unified, organized, and coherent. It has a **topic sentence** (the first sentence, which briefly states the main idea of the paragraph). It uses **transitional devices** ("while," "as well," "Darwin himself") and, as is often helpful, it **repeats key words**. But notice also that it is wordy, vague, and inflated ("in the field of," "many factors," "qualities and characteristics," "circumstances and events," "precisely because," "educational experience," "similar to if not more valuable than"). It is, in short, thin and boring. To whom does it teach what?

Consider, by contrast, these paragraphs from another essay on Darwin:

> Charles Darwin's youth was unmarked by signs of genius. Born in 1809 into the well-to-do Darwin and Wedgwood clans (his mother was a Wedgwood, and Darwin himself was to marry another), he led a secure and carefree childhood, happy with his family, indifferent to books, responsive to nature. The son and grandson of impressively successful physicians, he eventually tried medical training himself, but found the studies dull and surgery (before anesthesia) too ghastly even to watch. So, for want of anything better, he followed the advice of his awesome father (6' 2", 336 pounds, domineering in temperament) and studied for the ministry, taking his B.A. at Christ's College, Cambridge, in 1831.

> Then a remarkable turn of events saved Darwin from a country parsonage. His science teacher at Cambridge, John Stevens Henslow, arranged for Darwin the invitation to be naturalist on H.M.S. Beagle during a long voyage of exploration. Despite his father's initial reluctance, Darwin got the position, and at the end of 1831 left England for a five-year voyage around the globe that turned out to be not only a crucial experience for Darwin himself, but a passage of consequence for the whole world.

> *—Philip Appleman*

Notice how full of life these paragraphs are, compared to the paragraph that begins by asserting that "Charles Darwin's great accomplishments in the field of natural science resulted from many factors." These far more interesting paragraphs are filled with specific details, facts, and names that combine to convey ideas. We finish reading them with a sense of having learned something worth knowing, from someone fully engaged not only with the topic but also with conveying it to someone else.

The one indispensable quality of a good paragraph is **substance**. A paragraph may

- define a term,
- describe a person or a place,
- make a comparison,
- analyze a point,
- summarize an opinion,
- draw a conclusion.

It may do almost anything provided that it holds the readers' attention by telling them something they want or need to know, or are reminded of with pleasure.

But even a substantial paragraph does not guarantee that you'll hold the attention of your readers, because readers, like writers, are often lazy and impatient. If readers find that they must work too hard to understand you, if they are confused by what you write, they can and will stop reading. The art of writing is in large part the art of keeping your readers' goodwill while you teach them what you want them to learn. Now, experienced writers can usually tell what makes a satisfactory unit, and their paragraphs do not always exactly follow the principles we are going to suggest. But we think that if you follow these principles you will develop a sense of paragraphing. Or, to put it another way, you will improve your sense of how to develop an idea.

## The Shape of a Paragraph

The shape of a paragraph—the way in which its idea is set forth—will largely depend not only on the content but also on the position of the paragraph in the essay.

- The **content** of a paragraph explaining something may move from cause to effect, or from effect to cause; the content of a paragraph arguing a point may move from evidence to conclusion, or from conclusion to evidence.
- The **position** of the paragraph, its place in the essay as a whole, will also determine its shape. An opening paragraph will in one way or another lead into the topic. (Its main point may therefore come at the end.) A middle paragraph should follow easily from the preceding paragraph, and it should also lead into the next paragraph—so a middle paragraph might begin with a transitional sentence (a sentence that begins with a "Furthermore" or a "Nevertheless") and announce its main point in the second sentence. Or even in its last sentence.

We will discuss such matters in detail in the following pages. But here we can say that when you revise a draft, you want to make certain not only that each paragraph is clear in itself but also that it fits neatly into your essay.

# Paragraph Unity: Topic Sentences, Topic Ideas

The idea developed in each paragraph often appears, briefly stated, as a topic sentence. Topic sentences are most useful, and are therefore especially common, in paragraphs that offer arguments; they are much less useful, and therefore less common, in narrative and descriptive paragraphs.

The topic sentence usually is the first sentence in the paragraph—or the second, if the first sentence is transitional—because writers usually want their readers to know from the start where the paragraph is going. Sometimes, though, you may not wish to forecast what is to come; you may prefer to put your topic sentence at the end of the paragraph, summarizing the points that earlier sentences have made, or drawing a generalization based on the earlier details. Even if you do not include a topic sentence anywhere in the paragraph, the paragraph should have a **topic idea**, an idea that holds the sentences together.

## Examples of Topic Sentences at Beginning and at End, and of Topic Ideas

1. The following paragraph, from an essay in which a professor of physiology compares Darwin and Freud, begins with a topic sentence.

> To begin with, Darwin and Freud were both multifaceted geniuses with many talents in common. Both were great observers, attuned to perceiving in familiar phenomena a significance that had escaped almost everyone else. Searching with insatiable curiosity for underlying explanations, both did far more than discover new facts or solve circumscribed problems, such as the structure of DNA: they synthesized knowledge from a wide range of fields and created new conceptual frameworks, large parts of which are still accepted today. Both were prolific writers and forceful communicators who eventually converted many or most of their contemporaries to their positions.
>
> —*Jared Diamond*

The first sentence announces the topic the rest of the paragraph will develop—the talents Darwin and Freud had in common. Each sentence that follows this topic sentence develops or amplifies it by considering one of the talents the two men shared. The second sentence concerns their powers of observation. The third sentence concerns their curiosity about "underlying explanations" and their ability to create "new conceptual frameworks." Note also the logical order of subtopics in the paragraph: The discussion moves from *observation*, to *analysis* and *synthesis*, to *communication*.

2. The next paragraph has its topic sentence at the end:

If we try to recall Boris Karloff's face as the monster in the film of *Frankenstein* (1931), most of us probably think of the seams holding the pieces together, and if we cannot recall other details we assume that the face evokes horror. But when we actually look at a picture of the face rather than recall a memory of it, we are perhaps chiefly impressed by the high, steep forehead (a feature often associated with intelligence), by the darkness surrounding the eyes (often associated with physical or spiritual weariness), and by the gaunt cheeks and the thin lips slightly turned down at the corners (associated with deprivation or restraint). The monster's face is of course in some ways shocking, but probably our chief impression as we look at it is that this is not the face of one who causes suffering but of one who himself is heroically undergoing suffering.

—*Sylvia Rodriguez*

When the topic sentence is at the end, the paragraph usually develops from the particular to the general, the topic sentence serving to generalize or summarize the information that precedes it. Such a topic sentence can be especially effective in presenting an argument: The reader hears, considers, and accepts the evidence before the writer explicitly states the argument, and if the writer has effectively presented the evidence, the reader willingly accepts the conclusion.

3. The next paragraph has no topic sentence:

A few years ago when you mentioned Walt Disney at a respectable party—or anyway this is how it was in California, where I was then—the standard response was a headshake and a groan. Intellectuals spoke of how he butchered the classics—from

*Pinocchio* to *Winnie the Pooh*, how his wildlife pictures were sadistic and coy, how the World's Fair sculptures of hippopotamuses were a national if not international disgrace. A few crazies disagreed, and since crazies are always the people to watch, it began to be admitted that the early Pluto movies had a considerable measure of *je ne sais quoi*, that the background animation in *Snow White* was "quite extraordinary," that *Fantasia* did indeed have *one* great sequence (then it became two; now everyone says three, though there's fierce disagreement on exactly which three).

—*John Gardner*

The topic idea here is, roughly, "Intellectuals used to scorn Disney, but recently they have been praising him." Such a sentence could easily begin the paragraph, but it is not necessary because even without it the reader has no difficulty following the discussion. The first two sentences talk about Disney's earlier reputation; then the sentence about the "crazies" introduces the contrary view and the rest of the paragraph illustrates the growing popularity of this contrary view. The paragraph develops its point so clearly and consistently (it is essentially a narrative, in chronological order) that the reader, unlike the reader of a complex analytic paragraph, does not need the help of a topic sentence either at the beginning, to prepare for what follows, or at the end, to pull the whole together.

## Unity in Paragraphs

Although we emphasize **unity** in paragraphs, don't assume that every development or refinement or alteration of your thought requires a new paragraph. Such an assumption would lead to an essay consisting entirely of one-sentence paragraphs. A good paragraph may, for instance,

- ask a question *and* answer it, or
- describe an effect *and* then explain the cause, or
- set forth details *and* then offer a generalization.

Indeed, if the question or the effect or the details can be set forth in a sentence or two, and the answer or the cause or the generalization can be set forth in a sentence or two, the two halves of the topic should be pulled together into a single paragraph. Only if, for example, the question is long and complex and the answer equally long or longer will you need two or more paragraphs.

The following paragraph, from a book on athletic coaching, lacks unity, and the effect is disconcerting.

Leadership qualities are a prerequisite for achievement in coaching. A leader is one who is respected for what he says and does, and whom does his team admire. The coach gains respect by giving respect, and by possessing knowledge and skills associated with the sport. There are many "successful" coaches who are domineering, forceful leaders, gaining power more through fear and even hate than through respect. These military-type men are primarily from the old school of thought, and many younger coaches are achieving their goals through more humanistic approaches.

Something is wrong here. The first half of the paragraph tells us that "a leader is one who is respected for what he says and does," but the second half of the paragraph contradicts that assertion, telling us that "many" leaders hold their position "more through fear and even hate than through respect." The trouble is not that the writer is talking about two kinds of leaders; a moment ago we saw that a writer can in one paragraph talk about two kinds of balloons. The trouble here is that we need a unifying idea if these two points are to be given in one paragraph. The idea might be: There are two kinds of leaders, those who are respected and those who are feared. This idea might be developed along these lines:

Leadership qualities are a prerequisite for achievement in coaching, but these qualities can be of two radically different kinds. One kind of leader is respected and admired by his team for what he says and does. The coach gains respect by giving respect, and by possessing knowledge and skills associated with the sport. The other kind of coach is a domineering, forceful leader, gaining power more through fear than through respect. These military-type men are primarily from the old school of thought, whereas most of the younger coaches achieve their goals through the more humane approaches of the first type.

## Organization in Paragraphs

A paragraph needs more than a unified point; it needs a reasonable **organization** or sequence. Exactly how the parts of a paragraph will fit together depends on what the paragraph is doing.

- If it is *describing* a place, it may move from a general view to the significant details—or from immediately striking details to some less obvious but perhaps more important ones. It may move from near to far, or from far to near, or from the past to the present.

- If it is *explaining*, it may move from cause to effect, or from effect to cause, or from past to present; or it may offer an example.
- If it is *arguing*, it may move from evidence to conclusion, or from a conclusion to supporting evidence; or it may offer one piece of evidence—for instance, an anecdote that illustrates the argument.
- If it is *narrating*, it will likely move chronologically.
- If a paragraph is *classifying* (dividing a subject into its parts), it may begin by enumerating the parts and go on to study each, perhaps in climactic order.

The way in which a paragraph is organized, then, will depend on the writer's purpose. Almost always, one purpose is to make something clear to a reader, which means that the writer must present information in an orderly way. Writers use several common methods to organize a paragraph and to keep things clear:

1. General to particular (topic sentence usually at the beginning)
2. Particular to general (topic sentence usually at the end)
3. Enumeration of parts or details or reasons (probably in climactic order)
4. Question and answer
5. Cause and effect
6. Comparison and contrast
7. Analogy
8. Chronology
9. Spatial order (e.g., near to far, or right to left)

The only rule that can cover all paragraphs is this: Readers must never feel that they are wandering in a maze as they follow the writer to the end of the paragraph.

## Coherence in Paragraphs

In addition to having a unified point and a reasonable organization, a good paragraph is **coherent**—that is, the connections between ideas in the paragraph are clear. Coherence can often be achieved by inserting the right transitional words or by taking care to repeat key words.

## Transitions

Richard Wagner, commenting on his work as a composer of operas, said, "The art of composition is the art of transition," for his art moves from note to note, measure to measure, scene to scene. **Transitions** establish connections between ideas; they alert readers to what will follow. Here are some of the most common transitional words and phrases, categorized by their function:

1. **Amplification or likeness:** similarly, likewise, and, also, again, second, third, in addition, furthermore, moreover, finally
2. **Emphasis:** chiefly, equally, indeed, even more important
3. **Contrast or concession:** but, on the contrary, on the other hand, by contrast, of course, however, still, doubtless, no doubt, nevertheless, granted that, conversely, although, admittedly
4. **Example:** for example, for instance, as an example, specifically, consider as an illustration, that is, such as, like
5. **Consequence or cause and effect:** thus, so, then, it follows, as a result, therefore, hence
6. **Restatement:** in short, that is, in effect, in other words
7. **Place:** in the foreground, further back, in the distance
8. **Time:** afterward, next, then, as soon as, later, until, when, finally, last, at last
9. **Conclusion**: finally, therefore, thus, to sum up

Consider the following paragraph:

> Folklorists are just beginning to look at Africa. A great quantity of folklore materials has been gathered from African countries in the past century and published by missionaries, travelers, administrators, linguists, and anthropologists incidentally to their main pursuits. No fieldworker has devoted himself exclusively or even largely to the recording and analysis of folklore materials, according to a committee of the African Studies Association reporting in 1966 on the state of research in the African arts. Yet Africa is the continent supreme for traditional cultures that nurture folklore. Why this neglect?
>
> —*Richard M. Dorson*

The reader gets the point, but the second sentence seems to contradict the first: The first sentence tells us that folklorists are just beginning to look at Africa, but the next tells us that lots of folklore has been collected.

An "although" between these sentences would clarify the author's point, especially if the third sentence were hooked on to the second, thus:

> Folklorists are just beginning to look at Africa. Although a great quantity of folklore materials has been gathered from African countries in the past century by missionaries, travelers, administrators, linguists, and anthropologists incidentally to their main pursuits, no fieldworker has devoted himself . . .

But this revision gives us an uncomfortably long second sentence. Further revision would help. The real point of the original passage, though it is smothered, is that *although* many people have incidentally collected folklore materials in Africa, *professional* folklorists have not been active there. The contrast ought to be sharpened:

> Folklorists are just beginning to look at Africa. True, missionaries, travelers, administrators, linguists, and anthropologists have collected a quantity of folklore materials incidentally to their main pursuits, but folklorists have lagged behind. No fieldworker . . .

In this revision the words that clarify are the small but important words "true" and "but." The original paragraph is like a jigsaw puzzle that's missing some tiny but necessary pieces.

## Repetition

Coherence is also achieved through the **repetition** of key words. When you repeat words or phrases, or when you provide clear substitutes, such as pronouns and demonstrative adjectives, you are helping the reader to keep step with your developing thoughts. Grammatical constructions too can be repeated, the repetitions or parallels linking the sentences or ideas.

In the following example, notice how the repetitions provide continuity.

> In the movement from the miraculous prose of Toni Morrison to the screen, the story of Beloved has lost some of its breadth, complexity, and imaginative range. But its central messages—historical and human—have been sustained and, in some ways, enhanced by the gifts of the innovative Jonathan Demme and his associates and by the talent and commitment of the actors. We see in the film the wounds of slavery, inflicted and then self-inflicted through resistance—or, rather, we see the memories of these wounds as they still disturb the free. We see the resources of an African-American community for defining those wounds,

for quarreling about them, and for healing them. The story of trauma and recovery is distinctive, but it is told so as to invite others in, into the haunted house at 124 Bluestone and into Baby Sugg's clearing in the woods.

—*Natalie Zemon Davis*

Notice not only the exact repetitions ("wounds," "we see," "them") but also the slight variations, such as "inflicted" and "self-inflicted"; and the parallel construction of the last phrases of the last sentence ("into the haunted house . . . into Baby Sugg's clearing"), which brings a sense of closure to the paragraph.

# Linking Paragraphs Together

Since each paragraph in an essay generally develops a single idea, a single, new aspect of the main point of the essay, as one paragraph follows another, readers should feel they are getting somewhere, smoothly and without stumbling. As you move from one paragraph to the next, from one step in the development of your main idea to the next, you probably can keep your readers with you if you link the beginning of each new paragraph to the end of the paragraph that precedes it. Often a transitional word or phrase (such as those listed on p. 39) will suffice; sometimes repeating key terms will help connect a sequence of paragraphs together and make your essay, as many writers put it, "flow."

Consider the movement of ideas in the following essay written in response to an assignment that asked students to analyze a family photograph.

```
Cheryl Lee
Writing 125
Ms. Medina
April 1, 2011


          The Story Behind the Gestures

1        At the close of my graduation ceremony,
    my entire family gathered together to immortal-
    ize the special moment on film. No one escaped
    the flash of my mother's camera because she was
    determined to document every minute of the occasion
    at every possible angle. My mother made sure that
```

she took pictures of me with my hat on, with my hat off, holding the bouquet, sitting, standing, and in countless other positions. By the time this family picture was taken, my smile was intact, frozen on my face. This is not to say that my smile was anything less than genuine, for it truly was a smile of thankfulness and joy. It is just that after posing for so many pictures, what initially began as a spontaneous reaction became a frozen expression.

2    The viewer should, however, consider not so much the frozen expressions of those in the photograph, but rather the fact that the picture is posed. A posed picture supposedly shows only what the people in the picture want the viewer to see— in this case, their happiness. But ironically the photograph reveals much more about its subjects than the viewer first imagines. The photograph speaks of relationships and personalities. It speaks about the more intimate details that first seem invisible but that become undeniable through the study of gestures.

3    In the photograph, the most prominent and symbolic of gestures is the use and position of the arms. Both my father and mother place an arm around me and in turn around each other. Their encircling arms, however, do more than just show affection; they unify the three figures into a close huddle that leads the viewer's eye directly to them as opposed to the background or the periphery. The slightly bended arms that rest at their sides act as arrows that not only reinforce the three figures as the focal point but also exclude the fourth figure, my brother, from sharing the spotlight. Unlike the other members of the family whose arms and hands are intertwined, Edwin stands with both hands down in front of him, latching onto no one. The lack of physical contact between the huddled figures and Edwin is again emphasized as he positions himself away from the viewer's eye as he stands in the periphery.

4    Edwin's position in the photograph is indicative of him as a person, for he always seems to isolate himself from the spotlight, from being the center of attention. Thus, it is his decision to

escape public scrutiny, not the force of my parents' arms that drives him to the side. His quiet,
humble nature directs him away from even being
the focal point of a picture and leads him towards
establishing his own individuality and independence
in privacy. His long hair and his "hand-me-down"
clothes are all an expression of his simply being
himself. The reason behind his physical independence is the emotional independence that he already
possesses at the age of sixteen. He stands alone
because he can stand alone.

5     While Edwin stands apart from the other three
figures, I stand enclosed and protected. The lock
of arms as well as the bouquet restrain me; they
dissuade me from breaking away in favor of independence. Although my mother wants me to achieve the
same kind of independence that Edwin has achieved,
she works to delay the time when I actually will
move away to the periphery. Perhaps my being the
only daughter, the only other female in the family,
has something to do with my mother's desire to keep
me close and dependent as long as possible. Her arm
reaches out with bouquet in hand as if to shield
me from the world's unpleasantness. Even though my
father also holds onto me with an encircling arm, it
is my mother's firm grip that alone persuades me to
stay within the boundary of their protective arms.

6     Her grip, which proves more powerful than my
father's hold, restrains not only me but also my
father. In the picture, he falls victim to the same
outstretched hand, the same touch of the bouquet.
Yet this time, my mother's bouquet does more than
just restrain; it seems to push my father back
"into line" or into his so-called place. The picture illustrates this exertion of influence well,
for my mother in real life does indeed assume the
role of the dominant figure. Although my father
remains the head of the household in title, it is
my mother around whom the household revolves; she
oversees the insignificant details as well as the
major ones. But my father doesn't mind at all. Like
me, he also enjoys the protection her restraining
arm offers. It is because of our mutual dependence
on my mother that my father and I seem to draw

*The Lee Family.*

closer. This dependence in turn strengthens both of our relationships with my mother.

7      At the time the picture was taken, I seriously doubt that my mother realized the significance of her position in the picture or the import of her gestures. All of us in fact seem too blinded by the festivity of the occasion to realize that this photograph would show more than just a happy family at a daughter's graduation. The family photograph would inevitably become a telling portrait of each member of the family. It would, in a sense, leave us vulnerable to the speculative eyes of the viewer, who in carefully examining the photograph would recognize the secrets hidden in each frozen expression.

A few observations on these paragraphs may be useful. First, notice that each paragraph in the sequence examines a different aspect of the photograph and introduces a new point into the discussion.

- Paragraph 1 gives background information (the photograph was taken at Cheryl's graduation).
- Paragraph 2 states the writer's point—that studying the gestures of her family members enables us to understand the "personalities and relationships."

Each succeeding paragraph treats one of these gestures, or one of the personalities or relationships:

- Paragraph 3 considers the "encircling arms" of Cheryl's parents.
- Paragraph 4 focuses on the writer's brother Edwin.
- Paragraph 5 focuses on Cheryl's relationship to her mother.
- Paragraph 6 focuses on her mother and father.

Second, notice how Cheryl makes the essay cohere. Although she uses some transitional words ("however" at the beginning of the second paragraph; "while" at the beginning of the fifth paragraph), she establishes coherence in this essay primarily by repeating the key terms of her discussion. The first sentence of each new paragraph picks up a word or phrase from the last sentence of the paragraph preceding it. The phrase "frozen expressions" links the end of the first paragraph to the beginning of the second; "gesture" links the second paragraph to the third; "position" links the third to the fourth; "stand" links the fourth to the fifth; and so on. These links are hardly noticeable on a first reading, but because Cheryl uses transitions and repetition effectively, the writing flows, and the reader never stumbles.

# Paragraph Length

Although a paragraph can contain any number of sentences, two is probably too few, and ten might be too many. It is not a matter, however, of counting sentences; paragraphs are coherent blocks, substantial units of your essay, and the spaces between them are brief resting-places allowing the reader to take in what you have said. One double-spaced, word-processed page of writing (approximately 250 words) is about as much as the reader can take before requiring a slight break. On the other hand, a single page with half a dozen paragraphs is probably faulty because the reader is too often interrupted with needless pauses and because the page has too few *developed* ideas: An assertion is made, and then another, and another. These assertions are unconvincing because they are not supported with detail.

## The Use and Abuse of Short Paragraphs

A short paragraph can be effective when it summarizes a highly detailed previous paragraph or group of paragraphs, or when it serves as a transition between two complicated paragraphs, but unless you are sure that the reader needs a break, avoid thin paragraphs. A paragraph that is nothing but a transition can usually be altered into a transitional phrase or clause or sentence that starts the next paragraph. But of course there are times when a short paragraph is exactly right. Notice the effect of the two-sentence paragraph between two longer paragraphs:

> After I returned to prison, I took a long look at myself and, for the first time in my life, admitted that I was wrong, that I had gone astray—astray not so much from the white man's law as from being human, civilized—for I could not approve the act of rape. Even though I had some insight into my own motivations, I did not feel justified. I lost my self-respect. My pride as a man dissolved and my whole fragile moral structure seemed to collapse, completely shattered.
>
> That is why I started to write. To save myself.
>
> I realized that no one could save me but myself. The prison authorities were both uninterested and unable to help me. I had to seek out the truth and unravel the snarled web of my motivations. I had to find out who I am and what I want to be, what type of man I should be, and what I could do to become the best of which I was capable. I understood that what had happened to me had also happened to countless other blacks and it would happen to many, many more.
>
> —*Eldridge Cleaver*

If the content of the second paragraph were less momentous, it would hardly merit a paragraph. Here the brevity contributes to the enormous impact; those two simple sentences, set off by themselves, seem equal in weight, so to speak, to the longer paragraphs that precede and follow. They are the hinges on which the door turns.

When used for emphasis, short paragraphs can be effective.

Often, though, short paragraphs (like the one directly above) leave readers feeling unsatisfied, even annoyed. Consider these two consecutive paragraphs from a draft of a student's essay on Leonardo da Vinci's *Mona Lisa*:

> Leonardo's *Mona Lisa*, painted about 1502, has caused many people to wonder about the lady's expression. Different viewers see different things.
>
> The explanation of the puzzle is chiefly in the mysterious expression that Leonardo conveys. The mouth and the eyes are especially important.

Sometimes you can improve a sequence of short paragraphs merely by joining one paragraph to the next. But unsatisfactory short paragraphs usually cannot be repaired so simply: The source of the problem is usually not that sentences have been needlessly separated from each other, but that generalizations have not been supported by details, or that claims have not been supported by evidence. Here is the student's revision, strengthening the two thin paragraphs of the draft.

> Leonardo's *Mona Lisa*, painted about 1502, has caused many people to wonder about the lady's expression. Doubtless she is remarkably lifelike but exactly what experience of life, what mood, does she reveal? Is she sad, or gently mocking, or uncertain or self-satisfied, or lost in daydreams? Why are we never satisfied when we try to name her emotion?
> Part of the uncertainty may of course be due to the subject as a whole. What can we make out of the combination of this smiling woman and that utterly unpopulated landscape? But surely

*Mona Lisa, La Gioconda.*
Leonardo da Vinci
(1452–1519). Louvre, Paris,
France. Alinari/Art Resource.

a large part of the explanation lies in the way that Leonardo painted the face's two most expressive features, the eyes and the mouth. He slightly obscured the corners of these, so that we cannot precisely characterize them: although on one viewing we may see them one way, on another viewing we may see them slightly differently. If today we think she looks detached, tomorrow we may think she looks slightly threatening.

This revision is not simply a padded version of the earlier paragraphs; it is a necessary clarification of them, for without the details the generalizations mean almost nothing to a reader.

## Introductory Paragraphs

As the poet Byron said, at the beginning of a long part of a long poem, "Nothing so difficult as a beginning." Almost all writers find that the first paragraphs in their drafts are false starts. As we suggest in Chapter 1, we think you shouldn't worry too much about the opening paragraph of your draft; you'll almost surely want to revise your opening later anyway.

When writing a first draft, you merely need something to break the ice. But in your finished paper the opening cannot be mere throat-clearing. The opening should be interesting. Here are some common *un*interesting openings to avoid:

- A dictionary definition ("Webster says . . .").
- A restatement of your title. The title is (let's assume) "Anarchism and the Marx Brothers," and the first sentence says, "This essay will study the anarchic acts of the Marx Brothers." True, the sentence announces the topic of the essay, but it gives no information about the topic beyond what the title already offers, and it provides no information about you either—that is, no sense of your response to the topic, such as might be present in, say, "The Marx Brothers are funny, but one often has the feeling that under the fun the violence has serious implications."
- A broad generalization, such as "Ever since the beginning of time, human beings have been violent." Again, such a sentence may be fine if it helps you to start drafting, but it should not remain in your final version: It's dull—and it tells your readers almost nothing

about the essay they're about to read. (Our example, after all, could begin anything from an analysis of *Fight Club* to a term paper on Libya.) To put it another way, the ever-since-the-beginning-of-time opening lacks substance—and if your opening lacks substance, it will not matter what you say next. You've already lost your reader's attention.

What is left? What *is* a good way for an introductory paragraph to begin?

- It will be at least moderately interesting if it provides information.
- It will be pleasing if the information provides **focus**—that is, if it lets the reader know exactly what your topic is and what you will say about it.
- And it will capture a reader's attention if it articulates a problem and suggests why the essay is worth reading.

When you write, *you* are the teacher; it won't do to begin with a vague statement:

```
George Orwell says he shot the elephant because...
```

We need some information, identifying the text you are writing about:

```
George Orwell, in "Shooting an Elephant," says he
shot the elephant because...
```

Even better is,

```
     In "Shooting an Elephant," George Orwell sets
forth his reflections on his service as a policeman
in Burma. He suggests that he once shot an elephant
because...but his final paragraph suggests that we
must look for additional reasons.
```

Why is this opening better? Because it begins to suggest why the essay is worth reading. It points to a contradiction in the Orwell piece, a problem worth examining: Orwell says one thing, but that thing may not be entirely true.

Compare, for example, the opening sentences from three essays written by students on Anne Moody's *Coming of Age in Mississippi*. The book is the autobiography of an African American woman, covering her early years with her sharecropper parents, her schooling, and finally her work in the civil rights movement.

> The environment that surrounds a person from an early age tends to be a major factor in determining their character.

This is an all-purpose sentence that serves no specific purpose well; it could conceivably begin an essay on almost any topic: a study of the moral development of children, an analysis of the film *Slumdog Millionaire*, or a biography of Napoleon. Notice also the faulty reference of the pronoun (the plural "their" refers to the singular "a person"), the weaseling of "tends to be a major factor," and the vagueness of "early age" and "environment" and "character." These all warn us that the writer will waste our time.

> It is unfortunate but true that racial or color prejudice shows itself early in the life of a child.

Less pretentious than the first example, but it labors the obvious, sounds preachy, and still doesn't say much about the topic at hand.

> Anne Moody's autobiography, *Coming of Age in Mississippi*, vividly illustrates how she discovered her identity as an African American.

Surely this is the best of the three openings. Informative and focused, it identifies the book's theme and method, and it offers an evaluation. The essayist has been considerate of her readers: If we are interested in women's autobiographies or life in the South, we will read on. If we aren't, we are grateful to her for letting us off the bus at the first stop.

Let's look now not simply at an opening sentence but at an entire first paragraph, the opening paragraph of an analytic essay. Notice how the student provides necessary information about the book she is discussing (the diary of a man whose son has autism) and also focuses the reader's attention on the essay's topic (the quality that distinguishes this diary from others).

> Josh Greenfeld's diary, *A Place for Noah*, records the attempts of a smart, thoughtful man to reconcile himself to his son's autism, which

in Noah's case has left him nearly unable to communicate. Most diaries function as havens for secret thoughts, and Greenfeld's diary does frequently supply a voice to his darkest fears about who will ultimately care for Noah. It provides, too, an intimate glimpse of a family striving to remain a coherent unit despite their son's disorder. But beyond affording such urgent and personal revelations, *A Place for Noah*, in chronicling the isolation of the Greenfelds, reveals how inadequate and ineffectual our medical systems can be in responding to families with children diagnosed with autism—which even now is not fully understood.

This example is engaging, in part because it indicates why a reader might be interested in reading the essay it begins: Greenfeld's book is more than just a diary; it also explores the consequences of a problem that could affect any family.

Of course you can provide interest and focus by other means, among them the following:

- A quotation
- An anecdote or other short narrative
- An interesting fact (a statistic, for instance, showing the reader that you know something about your topic)
- A definition of an important term—but not merely one derived from a dictionary
- A question—but an interesting one, such as "Why do we call some words obscene?"
- A glance at the opposition
- An assertion that a problem exists

Many excellent opening paragraphs do not use any of these devices, and you need not use any of them if they feel forced. But in your reading you may observe that these devices are used widely. Here is an example of the second device, **an anecdote**, which makes an effective, indeed an unnerving, introduction to an essay on aging.

> There is an old American folk tale about a wooden bowl. It seems that Grandmother, with her trembling hands, was guilty of occasionally breaking a dish. Her daughter angrily gave her a wooden bowl, and told her that she must eat out of it from now on. The young granddaughter, observing this, asked her mother why

Grandmother must eat from a wooden bowl when the rest of the family was given china plates. "Because she is old!" answered her mother. The child thought for a moment and then told her mother, "You must save the wooden bowl when Grandma dies." Her mother asked why, and the child replied, "For when you are old."

*—Sharon R. Curtin*

The third strategy, **an interesting detail**, shows the reader that you know something about your topic and that you are worth reading. We have already seen (p. 32) a rather quiet example of this device, in a paragraph about Charles Darwin, which begins "Charles Darwin's youth was unmarked by signs of genius." Here is a more obvious example, from a student essay on blue jeans:

> That blue jeans or denims are not found only in Texas is not surprising if we recall that jeans are named for Genoa (Gene), where the cloth was first made, and that denim is cloth de Nîmes, that is, from Nîmes, a city in France.

(Such information is to be had by spending about a minute with a dictionary or three seconds with Google. Try googling "denim origin.")

The fourth strategy, **a definition**, is fairly common in analytic essays; the essayist first clears the ground by specifying the topic. Here is the beginning of a student's essay on bilingual education:

> Let's begin by defining "bilingual education."
> As commonly used today, the term does *not* mean
> teaching students a language other than English.
> Almost everyone would agree that foreign-language
> instruction should be available, and that it is
> desirable for Americans to be fluent not only in
> English but also in some other language. Nor does
> "bilingual education" mean offering courses in
> English as a second language to students whose na-
> tive language is, for example, Chinese or Spanish
> or Navajo or Aleut. Again, almost everyone would
> agree that such instruction should be offered where
> economically possible. Rather, it means offering
> instruction in such courses as mathematics, his-
> tory, and science *in the student's native language*,
> while also offering courses in English as a second

language. Programs vary in details, but the idea
is that the nonnative speaker should be spared the
trauma of total immersion in English until he or
she has completed several years of studying English
as a second language. During this period, instruction in other subjects is given in the student's
native language.

—Tina Bakka

The fifth strategy, **a question**, is briefly illustrated by the opening paragraph of an essay about whether it is sometimes permissible for doctors to lie to their patients.

> Should doctors ever lie to benefit their patients—to speed recovery or to conceal the approach of death? In medicine as in law, government, and other lines of work, the requirements of honesty often seem dwarfed by greater needs: the need to shelter from brutal news or to uphold a promise of secrecy; to expose corruption or to promote the public interest.

*—Sissela Bok*

The sixth strategy, **a glance at the opposition**, is especially effective if the opposing view is well established, but while you state it, you should manage to convey your distrust of it. Here is an example:

> One often hears, correctly, that there is a world food crisis, and one almost as often hears that not enough food is produced to feed the world's entire population. The wealthier countries, it is said, jeopardize their own chances for survival when they attempt to subsidize all of the poorer countries in which the masses are starving. Often the lifeboat analogy is offered: There is room in the boat for only X people, and to take in X+1 is to overload the boat and to invite the destruction of all. But is it true that the world cannot and does not produce enough food to save the whole population from starving?

*—V. Nagarajan*

The seventh strategy, **an assertion that a problem exists**, is common in essays that make proposals. The following example is the first paragraph of a grant proposal written by biomedical engineers seeking government funding for their research project, a new method for treating liver cancer. Notice that the paragraph does not offer the authors' proposal; it simply points out that there is an unsolved problem, and the reader infers that the proposal will offer the solution.

Liver cancer, especially metastatic colorectal cancer, is a significant and increasing health concern. In the United States, half of the 157,000 new cases of colorectal cancer will develop metastases in the liver. These metastases will lead to over 17,000 deaths annually. And while not as significant a health risk as colorectal metastasis, hepatocellular carcinoma is being diagnosed with increasing frequency. The current standard of practice for treating liver cancer is surgical resection, but only 10% of patients are eligible for this procedure. (Circumstances limiting eligibility include the tumor location, the number of lobes affected by the cancer, the patient's general poor health, and cirrhosis.) Moreover, fewer than 20% of those patients who undergo resection survive for three years without recurrence. Transplantation is an alternative to resection, but this technique is not appropriate for metastatic disease or for larger cancers, and the shortage of liver grafts limits the usefulness of this technique. Systemic chemotherapy has been shown to have a therapeutic effect on metastases, but it has also been shown to have no effect on long-term survival rates.

*—Michael Curley and Patrick Hamilton*

Clearly, there is no one way to write an opening paragraph, but we want to add that you cannot go wrong in beginning your essay—especially if it's an analytic essay written for a course in the humanities—with a paragraph that includes **a statement of your thesis**. A common version of this kind of paragraph follows this pattern:

- It offers some background (if you're writing about a novel, for example, you'll give the author and title as well as relevant information about the novel's plot).
- It suggests the problem the essay will address (in the paragraph below, the problem is implied: In *Frankenstein* similar characters meet very different fates; how can we account for the difference?).
- It ends with a sentence that states the main point, or thesis, of the essay.

In *Frankenstein*, Mary Shelley frames the novel with narratives of two similar characters who meet markedly different fates. Frankenstein, the medical researcher, and Walton, the explorer, are both passionately determined to push forward the boundaries of human knowledge. But while Walton's ambition to explore unknown regions of the earth is directed by reason and purpose, Frankenstein's ambition to create life is unfocused and misguided. This difference in the nature of their ambitions determines their fates. Walton's controlled ambition leads him to abandon his goal in order to save the lives of his crew members. When we last see him, he is heading toward home and safety. Frankenstein's unchecked ambition leads to his own death and the self-destruction of his creature.

## Concluding Paragraphs

Concluding paragraphs, like opening paragraphs, are especially difficult if only because they are so conspicuous. Fortunately, you are not always obliged to write one. Descriptive essays, for example, may end merely with a final paragraph, not with a paragraph that draws a conclusion. In an expository essay explaining a process or mechanism, you may simply stop when you have finished.

But if you do have to write a concluding paragraph, say something interesting. It is not of the slightest interest to say "Thus we see . . ." and then echo your title and first paragraph. There is some justification for a summary at the end of a long essay because the reader may have half forgotten some of the ideas presented 30 pages earlier, but an essay that can easily be held in the mind needs something more. A good concluding paragraph rounds out the previous discussion. Such a paragraph may offer a few sentences that summarize (it should not begin with the dull phrase "in summary"); but it will probably also draw an inference that has not previously been expressed. To draw such an inference is not to introduce an entirely new idea—the end of an essay is hardly the place for that. Rather it is to see the previous material in a fresh perspective, to take the discussion perhaps one step further.

Because all writers have to find out what they think about any given topic, and have to find the strategies appropriate for presenting these thoughts to a particular audience, we hesitate to offer a do-it-yourself kit for final paragraphs, but the following simple devices often work:

■ End with a quotation, especially a quotation that amplifies or varies a quotation used in the opening paragraph.

- End with some idea or detail from the beginning of the essay and thus bring it full circle.
- End with a new (but related) point, one that takes your discussion a step further.
- End with an allusion, say to a historical or mythological figure or event, putting your topic in a larger framework.
- End with a glance at the readers—not with a demand that they mount the barricades, but with a suggestion that the next move is theirs.

If you adopt any of these devices, do so quietly; the aim is not to write a grand finale, but to complete or round out a discussion.

All essayists must find their own ways of ending each essay; the five strategies we have suggested are common, but they are not for you if you don't find them useful. And so, rather than ending this section with rules about how to end essays, we suggest how not to end them: Don't merely summarize, don't say "in conclusion," don't introduce a totally new point, and don't apologize.

### CHECKLIST for Revising Paragraphs

☐ Does the paragraph *say* anything? Does it have substance? (See pp. 32–33.)

☐ Does the paragraph have a topic sentence? If so, is it in the best place? If the paragraph doesn't have a topic sentence, might one improve the paragraph? Does the paragraph have a clear topic idea? (See pp. 32–33.)

☐ If the paragraph is an opening paragraph, is it interesting enough to attract and to hold a reader's attention? (See pp. 48–55.) If it is a later paragraph, does it easily evolve out of the previous paragraph and lead into the next paragraph? (See pp. 41–45.)

☐ Does the paragraph contain some principle of development— for instance, from cause to effect or from general to particular? What is the purpose of the paragraph? Does the paragraph fulfill the purpose? (See pp. 37–38.)

☐ Does each sentence clearly follow from the preceding sentence? Have you provided transitional words or cues to guide your reader? Would it be useful to repeat certain key words for clarity? (See pp. 38–41.)

☐ Is the closing paragraph effective, or is it an unnecessary restatement of the obvious? (See pp. 55–56.)

# CHAPTER 4

# Revising for Conciseness

Excess is the common substitute for energy.

—Marianne Moore

WRITERS WHO WANT TO KEEP THE ATTENTION AND confidence of their audience revise for conciseness. The general rule is to say everything relevant in as few words as possible. The conclusion of the Supreme Court's decision in *Brown v. Board of Education of Topeka*, for example—"Separate educational facilities are inherently unequal"—says it all in six words.

The writers of the following sentences bore us because they don't make every word count.

```
There are two pine trees which grow behind this
house.

On his left shoulder is a small figure standing.
He is about the size of the doctor's head.
```

Compare those two sentences with these revisions:

```
Two pine trees grow behind this house.

On his left shoulder stands a small figure, about
the size of the doctor's head.
```

The time to begin revising for conciseness is when you think you have an acceptable draft in hand—something that pretty much covers your topic and comes reasonably close to saying what you believe about it. As you go over your draft, study each sentence to see what can be deleted without loss of meaning. Read each paragraph, preferably aloud, to see if each sentence supports the topic sentence or idea and clarifies the point you are making. Leave in the concrete details and examples that support your ideas, but cut out all the deadwood that chokes them:

- Extra words
- Empty or pretentious phrases
- Weak intensifiers
- Redundancies
- Negative constructions
- Wordy uses of the verb *to be*
- Other extra verbs and verb phrases

THE WRITING PROCESS

58

# Instant Prose

Here are some examples of Instant Prose from students' essays:

> Frequently a chapter title in a book reveals to the reader the main point that the author desires to bring out during the course of the chapter.

We could try revising this, cutting the twenty-seven words down to seven:

> A chapter's title often reveals its thesis.

But why bother? Unless the title is an exception, is the point worth making?

> The two poems are basically similar in many ways, yet they have their significant differences.

True, all poems are both similar to and different from other poems. Start over with your next sentence, perhaps something like:

> The two poems, superficially similar in rough paraphrase, are strikingly different in diction.

The following examples fall into the category of Unadulterated Instant Prose. Not even the writers of these sentences now know what they mean.

> Cassell only presents a particular situation concerning the issue, and with clear descriptions and a certain style sets up an interesting article.

> During the period of the post-Civil War era and
> Reconstruction, it was felt that the negative
> circumstances might never be productively resolved.

Writing Instant Prose is an acquired habit. It often begins in high school, sometimes earlier, when the victim is assigned a ten-page paper, or is told that a paragraph *must* contain at least three sentences, or that a thesis is stated in the introduction to an essay, elaborated in the body, and repeated in the conclusion. If the instructions appear arbitrary, and the student is bored or intimidated by them, the response is likely to be meaningless and mechanical.

Such students have forgotten the true purpose of writing—the discovery and communication of ideas, attitudes, and judgments. They concentrate instead on the word count: stuffing sentences, padding paragraphs, repeating points, and adding flourishes. Rewarded by a satisfactory grade, they repeat the performance, and in time, through practice, develop some fluency in spilling out words without thought or commitment, and almost without effort. Such students may enter college feeling somehow inauthentic, perhaps even aware that they don't really mean what they write—a sure symptom of habitual use of, or addiction to, Instant Prose.

## How to Avoid Instant Prose

1. **Trust yourself**. Writing Instant Prose is not only a habit; it's also a form of alienation. If you habitually resort to Instant Prose, you probably don't think of what you write as your own but as something you produce on demand for someone else, most likely that unreasonable authority, the teacher, whose mysterious whims and insatiable appetite for words must somehow be satisfied. Breaking the habit begins with recognizing it. It means learning to respect your ideas and experiences, and determining that when you write, you'll write what you mean. This involves taking some risks, of course; habits offer some security or they would have no grip on us. Moreover, we all have moments when we doubt that our ideas are worth taking seriously. Keep writing honestly anyway. The self-doubts will pass; accomplishing something—writing one clear sentence—can help make them pass.

2. **Learn to recognize Instant Prose Additives in your writing and in what you read**. And you *will* find them in what you read—in

textbooks and in academic journals, notoriously. Here's an example from a recent book on contemporary theater:

> One of the principal and most persistent sources of error that tends to bedevil a considerable proportion of contemporary literary analysis is the assumption that the writer's creative process is a wholly conscious and purposive type of activity.

Notice all the extra stuff in the sentence: "principal and most persistent," "tends to bedevil," "considerable proportion," "type of activity." Cleared of deadwood the sentence might read:

> The assumption that the writer's creative process is wholly conscious bedevils much contemporary criticism.

3. **Acquire two things: a new habit, Revising for Conciseness; and what Isaac Singer calls "the writer's best friend," a wastebasket**.

# Extra Words and Empty Words

Delete extra words; replace vague, empty, or pretentious words and phrases with specific and direct language. Notice how, in the examples provided, the following words crop up: *significant, situation, involving, effect*. These words have legitimate uses but are often no more than Instant Prose Additives. Delete them whenever you can. Similar words to watch out for: *aspect, basically, facet, factor, fundamental, manner, nature, type, ultimate, utilization, viable, virtually, vital*. If they make your writing sound good, don't hesitate—cross them out at once.

### Wordy

However, it must be remembered that Ruth's marriage could have positive effects on Naomi's situation.

### Concise

Ruth's marriage, however, will also provide security for Naomi.

In the revision, the unnecessary "it must be remembered that" has been struck out. For the vague words "positive effects" and "situation," specific words have been substituted. The revision, though briefer, says more.

### Wordy

In high school, where I had the opportunity for three years of working with the student government, I realized how significantly a person's enthusiasm could be destroyed merely by the attitudes of his superiors.

**Concise**

In high school, during three years on the student council, I saw students' enthusiasm destroyed by insecure teachers and cynical administrators.

Again, the revised sentence gives more information in fewer words. How?

## Weak Intensifiers

Words like *very, quite, rather, completely, definitely,* and *so* can usually be struck from a sentence without loss. Paradoxically, sentences are often more emphatic without intensifiers. Try reading the following sentences both with and without the bracketed words:

At that time I was [very] idealistic.
We found the proposal [quite] feasible.
The scene was [extremely] typical.

Always avoid using intensifiers with *unique.* Either something is unique—the only one of its kind—or it is not. It can't be very, quite, so, pretty, or fairly unique.

## Circumlocutions

Roundabout or long-winded ways of saying things weaken your prose and tire your reader. Notice how each circumlocution in the first column is matched by a concise expression in the second.

| | |
|---|---|
| I came to the realization that | I realized that |
| She is of the opinion that | She thinks that |
| The quotation is supportive of | The quotation supports |
| Concerning the matter of | About |
| During the course of | During |
| For the period of a week | For a week |
| In the event that | If |
| In the process of | During, while |
| Regardless of the fact that | Although |
| Due to the fact that | Because |

| | |
|---|---|
| The fact that | That |
| It is often the case that | Often |
| In all cases | Always |
| At that point in time | Then |
| At this point in time | Now |

Now try revising this sentence:

> These movies have a large degree of popularity for the simple reason that they give the viewers insight in many cases.

## Wordy Beginnings

Vague words and phrases sometimes clog the beginnings of sentences. They're like elaborate windups before the pitch.

**Wordy**

What the cartoonist is illustrating and trying to get across is the greed of the oil producers.

**Concise**

The cartoon illustrates the greed of the oil producers.

**Wordy**

In opposition to the situation of the younger son is that of the elder who remained in his father's house, working hard and handling his inheritance wisely.

**Concise**

The elder son, by contrast, remained in his father's house, worked hard, and handled his inheritance wisely.

Notice that when the deadwood is cleared from the beginning of the sentence, the subject appears early, and the main verb appears close to it:

> The cartoon illustrates . . .
> The elder son . . . remained . . .

Locating the right noun for the subject, and the right verb for the predicate, is the key to revising sentences with wordy beginnings.

## Empty Conclusions

Often a sentence that begins well has an empty conclusion. The words go on but the sentence seems to stand still; if it's not revised, it requires another sentence to explain it.

### Empty

"Those Winter Sundays" is composed so that a reader can feel what the poet was saying. [How is it composed? What is he saying?]

### Informative

"Those Winter Sundays" describes the speaker's anger as a child, and his remorse as an adult.

### Empty

In both Orwell's and Baldwin's essays the feeling of white supremacy is very important. [Why is white supremacy important?]

### Informative

Both Orwell and Baldwin trace the insidious consequences of white supremacy.

## Wordy Uses of the Verbs To Be, To Have, and To Make

Notice that in the preceding unrevised sentences, a form of the verb *to be* introduces the empty conclusion: "*was* saying," "*is* very important." In each revision, the right verb added and generated substance. In the following sentences, substitutions for the verb *to be* both invigorate and shorten otherwise substantial sentences. (The wordy expressions are italicized, and so are the revisions.)

### Wordy

The scene *is taking place* at night, in front of the court house.

### Concise

The scene *takes place* at night, in front of the court house.

### Wordy

The words "flashing," "rushing," "plunging," and "tossing" *are suggestive of* excitement.

### Concise

The words "flashing," "rushing," "plunging," and "tossing" *suggest* excitement.

## A RULE FOR WRITERS

Whenever you can, replace a form of the verb *to be* with a stronger verb.

| To Be | Strong Verb |
|---|---|
| and a participle (*is taking*) | *takes* |
| and a noun (*are indications*) | *indicate* |
| and an adjective (*are suggestive*) | *suggest* |

In the following examples, substitutions for the verbs *to have* and *to make* shorten and enliven the sentence.

### Wordy

The Friar *has knowledge* that Juliet is alive.

### Concise

The Friar *knows* that Juliet is alive.

### Wordy

The law *makes a very sharp distinction* between manslaughter and murder.

### Concise

The law *distinguishes sharply* between manslaughter and murder.

Like all rules, this one has exceptions. We don't list them here; you'll discover them by listening to your sentences.

## Redundancy

*Redundancy* refers to unnecessary repetition in the expression of ideas. "Future plans," after all, are only plans, and "to glide smoothly" or "to scurry rapidly" is only to glide or to scurry. Unlike repetition, which often provides emphasis or coherence (for example, "government of the people, by the people, for the people"), redundancy can always be eliminated.

### Redundant

Any student could randomly sit anywhere. (If the students could sit anywhere, the seating was random.)

### Concise

Students could sit anywhere.
Students chose their seats at random.

### Redundant

In the orthodox Cuban culture, the surface of the female role seemed degrading. [Perhaps this sentence means what it says. More probably "surface" and "seemed" are redundant.]

### Concise

In the orthodox Cuban culture, the female role seemed degrading. In the orthodox Cuban culture, the female role was superficially degrading.

What words can be crossed out of the following phrases?

throughout the entire article
her attitude of indifference
his own personal opinion
elements common to both of them
shared together

Many phrases in common use are redundant. For example, there is no need to write "blare noisily," since the meaning of the adverb "noisily" is conveyed in the verb "blare." Watch for phrases like these when you revise:

round in shape          resulting effect
must necessarily        connected together
very unique             true fact
free gift               the reason why is because

## Negative Constructions

Negative constructions are often wordy and sometimes pretentious.

### Wordy

Housing for married students is *not unworthy of* consideration.

### Concise

Housing for married students is worth considering.

### Better

The trustees should earmark funds for married students' housing. [Probably what the author meant.]

*"See what I mean? You're never sure just where you stand with them."*
© The New Yorker Collection 1971. Al Rossi from cartoonbank.com. All Rights Reserved.

### A (GOLDEN) RULE FOR WRITERS

Write for others as you would have them write for you (not "Write for others in a manner not unreasonably dissimilar to the manner in which you would have them write for you").

## Extra Sentences, Extra Clauses: Subordination

Sentences are sometimes wordy because ideas are given more elaborate grammatical constructions than they need. When revising, try to reduce these constructions. Two sentences, for example, may be reduced to one, or a clause may be reduced to a phrase.

### Wordy

Facebook was born in 2004. It was a time when social networking was still in its infancy.

### Concise

Facebook was born in 2004, when social networking was still in its infancy.

**Wordy**

The first group was the largest. This group was seated in the center of the dining hall.

**Concise**

The first group, the largest, was seated in the center of the dining hall.

## Who, Which, That

Watch for clauses beginning with *who*, *which*, and *that*.

**Wordy**

Lady Gaga is the stage name of Stefani Germanotta, *who is* an American pop star.

**Concise**

Lady Gaga is the stage name of Stefani Germanotta, an American pop star.

**Wordy**

They are seated at a table *which is* covered with a patched and tattered cloth.

**Concise**

They are seated at a table covered with a patched and tattered cloth.

**Wordy**

There is one feature *that is* grossly out of proportion.

**Concise**

One feature is grossly out of proportion.

For further discussion of *which* clauses, see "Using the Right Word," Chapter 12 (p. 292).

## It Is, This Is, There Are

Watch for sentences and clauses beginning with *it is*, *this is*, *there are* (again, wordy uses of the verb *to be*). These expressions often lead to a *which* or a *that*, but even when they don't, they may be wordy.

**Wordy**

*This is* a quotation from Black Elk's autobiography *which* discloses his prophetic powers.

**Concise**

This quotation from Black Elk's autobiography discloses his prophetic powers.

**Wordy**

In Notman's photograph of Buffalo Bill and Sitting Bull *there are* definite contrasts between the two figures.

**Concise**

Notman's photograph of Buffalo Bill and Sitting Bull contrasts the two figures.

# Some Concluding Remarks About Conciseness

We spoke earlier about how high school students succumb to Instant Prose and acquire other wordy habits—by writing what they think the teacher has asked for. We haven't forgotten that instructors assign papers of a certain length in college too. But the length given is not an arbitrary limit that must be reached—the instructor who asks for a ten-page paper is probably trying to tell you that it's likely to take you ten pages to develop your ideas on the topic at hand. Such, apparently, was the intention of William Randolph Hearst, the newspaper publisher, who cabled an astronomer, "Is there life on Mars? Cable reply 1000 words." The astronomer's reply was, "Nobody knows," repeated 500 times.

What do you do when you've been asked to produce a ten-page paper and after diligent writing and revising you find you've said everything relevant to your topic in seven and a half pages? Our advice is, hand it in. We can't remember ever counting the words or pages of a substantial, interesting essay; we assume that our colleagues elsewhere are equally reasonable and equally overworked. If we're wrong, tell us about it—in writing, and in the fewest possible words.

**CHECKLIST for Revising for Conciseness**

☐ Does every word count? Can any words or phrases be cut without loss of meaning?

☐ Are there any empty or pretentious words such as *situation, factor, virtually, significant,* and *utilize*? (See pp. 60–65.)

- Do intensifiers such as *very, truly*, and *rather* weaken your sentences? (See p. 61.)
- Are there any roundabout or long-winded locutions? Do you say, for example, *at that point in time* when you mean *then*, or *for the simple reason that* when you mean *because*? (See pp. 61–62.)
- Do sentences get off to a fast start? Can you cut any sentences that open with "it is . . . that"? (See pp. 67–68.)
- Can you replace forms of the verbs *to be, to have*, and *to make* with precise and active verbs? (See pp. 63–64.)
- Are there any redundancies or negative constructions? (See pp. 64–65.)
- Can any sentences be combined using subordination? (See pp. 66–68.)

# Revising for Clarity

Here's to plain speaking and clear understanding.
—Sidney Greenstreet, in *The Maltese Falcon*

## Clarity

First, read the following two passages:

> We have seen new realities created by the advance of physics. But this chain of creation can be traced back far beyond the starting point of physics. One of the most primitive concepts is that of an object. The concepts of a tree, a horse, any material body, are creations gained on the basis of experience, though the impressions from which they arise are primitive in comparison with the world of physical phenomena. A cat teasing a mouse also creates, by thought, its own primitive reality. The fact that the cat reacts in a similar way toward any mouse it meets shows that it forms concepts and theories which are its guide through its own world of sense impressions.

> —*Albert Einstein and Leopold Infeld*

> Skills constitute the manipulative techniques of human goal attainment and control in relation to the physical world, so far as artifacts or machines especially designed as tools do not yet supplement them. Truly human skills are guided by organized and codified knowledge of both the things to be manipulated and the human capacities that are used to manipulate them. Such knowledge is an aspect of cultural-level symbolic processes, and, like other aspects to be discussed presently, requires the capacities

of the human central nervous system, particularly the brain. This organic system is clearly essential to all of the symbolic processes; as we well know, the human brain is far superior to the brain of any other species.

*—Talcott Parsons*

Why is the first passage easier to understand than the second?

Both passages discuss the relationship between the brain and the physical world it attempts to understand. The first passage, by Einstein and Infeld, is, if anything, more complex both in what it asserts and in what it suggests than the second, by Parsons. Both passages explain that the brain organizes sense impressions. But Einstein and Infeld further explain that the history of physics can be understood as an extension of the simplest sort of organization, such as we all make in distinguishing a tree from a horse, or such as even a cat makes in teasing a mouse. Parsons only promises that "other aspects" will "be discussed presently." How many of us are eager for those next pages?

Good writing is clear, not because it presents simple ideas but because it presents ideas in the simplest form the subject permits. A clear analysis doesn't falsely reduce a complex problem to a simple one; it breaks it down into its simple, comprehensible parts and discusses them, one by one. A clear paragraph explains one of these parts coherently, and in language as simple and as particular as the reader's understanding requires and the context allows. Where Parsons writes of "organized and codified *knowledge* of . . . the things to be manipulated," Einstein and Infeld write simply of the concept of an object. And even "object," a simple but general word, is further clarified by the specific, familiar examples, "tree" and "horse." Parsons writes of "the manipulative techniques of . . . goal attainment and control in relation to the physical world, so far as artifacts or machines especially designed as tools do not yet supplement them." Einstein and Infeld show us a cat teasing a mouse.

## A RULE FOR WRITERS

Present ideas in the simplest form the subject permits.

Notice also the clear organization of Einstein and Infeld's paragraph. The first sentence, clearly transitional, refers to the advance of physics traced in the preceding pages. The next sentence, introduced by "But," reverses our direction: We are now going to look not at an advance, but at primitive beginnings. And the following sentences, to the end of the paragraph, fulfill that promise. We move back to primitive human concepts, clarified by examples, and finally to the still more primitive example of the cat. Parson's paragraph is also organized, but the route is much more difficult to follow.

Why do people write obscurely? It's difficult to write clearly.[1] Authorities may be obscure not because they want to tax you with unnecessary problems, but because they don't know how to avoid them. If you have ever tried to assemble a piece of furniture by following the "easy instructions," you know that the simplest kind of expository writing, giving instructions, can foil the writers most eager for your goodwill (that is, those who want you to use their products). Few instructions, unfortunately, are as unambiguous as "Go to jail. Go directly to jail. Do not pass Go. Do not collect $200."

You can, though, learn to write clearly by learning to recognize common sources of obscurity in writing and by consciously revising your own work. We offer, to begin with, three general rules:

- Use the simplest, most exact, most specific language your subject allows.
- Put together what belongs together, in the essay, in the paragraph, and in the sentence.
- Keep your reader in mind, particularly when you revise.

Now for more specific advice and examples—the cats and mice of revising for clarity.

# Clarity and Exactness: Using the Right Word

## Denotation

Be sure the word you choose has the right explicit meaning, or *denotation*. Did you mean *sarcastic* or *ironic? Fatalistic* or *pessimistic? Disinterested* or *uninterested? Biannual* or *semiannual? Enforce* or *reinforce? Use* or *usage?* If you're not sure, check the dictionary. You'll find some of the most commonly misused words discussed in "Using

---

[1]"Our first draft of this sentence read "Writing clearly is difficult." Can you see why we changed it?

the Right Word," Chapter 12, pages 268–93. Here are examples of a few others:

He faces a dilemma between his humane feelings and his conceptions of justice. [Strictly speaking, a *dilemma* requires a choice between two equally unattractive alternatives. *Conflict* would be a better word here.]

However, as time dragged on, exercising seemed to lose its charisma. [What is charisma? Why is it inexact here?]

When I run, I don't allow myself to stop until I have reached my destiny. [What is the difference between destiny and destination?]

## Connotation

Be sure the word you choose has the right *connotation* (association, implication). As Mark Twain said, the difference between the right word and the almost right word is the difference between lightning and the lightning bug.

Boston politics has always upheld the reputation of being especially crooked. [*Upheld* inappropriately suggests that Boston has proudly maintained its reputation. *Has always had* would be appropriate here, but pale. *Deserved* would, in this context, be ironic, implying—accurately—the writer's scorn.]

This book, unlike many other novels, lacks tedious descriptive passages. [*Lacks* implies a deficiency. How would you revise the sentence?]

New Orleans, notorious for its good jazz and good food . . . [Is *notorious* the right word here, or *famous?*]

Sunday, Feb. 9. Another lingering day at Wellesley. [In this entry from a student's journal, *lingering* strikes us as right. What does *lingering* imply about Sundays at Wellesley that *long* would not?]

Because words have connotations, most writing—even when it pretends to be objective—conveys attitudes as well as facts. Consider, for example, this passage by Jessica Mitford, describing part of the procedure used for embalming:

A long, hollow needle attached to a tube . . . is jabbed into the abdomen, poked around the entrails and chest cavity, the contents of which are pumped out . . .

Here, as almost always, the writer's *purpose* in large measure determines the choice of words. Probably the sentence accurately describes part of the procedure, but it also, of course, records Mitford's contempt for the procedure. Suppose she wanted to be more respectful—suppose, for example, she were an undertaker writing an explanatory pamphlet. Instead of the needle being "jabbed" it would be "inserted," and instead of being "poked around the entrails" it would be "guided around the viscera," and the contents would not be "pumped out" but would be "drained." Mitford's words would be the wrong words for an undertaker explaining embalming to apprentices or to the general public, but, given her purpose, they are exactly the right ones because they clearly convey her attitude.

Notice, too, that many words have social, political, or sexist overtones. What is implied by the distinction? Consider the differences in *connotation* in each of the following series:

underdeveloped nations, developing nations, emerging nations
preference, bias, prejudice
upbringing, conditioning, brainwashing
intelligence gathering, espionage, spying
antiabortion, pro-life, pro-abortion, pro-choice

## Avoiding Sexist Language

Traditionally, the pronouns *he* and *his* have been used as generic pronouns when both men and women are implied: "A historian must consider the context of *his* source." But contemporary writers avoid the generic use of male pronouns, because such usage is sexist (our example excludes women historians from the discussion), and because it can be misleading and unclear (the example may suggest that there are no women historians, or that women historians do something different from the men). They commonly turn to three remedies in their writing:

- Using both male and female pronouns: "A historian must consider the context of *his* or *her* source."
- Substituting the plural form: "*Historians* must consider the context of *their* source."
- Eliminating the pronoun: "Historians must consider a source's context."

**Note:** Writers and speakers sometimes attempt to correct sexist language by using a plural pronoun with a singular subject: "A *historian* must consider *their* source's context." But this approach produces ungrammatical sentences: The pronoun doesn't agree with its antecedent. (For more on agreement, see pp. 93–95.) Writers also sometimes use such constructions as "his/her," "him/her," or "s/he": "A historian must consider his/her source." While not incorrect, we think that this approach produces ugly sentences, and we recommend that you use one of the three remedies above.

### A RULE FOR WRITERS

Avoid using *he* and *him* as generic pronouns to refer to both men and women.

Likewise, avoid using "man" and "mankind" generically:

Man's need for approval . . .

Substitute gender-neutral terms for gender-specific terms whenever possible—unless, of course, your sentence refers specifically to one gender. The sentence above could thus be revised:

Humanity's need for approval . . .
Our need for approval . . .

Here are more examples of gender-specific or sexist terms, with possible replacements:

| Sexist Term | Gender-Neutral Term |
| --- | --- |
| chairman | chairperson, chair, head |
| manpower | personnel |
| stewardess | flight attendant |
| freshman | first-year student |
| mailman | mail carrier |

## Quotation Marks as Apologies

When you have used words with exact meanings (denotations) and appropriate associations (connotations) for your purpose, don't apologize for them by putting quotation marks around them. If the words *copped a plea, ripped off,* or *kids* suit your purpose better than *plea-bargained, stolen,* or *children,* use them. If they are inappropriate, don't put them in quotation marks; find the right words.

"Please stop doing that annoying quote marks thing."

www.CartoonStock.com

### Being Specific

When writing descriptions, catch the richness, complexity, and unique-ness of things. Suppose, for example, you are describing a scene from your childhood, a setting you loved. There was, in particular, a certain tree . . . and you write: "Near the water there was a big tree that was rather impressive." Most of us would produce something like that sen-tence. Here is the sentence Ernesto Galarza wrote in *Barrio Boy*:

> On the edge of the pond, at the far side, there was an enormous walnut tree, standing like an open umbrella whose ribs extended halfway across the still water of the pool.

We probably could not have come up with the metaphor of the umbrella because we wouldn't have seen the similarity. (As Aristotle observed, the gift for making metaphors distinguishes the poet from the rest of us.) But we can all train ourselves to be accurate observers and reporters. For "the water" (general) we can specify "pond"; for "near" we can say how near, "on the edge of the pond," and add the specific location, "at the far side"; for "tree" we can give the species, "walnut tree"; and for "big" we can provide a picture, its branches "extended halfway across" the pond: It was, in fact, "enormous."

Galarza does not need to add limply, as we did, that the tree "was rather impressive." The tree he describes *is* impressive. That he accurately remembered it persuades us that he was impressed, without his having to tell us he was. For writing descriptions, a good general rule is: Show, don't tell.

Be as specific as you can be in all forms of exposition too. Take the time, when you revise, to find the exact word to replace vague phrases or clichés. In the following examples, we have to guess or invent what the writer means.

**Vague**

The clown's part in *Othello* is very small.

**Specific**

The clown appears in only two scenes in *Othello*.

The clown in *Othello* speaks only thirty lines. [Notice the substitution of the verb *appears* or *speaks* for the frequently debilitating *is*. And in place of the weak intensifier *very*, we have specific details to tell us how small the role is.]

**Vague**

He feels uncomfortable at the whole situation. [Many feelings are uncomfortable. Which one does he feel? What's the situation?]

**Specific**

He feels guilty for having distrusted his father.

**Vague Cliché**

Then she criticized students for living in an ivory tower. [Did she criticize them for being detached or for being secluded? For social irresponsibility or studiousness?]

**Specific**

Then she criticized students for being socially irresponsible.

## Using Examples

In addition to exact words and specific details, illustrative examples make for clear writing. Einstein and Infeld, in the passage quoted on page 70, use as an example of a primitive concept a cat teasing not only its first mouse but also "any mouse it meets." Here is another passage from *Barrio Boy*; like the paragraph from Einstein and Infeld, this paragraph clarifies and develops its topic through examples:

> In Jalco people spoke in two languages—Spanish and with gestures. These signs were made with the face or hands or a combination of both. If you bent one arm and tapped the elbow with the other hand, it meant "He is stingy." When you sawed one arm across the other you were saying that someone you knew played the fiddle terribly. To say that a man was a tippler you made a set of cow's horns with the little finger and the thumb of one hand, bending the three middle fingers to the palm and pointing the thumb at your mouth. And if you wanted to indicate, without saying so for the sake of politeness, that a mutual acquaintance was daffy, you tapped three times on your forehead with your middle finger.
>
> *—Ernesto Galarza*

Now look at a student's paragraph, here printed in the left column, from an essay whose thesis is that rage can be a useful mechanism for effecting change. Then compare the left-hand paragraph with the same paragraph, revised, at the right. Note the specific ways, sentence by sentence, the student revised for clarity.

In my high school we had little say in the learning processes that were used. The subjects that we were required to take were irrelevant. One had to take them to earn enough points to graduate. Some of the teachers were sympathetic to our problem. They would tell us about when they were young, how they tried to oppose their school system. But when they were young it was a long time ago, for most of them. The

In my high school we had little say about our curriculum. We were required, for example, to choose either American or European History to earn enough points for graduation. We wanted, but were at first refused, the option of Black History. Some of our teachers were sympathetic with us; one told me about her fight opposing the penmanship course required in her school. Nor was the principal totally principal would call assemblies to speak on the subject. They were entitled "The Value of an Education" or "Get a Good Education to Have a Bright Future." The titles were not inviting. They had nothing to do with our plight. Most students never came to any agreements with the principal because most of his thoughts and views seemed old and outdated.

indifferent—he called assemblies. I remember one talk he gave called "The Value of an Education in Today's World," and another, "Get a Good Education to Have a Bright Future." I don't recall hearing about a Black History course in either talk. Once, he invited a group of us to meet with him in his office, but we didn't reach any agreement. He solemnly showed us an American History text (not the one we used) that had a whole chapter devoted to Black History.

## Jargon and Technical Language

Most dictionaries give three meanings for *jargon*:

- Technical language
- Meaningless language
- Inflated or pretentious language

The members of almost every profession or trade—indeed, almost all people who share any specialized interest—use the jargon of their field. And this is certainly true of members of academic disciplines. In fact, learning a new discipline involves learning a new vocabulary, a new set of technical terms. Art historians talk of *cubism, iconography,* and *formalism*; Freudians talk of *cathect, libido,* and the *oral phase*; film critics and theorists talk of *anamorphic lenses, optical printers,* and *silent speed.*

Properly used, technical language communicates information concisely and clearly, and it can create a comfortable bond between speakers, or between the writer and the reader.

On the other hand, jargon sometimes *is* inflated and pretentious. Consider, for example, the following sentence by an art historian writing on American Indian baskets made for whites in the early twentieth century:

> Native curios were privileged in bourgeois parlor decoration as metonymic representations of the premodern, their significations enhanced by hand-made production and utilitarian function, two aspects of the premodern also valorized in the contemporary American Arts and Crafts Movement.

This sentence does communicate information to specialists—and perhaps even to general readers who are patient enough to work their way through it. In fact, some academic prose can sound a lot like the quoted sentence. Nevertheless, we believe that such language doesn't communicate clearly and efficiently. One problem with the sentence is that the level of abstraction is very high; the terms "premodern," "significations," and "valorized" don't call to mind specific, concrete things. Another problem with such language is that it is more complicated than it needs to be. Reading it can be alienating; the writer of such sentences risks losing readers' attention. A plainer style is far more inviting. Consider the following paraphrase of the sentence on baskets:

> Middle-class whites valued native curios and displayed them in their parlors. Because these objects were handmade and because they had been used in daily life, they stood for a pre-industrial world, a world celebrated also in the contemporary American Arts and Crafts Movement.

In general, it's best to use plain English—or, at least, the plainest English possible. After all, in an essay you wouldn't speak of a "preliminary overall strategizing concept" when "plan" would do. Don't use abstract, inflated language simply in order to sound impressive. On the other hand, do use the specialized terms of your field if you have come to know what they mean, if they are the best way to make your point, and if you are fairly confident that your imagined reader is familiar with them. If you're unsure, define them.

## Clichés

Clichés (literally, in French, molds from which type is cast) are trite expressions, mechanically reproduced. Since they are available without thought, they are great Instant Prose Additives (see pp. 59–60). Writers who use clichés are usually surprised to be criticized: They find the phrases attractive and may even think them exact. (Phrases become clichés precisely because they have wide appeal and therefore wide use.) But clichés, by their very nature, cannot communicate the uniqueness of your thoughts. Furthermore, because they come instantly to mind, they tend to block the specific detail or exact expression that will let the reader know what precisely is in your mind. In revising, when you strike out a cliché, you force yourself to do the work of writing clearly. How many clichés can you spot in the following example?

> Finally, the long-awaited day arrived. Up bright and early. . . . She peered at me with suspicion; then a faint smile crossed her face.

Here are some other worn-out phrases to avoid:

| | |
|---|---|
| first and foremost | the acid test |
| bustled to and fro | fatal flaw |
| short but sweet | few and far between |
| slowly but surely | little did I know |
| sigh of relief | the big moment |
| last but not least | |

In attempting to avoid clichés, however, don't go to the other extreme of wildly original, super-vivid writing—"'Well then, say something to her,' he roared, his whole countenance gnarled in rage." It's better to write, "he said." (Anyone who intends to write dialogue should memorize Ring Lardner's intentionally funny line, "'Shut up!' he explained.")

## Metaphors and Mixed Metaphors

Ordinary speech abounds with metaphors. We speak or write of the *foot of a mountain*, the *germ of an idea*, the *root of a problem*. Metaphors so deeply embedded in the language that they no longer evoke pictures in our minds are called **dead metaphors**. Usually they offer us, as writers, no problems: We need neither seek them nor avoid them; they are simply there. (Notice, for example, "embedded" two sentences back.) Such metaphors become problems, however, when we unwittingly call them back to life, as Howard Nemerov observes: "That these metaphors may be not dead but only sleeping, or that they may arise from the grave and walk in our sentences, is something that has troubled everyone who has ever tried to write plain expository prose."

Dead metaphors are most likely to haunt us when they are embodied in clichés. Since we use clichés without attention to what they literally say or point to, we are unlikely to be aware of the dead metaphors buried in them. But when we attach one cliché to another, we may raise

"*You're right as rain. It's the dawn of history, and there are no clichés as yet. I'll drink to that.*"

©The New Yorker Collection 1972. J. B. Handelsman from cartoonbank.com. All Rights Reserved.

the metaphors from the grave. The result is likely to be a **mixed metaphor**; the effect is almost always absurd.

Water seeks its own level whichever way you want to slice it.

Traditional liberal education has run out of gas and educational soup kitchens are moving into the vacuum.

The low ebb has been reached and hopefully it's turned the corner.

Her energy, drained through a stream of red tape, led only to closed doors.

As comedian Joe E. Lewis observed, "Show me a man who builds castles in the air and I'll show you a crazy architect."

Fresh metaphors, on the other hand, imaginatively combine accurate observations. They are not prefabricated ideas; they are a means of discovering or inventing new ideas. They enlarge thought and enliven prose. Here are two examples from students' journals:

> I have some sort of sporadic restlessness in me, like the pen on a polygraph machine. It moves along in curves, then suddenly shoots up, blowing a bubble in my throat, making my chest taut, forcing me to move around. It becomes almost unbearable and then suddenly it will plunge, leaving something that feels like a smooth orange wave.

> Time is like wrapping papers. It wraps memories, decorates them with sentiment. No matter (almost) what's inside, it's remembered as a beautiful piece of past time. That's why I even miss my high school years, which were filled with tiredness, boredom, confusion.

And here is a passage from an essay in which a student analyzes the style of a story he found boring:

> Every sentence yawns, stretches, shifts from side to side, and then quietly dozes off.

Experiment with metaphors, let them surface in the early drafts of your essays and in your journals, and by all means, introduce original and accurate comparisons in your essays. But leave the mixed metaphors to politicians and comedians.

## Euphemisms

**Euphemisms** are words substituted for other words thought to be offensive. In deodorant advertisements there are no *armpits*, only *underarms*, which may *perspire*, but not *sweat*, and even then they don't *smell*. A parent reading a report card is likely to learn not that his child got an F in conduct but that she "experiences difficulty exercising self-control: (a) verbally; (b) physically." And where do old people go? To Sun City, "a retirement community for senior citizens."

We do not advise you to write or speak discourteously; we do advise you, though, to use euphemisms sparingly, when tact recommends them. It's customary in a condolence letter to avoid the word *death*, and, depending both on your own feelings and those of the bereaved, you may wish to follow that custom. But there's no reason on earth to write "Hamlet passes on." You should be aware, moreover, that some people find euphemisms themselves offensive. Margaret Kuhn, for instance, argues that the word *old* is preferable to *senior*. "Old," she says "is the right word. . . . I think we should wear our gray hair, wrinkles, and crumbling joints as badges of distinction. After all, we worked damn hard to get them."

### A RULE FOR WRITERS

When revising, replace needless euphemisms with plain words.

## Passive or Active Voice?

Verbs appear in either the active or passive voice. In the active voice, the subject acts on the object: "I wrote the review." ("I" is the subject.) In the passive voice, the subject receives the action: "The review was written by me." (Here, "the review" is the subject.) In general, prefer the active voice. The passive voice is often vague and sentences using it are needlessly wordy.

Consider the following passage, the opening paragraph of an analytic essay on the classical aspects of a library at a women's college:

> A person walking by Margaret Clapp Library
> (1908-1913) is struck by its classical design.
> The symmetry of the façade is established by the
> regularly spaced columns of the Ionic order on the
> first story of the building and by pilasters on
> the second level. In the center of the lower tier
> are two bronze doors: On the left door a relief
> is seen, depicting Sapientia (Wisdom), and on the
> right is seen the image of Caritas (Charity).
> The Greco-Roman tradition is furthered by the
> two bronze statues on either side of the entrance.
> On the left is Vesta (goddess of the hearth) and
> on the right Minerva (goddess of wisdom). Through
> the use of classical architecture and Greco-Roman
> images, an image is conveyed—one which Wellesley
> College hopes to create in its women.

Although the paragraph is richly informative, it is sluggish, chiefly because the writer keeps using the passive voice: "A person . . . is struck by"; "symmetry is established by"; "a relief is seen"; "on the right is seen"; "tradition is furthered by"; "an image is conveyed."

Converting some or all of these expressions into the active voice greatly improves the passage:

> The most striking feature of the Margaret
> Clapp Library is its classical design. Regularly
> spaced columns of the Ionic order on the first
> story, and pilasters on the second, establish the
> symmetry of the façade. In the center of the lower
> tier are two bronze doors: On the left door a re-
> lief depicts Sapientia (Wisdom), and on the right
> Caritas (Charity). A bronze statue on each side of
> the entrance (Vesta, goddess of the hearth, on the
> left, and Minerva, goddess of wisdom, on the right)
> furthers the Greco-Roman tradition. Wellesley
> College hopes, through the use of classical archi-
> tecture and Greco-Roman sculpture, to inspire in
> its students particular ideals.

There are, however, times when the passive is appropriate:

- When the doer is obvious ("Bush was elected president in 2000 and 2004.")
- When the doer is unknown ("The picture was stolen between midnight and 1 A.M.")
- When the doer is unimportant ("The medication always should be kept in the refrigerator.")

## A RULE FOR WRITERS

When revising, consider each sentence in which you have used the passive voice. If the passive suits your meaning, retain it; if it obscures your meaning, change it. More often than not, the passive voice obscures meaning.

### Passive Voice

The revolver given Daru by the gendarme *is left* in the desk drawer. [Left by whom? The passive voice here obscures the point.]

### Active Voice

Daru leaves the gendarme's revolver in the desk drawer.

### Passive Voice

Daru serves tea and the Arab *is offered* some. [Confusing shift from the active voice "serves" to the passive voice "is offered."]

### Active Voice

Daru serves tea and *offers* the Arab some.

Finally, avoid what has been called the Academic Passive: "In this essay it has been argued that . . ." This cumbersome form used to be common in academic writing (to convey scientific objectivity) but "I have argued" is usually preferable to such stuffiness.

## The Writer's "I"

It is seldom necessary in writing an essay (even on a personal experience) to repeat "I think that" or "in my opinion." Your reader knows that what you write is your opinion. Nor is it necessary, if you've done your job well, to apologize. "After reading the story over several times I'm not really sure what it is about, but . . ." Write about something you are reasonably sure of. Occasionally, though, when there is a real problem in the text—for example, the probable date of the Book of Ruth—it is not only permissible to disclose doubts and to reveal tentative conclusions, it may be necessary to do so.

Note also that there is no reason to avoid the pronoun *I* when you are in fact writing about yourself. Attempts to avoid *I* ("this writer," "we," expressions in the passive voice such as "it has been said above" and "it was seen") are noticeably awkward and distracting. And sometimes you may want to focus on your subjective response to a topic in order to clarify a point. The following opening paragraph of a movie review provides an example:

> I take the chance of writing about Bergman's *Persona* so long after its showing because this seems to me a movie there's no hurry about. It will be with us a long time, just as it has been on my mind for a long time. Right now, when I am perhaps still under its spell, it seems to me Bergman's masterpiece, but I can't imagine ever thinking it less than one of the great movies. This of course is opinion; what I know for certain is that *Persona* is also one of the most difficult movies I will ever see; and I am afraid that in this case there is a direct connection between difficulty and value. It isn't only that *Persona* is no harder than it has to be;

its peculiar haunting power, its spell, and its value come directly from the fact that it's so hard to get a firm grasp on.

—*Robert Garis*

Students who have been taught not to begin sentences with *I* often produce sentences that are eerily passive even when the verbs are in the active voice. For example:

> Two reasons are important to my active participation in dance.

> An eager curiosity overcame my previous feeling of fear to make me feel better.

But doesn't it make more sense to say:

> I dance for two reasons.

> I enrolled in the Health Careers Summer Program.

> My curiosity aroused, I was no longer afraid.

For more on the use of "I" in academic writing, see pages 99–101.

### A RULE FOR WRITERS
Make the agent of the action the subject of the sentence.

# Clarity and Coherence

Writing a coherent essay is hard work; it requires mastery of a subject and skill in presenting it; it always takes a lot of time. Writing a coherent paragraph often takes more fussing and patching than you expect, but once you have the hang of using transition and repetition to link ideas and sentences together, the work can be relatively straightforward. Writing a coherent sentence requires only that you stay awake until you get to the end of it.

We all do nod off sometimes, even over our own prose. But if you make it a practice to read over your work several times, at least once aloud, you give yourself a chance to spot the incoherent sentence before your reader does, and to revise it. When you see—or hear—that a sentence is incoherent, it's usually easy to recast it.

## Cats Are Dogs

Looking at a picture of a woman, a man once said to the painter Henri Matisse, "That woman's arm is too long." "That's not a woman," Matisse replied, "it's a painting."

In some sentences a form of the verb *to be* mistakenly asserts that one thing is in a class with another. Is a picture a woman? Are cats dogs? Students did write the following sentences:

**Incoherent**

X. J. Kennedy's poem "Nothing in Heaven Functions as It Ought" is a contrast between Heaven and Hell.

As soon as you ask yourself the question "Is a poem a contrast?" you have, by bringing the two words close together, isolated the problem. A poem may be a sonnet, an epic, an ode—but not a contrast. The writer was trying to say what the poem does, not what it is.

**Coherent**

X. J. Kennedy's poem "Nothing in Heaven Functions as It Ought" contrasts Heaven and Hell.

**Incoherent**

Besides, he tells himself, a matchmaker is an old Jewish custom. [Is a matchmaker a custom?]

**Coherent**

Besides, he tells himself, consulting a matchmaker is an old Jewish custom.

**Incoherent**

He demonstrates many human frailties, such as the influence of others' opinions upon one's actions. [Is influence a frailty? How might this sentence be revised?]

## Items in a Series

If you were given a shopping list that mentioned apples, fruit, and pears, you would be puzzled and possibly irritated by the inclusion of "fruit." Don't puzzle or irritate your reader with a **false series** of this sort. Analyze sentences containing items in a series to be sure that the items are of the same order of generality. For example:

**False Series**

His job exposed him to the "dirty work" of the British and to the evils of imperialism. ["The 'dirty work' of the British" is a *specific* example of the more *general* "evils of imperialism." The false series makes the sentence incoherent.]

**Revised**

His job, by exposing him to the "dirty work" of the British, brought him to understand the evils of imperialism.

In the following sentence, which item in the series makes the sentence incoherent?

Why should one man, no matter how important, be exempt from investigation, arrest, trial, and law-enforcing tactics?

## Modifiers

A modifier should appear close to the word it modifies (that is, describes or qualifies). Three kinds of faulty modifiers are common: misplaced, squinting, and dangling.

### Misplaced Modifiers

A modifier that seems to modify the wrong word is called a **misplaced modifier**. Such faulty connections are often unintentionally funny. The judo parlor that advertised "For $20 learn basic methods of protecting yourself from an experienced instructor" probably attracted more amused readers than paying customers.

**Misplaced**

The biologist fabricated data under pressure. [The data wasn't under pressure, the biologist was.]

**Revised**

The biologist, under pressure, fabricated data.

**Misplaced**

The construction decision was based on steel's relative cost to aluminum. [The aluminum didn't cost the steel anything.]

**Revised**

The construction decision was based on the relative costs of steel and aluminum.

Sometimes other parts of sentences are misplaced:

**Misplaced**

We learn from the examples of our parents who we are. [The sentence appears to say we are our parents.]

**Revised**

We learn who we are from the examples of our parents.

**Misplaced**

It is up to the students to revise the scheme, not the administrators. [We all know you can't revise administrators. Revise the sentence.]

### Squinting Modifiers

If a modifier is ambiguous—that is, if it can be applied equally to more than one term—it is sometimes called a **squinting modifier**: It seems to look forward as well as backward.

**Squinting**

Being with Jennifer more and more enrages me. [Is the writer spending more time with Jennifer, or is the writer more enraged? Probably more enraged.]

**Revised**

Being with Jennifer enrages me more and more.

**Squinting**

Writing clearly is difficult. [Is this sentence about "writing" or about "writing clearly"?]

**Revised**

It is clearly difficult to write.
It is difficult to write clearly.

**Squinting**

Students only may use this elevator. [Does "only" modify students? If so, no one else may use the elevator. Or does it modify elevator? If so, students may use no other elevator.]

**Revised**

Only students may use this elevator.
Students may use only this elevator.

**Note:** The word *only* often squints, seeming to look in two directions. In general, put *only* immediately before the word or phrase it modifies. Often it appears too early in the sentence. (See "Using the Right Word," Chapter 12, p. 285.)

### Dangling Modifiers

If a modifier refers to a term that appears nowhere in the sentence, you have what is called a **dangling modifier**.

**Dangling**

Being small, his ear scraped against the belt when his father stumbled. [The writer meant that the boy was small, not the ear. But the boy is not in the sentence.]

**Revised**

Because the boy was small, his ear scraped against the belt when his father stumbled.
Being small, the boy scraped his ear against the belt when his father stumbled.

**Dangling**

A meticulously organized person, his suitcase could be tucked under an airplane seat. [How would you revise the sentence?]

---

**A RULE FOR WRITERS**

When you revise sentences, put together what belongs together.

---

## Reference of Pronouns

A pronoun is used in place of a noun. Because the noun usually precedes the pronoun, the noun to which the pronoun refers is called the *antecedent* (Latin: "going before"). For example:

antecedent          pronoun

When *Sheriff Johnson* was on a horse, *he* was a big man.

But the pronoun can also precede the noun:

pronoun                              noun
When *he* was on a horse, *Sheriff Johnson* was a big man.

The word *antecedent* can be used here too. In short, the antecedent is the word or group of words referred to by a pronoun.

**Whenever possible, make sure that a pronoun has a clear reference.** Sometimes it isn't possible: *It* is commonly used with an unspecified reference, as in "It's hot today," and "Hurry up please, it's time"; and there can be no reference for interrogative pronouns: "What's bothering you?" and "Who's on first?" But otherwise, always be sure that you've made clear what noun the pronoun is standing for.

### Vague Reference of Pronouns

**Vague**

Apparently, they fight physically and it can become rather brutal. ["It" doubtless refers to "fight," but "fight" in this sentence is the verb, not an antecedent noun.]

**Clear**

Their fights are apparently physical, and sometimes brutal.

**Vague**

I was born in Colón, the second largest city in the Republic of Panama. Despite this, Colón is still an undeveloped town. ["This" has no specific antecedent. It appears to refer to the writer's having been born in Colón.] For more on *this*, see "Using the Right Word," Chapter 12, p. 290.

**Clear**

Although Colón, where I was born, is the second largest city in Panama, it remains undeveloped.

### Shift in Pronouns

This common error is easily corrected.

In many instances the child was expected to follow the profession of your father. [Expected to follow the profession of whose father, "yours" or "his"?]

Having a tutor, you can get constant personal encouragement and advice that will help me budget my time. [If "you" have a tutor, will that help "me"?]

### Ambiguous Reference of Pronouns

A pronoun normally refers to the first appropriate noun or pronoun preceding it. Same-sex pronouns and nouns, like dogs, often get into scraps.

**Ambiguous**

Her mother died when she was eighteen. [Who was eighteen, the mother or the daughter?]

**Clear**

Her mother died when Mabel was eighteen.

Her mother died at the age of eighteen. [Note the absence of ambiguity in "His mother died when he was eighteen."]

**Ambiguous**

Caroline learned that she must follow her boss's advice against her better judgment. [Is the boss advising Caroline against using her better judgment? Or is it against Caroline's better judgment to listen to her boss's advice.]

**Clear**

Caroline learned that she must, against her better judgment, follow her boss's advice.

## Agreement

### Noun and Pronoun

Everyone knows that a singular noun requires a singular pronoun, and a plural noun requires a plural pronoun, but writers sometimes slip.

**Faulty**

singular                                              plural
A *dog* can easily tell if people are afraid of *them*.

**Correct**

singular                                              singular
A *dog* can easily tell if people are afraid of *it*.

**Faulty**

   singular                                           plural
*Every student* feels that Wellesley expects *them* to do their best.

**Correct**

   singular                                           singular
*Every student* feels that Wellesley expects *her* to do her best.

*Each, everybody, nobody, no one*, and *none* are especially troublesome. See the entries on these words in "Using the Right Word," Chapter 12.

### Subject and Verb

A singular subject requires a singular verb, a plural subject a plural verb.

**Faulty**

> **plural**                                          **singular**
> *Horror films* bring to light a subconscious fear and *shows* a character who succeeds in coping with it.

**Correct**

> **plural**                                          **plural**
> *Horror films* bring to light a subconscious fear and *show* a character who succeeds in coping with it.

The student who wrote "shows" instead of "show" thought that the subject of the verb was "fear," but the subject really is "Horror films," a plural.

**Faulty**

> The manager, as well as the pitcher and the catcher, were fined.

**Correct**

> The manager, as well as the pitcher and the catcher, was fined.

If the sentence had been "The manager and the pitcher . . .," the subject would have been plural and the required verb would be *were:*

> The manager and the pitcher were fined.

But in the sentence as it was given, "as well as" (like *in addition to, with,* and *together with*) does *not* add a subject to a subject and thereby make a plural subject. "As well as" merely indicates that what is said about the manager applies to the pitcher and the catcher.

### Three Additional Points

1. **A collective noun**—that is, a noun that is singular in form but that denotes a collection of individuals, such as *mob, audience, jury—* normally takes a *singular* verb:

**Correct**

> The mob is at the gate.

**Correct**

> An audience of children is easily bored. [The subject is "an audience," not "children."]

**Correct**

The jury is seated.

But when the emphasis is on the individuals within the group—for instance, when you are calling attention to a division within the group—you can use a plural verb:

The jury disagree.

Still, because this sounds a bit odd, it is probably better to recast the sentence:

The jurors disagree.

2. **Sometimes a sentence that is grammatically correct may nevertheless sound awkward:**

One of its most noticeable features is the lounges.

Because the subject is "one"—*not* "features"—the verb must be singular, "is," but "is" sounds odd when it precedes the plural "lounges." The solution: **Revise the sentence**.

Among the most noticeable features are the lounges.

3. **When a singular and a plural subject are joined by *or*, *either . . . or*, or *neither . . . nor*, use a verb that agrees in number with the subject closest to the verb**.

**Correct**

*Either* the teacher *or the students are* mistaken.

**Correct**

*Either* the students *or the teacher is* mistaken.

The first version uses "are" because the verb is nearer to "students" (plural) than to "teacher" (singular); the second uses "is" because the verb is nearer to "teacher" than to "students."

## Repetition and Variation

Sometimes repetition can help clarify or emphasize a point; sometimes repetition is simply unnecessary and dull. Here are five general rules on the subject.

1. **Don't be afraid to repeat a word if it is the best word**. The following paragraph repeats "joyful," "book," "moments," and "in its"; notice also "joyful" and "joy." Repetition, a device necessary for continuity and clarity, holds the paragraph together.

*The Brothers Karamazov* is a joyful book. Readers who know what it is about may find this an intolerably whimsical statement. It does have moments of joy, but they are only moments; the rest is greed, lust, squalor, unredeemed suffering, and sometimes terrifying darkness. But the book is joyful in another sense: in its energy and curiosity, in its formal inventiveness, in the mastery of its writing. And therefore, finally, in its vision.

—Richard Pevear

2. **Use pronouns, when their reference is clear, as substitutes for nouns**. Notice Pevear's use of pronouns; notice also that in the second and third sentences, he substitutes "it" for "book," and then uses "the book" again in the fourth sentence. Substitutions that neither confuse nor distract keep a paragraph from becoming dull.

3. **Do not, however, confuse the substitutions we have just spoken of with the fault called Elegant Variation**. A groundless fear of repetition sometimes leads students to write first, for example, of "Shakespeare" then of "the writer," then of "our author," then of "the playwright," and then of "the Bard of Avon." Such variations strike the reader as silly. They can, moreover, be confusing because they can suggest that the student is referring to different writers.

4. **Don't repeat a word if it is being used in two different senses**.

**Confusing**

My theme focuses on the theme of the book. [The first "theme" means "essay"; the second means "underlying idea" or "motif."]

**Clear**

My essay focuses on the theme of the book.

**Confusing**

Caesar's character is complex. The comic characters, however, are simple. [The first "character" means "personality"; the second means "persons" or "figures in the play."]

**Clear**

Caesar is complex; the comic characters, however, are simple.

5. **Eliminate words repeated unnecessarily**. The use of words like *surely, in all probability, it is noteworthy* may become habitual. If they don't help the reader to follow your thoughts, they are Instant Prose Additives. Cross them out.

### A RULE FOR WRITERS

When you revise, test sentences and paragraphs for both sound and sense to decide if a word should be repeated, varied, or eliminated.

# Clarity and Sentence Structure: Parallelism

Use parallels to clarify relationships. Few of us are likely to compose such deathless parallels as "I came, I saw, I conquered," or "of the people, by the people, for the people," but we can see to it that coordinate expressions correspond in their grammatical form. Consider the following sentence and the revisions:

### Awkward

He liked drawing and to paint.

### Parallel

He liked to draw and to paint.
He liked drawing and painting.

In the first version, "drawing" (a gerund) and "to paint" (an infinitive) are not grammatically parallel. The difference in grammatical form blurs the writer's point that there is a similarity between the two activities; the resulting sentence is fuzzy and awkward.

In the following examples, the parallel construction is italicized.

### Awkward

The dormitory rules needed revision, a common area was a necessity, and a generally more active role for the school in social affairs were all significant to her.

### Parallel

She recommended that the school *revise* its dormitory rules, *provide* a common area, and *organize* more social activities.

### Awkward

Many Chinese parents disapprove of interracial dating or they just do not permit it.

### Parallel

Many Chinese parents *disapprove* of interracial dating, and some *forbid* it.

In parallel constructions, be sure to check the consistency of articles, prepositions, and conjunctions. For example:

**Awkward**

He wrote papers on a play by Shakespeare, a novel of Dickens, and a short story by Oates.

**Parallel**

He wrote papers on a play by Shakespeare, a novel by Dickens, and a short story by Oates.

The shift from "by" to "of" and back to "by" serves no purpose and is merely distracting.

To sum up:

A pupil once asked Arthur Schnabel (the noted pianist) whether it was better to play in time or to play as one feels; his characteristic mordant reply was another question: "Why not feel in time?"

—David Hamilton

### CHECKLIST for Revising for Clarity

☐ Is word choice precise and specific? While writing the draft, did you feel that a particular word was close to what you meant, but not quite right? If so, replace that word with the *right* word. (See pp. 72–74.)

☐ Do you offer specific examples where necessary? (See pp. 76–78.)

☐ Are technical terms used appropriately and helpfully? Can any jargon be replaced with plain English? (See pp. 79–80.)

☐ Does your prose include any dead or mixed metaphors, or clichés? (See pp. 80–83.)

☐ Have you put together what belongs together? Do modifiers appear close to, and refer clearly to, the words they modify? (See pp. 89–91.)

☐ Have you eliminated sexist language? Have you replaced such words as "mankind" with gender-neutral terms, and eliminated the generic "he," "him," and "his"? (See pp. 74–75.)

☐ Have you replaced passive verbs with active verbs where appropriate? (See pp. 84–86.)

☐ Do pronouns have clear references, and do they agree in number with the nouns to which they refer? (See pp. 91–93.)

☐ Does the structure of your sentence reflect the structure of your thought? Are parallel ideas in parallel constructions? (See pp. 97–98.)

# CHAPTER 6

# Writing with Style

The friends that have it I do wrong
When ever I remake a song,
Should know what issue is at stake:
It is myself that I remake.

—William Butler Yeats

## Academic Styles, Academic Audiences

When you write an essay for a course, you are learning how people working in that academic discipline express themselves. To communicate with other people in the discipline, you must adapt your voice to the conventions of the discipline and to the audience's expectations about writing within that discipline. Some disciplines (literature, for example) frown on passive verbs. But in lab reports in the sciences, passive verbs are often acceptable, in part because they help focus the reader's attention on the experiment ("the vaccine was tested") rather than on the person who conducted it ("a technician tested the vaccine") and thereby help to establish authority.

To make matters even more complicated, the conventions are changing, and they vary to some degree from class to class, and instructor to instructor. For example, one literature instructor might accept an essay containing the word "we" (as in "we see here the author's fascination with landscape"); another might object to its use, arguing that the "we" falsely implies that all readers—regardless of race, class, gender, and so on—read all texts in the same way.

These differences frustrate some students. To these students, writing an essay becomes a game of figuring out What the Instructor Wants. (For what it's worth, such students can frustrate instructors a bit too.)

It may help both students and instructors to keep in mind that there isn't one *right* style—and that the differences among styles are a matter of disciplinary convention and (to some degree) theoretical approach, not arbitrary and inscrutable personal taste.

It is impossible to list here all the different conventions you'll encounter in college. You don't need to learn them all anyway. You simply need to be alert to the ways in which people talk to each other in the disciplines within which you're writing, and do your best to follow the conventions you observe. We illustrate a few of these differences below.

Here is the first paragraph of an article from an issue of the *Cambridge Journal of Economics:*

> In this paper I shall develop a framework which may be used to examine several alternative theories of the rate of interest. The four most widely accepted approaches are the Neoclassical Loanable Funds, Keynes's Liquidity Preference, Neoclassical Synthesis ISLM, and Basil Moore's Horizontalist (or endogenous money). I will use the framework developed here to present a fifth: an integration of liquidity preference theory with an endogenous money approach. I first briefly set forth the primary alternative approaches, then develop an analytical framework based on an asset or stock approach and use it to discuss several theories of the interest rate: those advanced by Keynes, by Moore, by neoclassical theory and the monetarists, by Kregel, and by Tobin. Finally, I shall use the framework to reconcile liquidity preference theory with an endogenous money approach.
>
> —L. Randall Wray

Note the use of the pronoun "I," the direct statement of what the writer will do ("In this paper I shall develop a framework . . ."), and the listing of the steps of his procedure ("I first briefly set forth," and so on). A literary critic would be unlikely to present his or her ideas so methodically, as the next example suggests.

Here is the first paragraph of a chapter from a study of Bram Stoker's *Dracula,* in which a literary critic analyzes the novel in its social and political context.

> "In obedience to the law as it then stood, he was buried in the centre of a *quadrivium,* or conflux of four roads (in this case four streets), with a stake driven through his heart. And over him drives for ever the uproar of unresting London!" No, not *Dracula*

(1897), but the closing lines of a much earlier nineteenth-century work, Thomas De Quincey's bleakly ironic essay "On Murder Considered as One of the Fine Arts" (1854). De Quincey is describing how in 1812 the London populace dealt with the body of one of its prize exhibits, a particularly grisly serial killer who had escaped the gallows by hanging himself in his cell in the dead of night. Yet it is difficult for us to read this gleefully chilling passage today without thinking of Bram Stoker's classic vampire novel. The quirky Christian symbolism, the mandatory staking down of the monster to keep it from roaming abroad, the sense of busily self-absorbed London unaware of its proximity to a murderous presence that haunts its most densely populated byways: together these features seem virtually to define a basic iconography for the vampire Gothic as it achieved canonical status in *Dracula*.

—David Glover

Note the absence of the pronoun "I" and the presence of the pronoun "we." Note also the playfulness of the style (the reference to a "gleefully chilling passage" and the "staking down of the monster"), the specificity of the language, and the variety in punctuation and sentence structure.

Here is the opening paragraph of a chemistry student's study of the enzyme calf alkaline phosphatase.

> Enzymes, protein molecules that catalyze reactions, are crucial for many biochemical reactions. This research project studies the actions of the enzyme calf alkaline phosphatase on the substrate p-nitrophenyl phosphate. The focus of this research project is the relation of alkaline phosphatase denaturation to temperature. Heat denaturation has been well documented in major biology and chemistry texts, but few textbooks mention how extreme cold affects enzyme structure and function. This study will examine how alkaline phosphatase responds to both high and low temperatures.
>
> —Hilary Suzawa

Note the absence of personal pronouns (the "*research project* studies"), the orderly and careful presentation of information (including the brief definition of the word "enzymes" in the first sentence), and the clear statement of purpose. (You might compare this writer's first sentence with Glover's—deliberately misleading—opening.)

# Defining Style

As we have suggested, style in academic writing is partly a matter of disciplinary conventions. But style also reflects the individual writer's mind, his or her values and sensibility. Style is not simply a flower here and some gilding there; it pervades the whole work. Van Gogh's style, or Walt Disney's, let us say, consists in part of features recurring throughout a single work and from one work to the next: angular or curved lines, hard or soft edges, strong or gentle contrasts, and so on. Pictures of a seated woman by Van Gogh and by Disney are utterly different, and if we have seen a few works by each, we can readily identify who did which one. Artists leave their fingerprints, so to speak, all over their work. Writers leave their voiceprints.

Although the word *style* comes from the Latin *stilus* and originally referred to a Roman writing instrument, even in Roman times *stilus* had acquired a figurative sense, referring not only to the instrument but also to the writer's choice of words and arrangement of words into sentences. But is it simply the choice and arrangement of words we comment on when we speak of a writer's style, or are we also commenting on the writer's mind? Don't we feel that a piece of writing, whether it's on Civil War photographs or on genetics and intelligence, is also about the writer? The writing, after all, sets forth the writer's views of a chosen topic. It sets forth perceptions and responses to something the writer has thought about. The writer has, from the start, from the choice of a topic, revealed that he or she found it worth thinking about. The essay, in attempting to persuade us to think as the writer does, reveals not only how and what the writer thinks, but also what he or she values. As E. B. White has noted, "No writer long remains incognito."

When we write about things "out there," our writing always reveals the form and likeness of our minds, just as every work of art reveals the creator as well as the ostensible subject. A portrait painting, for example, is not only about the sitter, it is also about the artist's perceptions of the sitter; hence the saying that every portrait is a self-portrait. Even photographs are as much about the photographer as they are about the subject. Richard Avedon said of his portraits of famous people, "They are all pictures of me, of the way I feel about the people I photograph." A student's essay similarly, if it is written truly, is not exclusively about "*La Causa* and the New Chicana"; it is also about the perceptions and responses of the writer to both racism and sexism.

# Style and Tone

Suppose we take a page of handwriting, or even a signature. We need not believe that graphology is an exact science to believe that the shape of the ink-lines on paper (apart from the meaning of the words) often tells us something about the writer. We look at a large, ornate signature, and we sense that the writer is confident; we look at a tiny signature written with the finest of pens, and we wonder why anyone is so self-effacing.

More surely than handwriting, the writer's style reveals an attitude toward the self, toward the reader, and toward the subject. The writer's attitudes are reflected in what is usually called *tone*. It is difficult to separate style from tone but we can try. Most discussions of style concentrate on what might be thought of as ornament: figurative language ("a sea of troubles"), inversion ("A leader he is not"), repetition and parallelism ("government of the people, by the people, for the people"), balance and antithesis ("It was the best of times, it was the worst of times"). Indeed, for centuries style has been called "the dress of thought," implying that the thought is something separate from the expression; the thought, in this view, is dressed up in stylistic devices. But in most of the writing that we read with interest and pleasure, the stylistic devices are not ornamental but integral. When we talk about wit, sincerity, tentativeness, self-assurance, aggressiveness, objectivity, and so forth—and certainly when we talk about clarity—we can say we are talking about style, but we should recognize that style now is not a matter of ornamental devices that dress up some idea, but part of the idea itself. And "the idea itself" includes the writer's unified yet appropriately varied tone of voice.

To take a brief example: The famous English translation of Caesar's report of a victory,

> I came, I saw, I conquered,

might be paraphrased thus:

> After getting to the scene of the battle, I studied the situation.
> Then I devised a strategy that won the battle.

But this paraphrase loses much of Caesar's message; the brevity and the parallelism of the famous version, as well as the alliteration (*came, conquered*), convey tight-lipped self-assurance—convey, that is, the tone that reveals Caesar to us. And this tone is a large part of Caesar's message. Caesar is really telling us not only about what he did but also about what sort of person he is. He is perceptive, decisive, and effective.

actions, Caesar in effect tells us, are (for a man like Caesar)
⸜ne Latin original is even more tight-lipped and more unified by
⸜eration: *veni, vidi, vici.*)

Let's look now at a longer example, the opening sentence of Lewis
Thomas's essay "On Natural Death":

> There are so many new books about dying that there are now
> special shelves set aside for them in bookstores, along with the
> health, diet and home-repair paperbacks and the sex manuals.

This sentence could have ended where the comma is placed: The words
after "bookstores" are, it might seem, not important. One can scarcely
argue that by specifying some kinds of "special shelves" Thomas clarifies
an otherwise difficult or obscure concept. What, then, do these additional words do? They tell us nothing about death and almost nothing
about bookshops, but they tell us a great deal about Thomas's *attitude*
toward the new books on death. He suggests that such books are faddish
and perhaps (like "the sex manuals") vulgar. After all, if he had merely
wanted to call up a fairly concrete image of a well-stocked bookstore, he
could have said "along with books on politics and the environment," or
some such thing. His next sentence runs:

> Some of them are so packed with detailed information and step-by-
> step instructions for performing the function that you'd think this
> was a new sort of skill which all of us are now required to learn.

Why "you'd think" instead of, say, "one might believe"? Thomas uses
a colloquial form, and a very simple verb, because he wants to convey to us his commonsense, homely, down-to-earth view that these
books are a bit pretentious—a pretentiousness conveyed in his use of
the words "performing the function," words that might come from
the books themselves. In short, when we read Thomas's paragraph we
are learning as much about Thomas as we are about books on dying.
We are hearing a voice, perceiving an attitude, and we want to keep
reading, not only because we are interested in death but also because
Thomas has managed to make us interested in Thomas, a thoughtful
but unpretentious fellow.

Now listen to a short paragraph from John Szarkowski's *Looking at
Photographs*. Szarkowski is writing about one of Alexander Gardner's
photographs of a dead Confederate sharpshooter.

> Among the pictures that Gardner made himself is the one re-
> produced here. Like many Civil War photographs, it showed that

Alexander Gardner, *The Home of a Rebel Sharpshooter, Gettysburg*

the dead of both sides looked very much the same. The pictures of earlier wars had not made this clear.

Try, in a word or two, to characterize the tone (the attitude, as we sense it in the inflection of the voice) of the first sentence. Next, the tone of the second, and then of the third. Suppose the second and third sentences had been written thus:

> It showed that the dead of both sides looked very much the same. This is made clear in Civil War photographs, but not in pictures of earlier wars.

How has the tone changed? What word can you find to characterize the tone of the whole, as Szarkowski wrote it?

## Acquiring Style

In the preceding pages we said that your writing reveals not only where you stand (your thesis) and how you think (the organization of your ideas) but also who you are and how you take yourself (your tone). To follow our argument to its limit, we might say that everything in this book—including rules on the comma (the place in a sentence where you breathe)—is about style. We do. What more is there to say?

## Clarity and Texture

Let's look first at a distinction Aristotle makes between two parts of style: that which gives clarity and that which gives texture. Exact words, concrete illustrations of abstractions, conventional punctuation, and so forth—matters we treat in some detail in the chapters on revising and editing—make for clarity. On the whole, this part of style is inconspicuous when present; when absent, the effect ranges from mildly distracting to ruinous. Clarity is the foundation of style. It can be achieved by anyone willing to make the effort.

Among the things that give texture, or individuality, are effective repetition, variety in sentence structure, wordplay, and so forth. This second group of devices, on the whole more noticeable, makes the reader aware of the writer's particular voice. These devices can be learned too, but seldom by effort alone. In fact, playfulness helps here more than doggedness. Students who work at this part of style usually enjoy hanging around words. At the same time, they're likely to feel that when they put words on paper, even in a casual letter to a friend, they're putting themselves on the line. Serious, as most people are about games they really care about, but not solemn, they'll come to recognize the rules of play in John Holmes's advice to young poets: "You must believe that your feelings and your words for your feelings are important. . . . That they are unique is a fact; that you believe they are unique is necessary."

## Originality and Imitation

We conclude with a paradox: One starts to acquire an individual style by studying and imitating the style of others. The paradox isn't limited to writing. Stylists in all fields begin as apprentices. The young ball player imitates the movements of Dustin Pedroia, the chess player hangs around the park or club watching the old pros, then finds a book that probably recommends beginning with Ruy Lopez's opening. When Millet was young he copied works by Michelangelo; when Van Gogh was young he copied works by Millet. The would-be writer may be lucky enough to have a teacher, one he can imitate; more likely he will, in W. H. Auden's words, "serve his apprenticeship in the library."

# PART TWO
# College Writing

# Using Sources

One must be a wise reader to quote wisely and well.
—Amos Bronson Alcott

I quote others only in order the better to express myself.
—Michel de Montaigne

## What Is a Source?

Academic writers use sources to enlarge and refine their ideas. These sources can include facts, opinions, and the ideas of others, recorded in print or in bytes, and in the form of books, articles, lectures, reports, reviews, and interviews.

Although, in college you may sometimes be asked to write from your own experience or observation, most often you'll be asked to write from sources. Sources vary by discipline and are generally designated *primary* or *secondary*. In a twentieth-century literature course, primary sources might include poems, novels, and plays (these are the chief subjects of your writing). Secondary sources might include articles by literary critics *about* those works. Sources in a Civil War history course might include letters written by soldiers to their families at home (primary); they might also include contemporary newspaper accounts of battles and casualties (primary) as well as current writing on the period by historians (secondary). Social science students work with data gathered from experiments (primary) as well as theories developed by other researchers (secondary). (For more on primary and secondary sources, see pp. 192–93.)

What do academic writers do with these sources? In general, they analyze and make arguments about them. To do these things, they must be able to present, in their own writing, the words and ideas of others.

They must also be able to distinguish clearly between their own ~~words~~ and ideas, and others' words and ideas. They must be able to **summarize**, **paraphrase**, **quote**, and **acknowledge** sources.

In this chapter, we will offer advice on using sources accurately and efficiently; we will also provide information on **plagiarism**: what it is, and how to avoid it.

# Summarizing Sources

A **summary** sets out the key ideas of a text, and academic writers write them all the time. A summary will

- always be **shorter** than the original text;
- be written **in your own words** (if any distinctive words or brief phrases from the text are used, they must be enclosed in quotation marks);
- generally be written in the **present tense**.

A student analyzing a short story might present a brief summary of its plot to enable a reader who isn't familiar with the text, or who had not read it recently, to follow the discussion. A student making an argument about the causes of the Civil War would probably offer a summary of each of several main lines of thought about those causes before presenting his or her own position. The summaries in this case would provide useful background and help to demonstrate that the writer has something new to say. Students in the sciences write and read abstracts—very brief accounts of longer papers that present the results of substantial research projects. Those abstracts make it possible for later researchers to tell quickly if the earlier projects are relevant to their own work. Sometimes students write summaries because the act of summarizing can help them see if they really understand the text in question. And sometimes students write summaries simply because their instructors tell them to.

## *Writing a Summary*

Perhaps the first steps when it comes to writing a summary are to read carefully and to annotate the text—with a pen or electronically:

- Underline or highlight **key terms**: These terms will usually be repeated several times and will likely appear in the title and in the thesis statement.

**main points**: They often appear at the beginnings of

When you're preparing to write a summary, it can be
ful to encapsulate the main point of each paragraph
brief sentence.

on: Do not allow yourself to highlight or underline whole
paragraphs. Before you start to mark a paragraph, read it to the
end and then go back and mark what you now see as the key word,
phrase, or passage. If you simply start marking a paragraph from the
beginning, you may end up marking everything, and you will thus
defeat your purpose, which is to make highly visible the basic points
of the essay.

Let's take for example a brief essay on new media by Steven Pinker,
a Professor of Psychology at Harvard University. We've annotated the
essay to illustrate what you might do in preparation for writing a summary of it.

---

STEVEN PINKER

# Mind over Mass Media

*Published: June 10, 2010*

1    NEW forms of (media) have always caused          *Key term*
moral panics: the printing press, newspapers,
paperbacks and television were all once denounced
as threats to their consumers' brainpower and
moral fiber.

*Power-*    2    So too with (electronic technologies.)          *Key term*
*Point*
*and*            PowerPoint, we're told, is reducing discourse to
*Twitter*        bullet points. Search engines lower our intel-
*are said*       ligence, encouraging us to skim on the surface
*to lower*                                                        *Panic un-*
*brain*          of knowledge rather than dive to its depths.      *realistic:*
*power*          Twitter is shrinking our attention spans.         *TV and*
                                                                   *Video do*
         3    But such panics often fail basic reality          *not lower*
checks. When comic books were accused of              *IQ*

turning juveniles into delinquents in the 1950s, crime was falling to record lows, just as the denunciations of video games in the 1990s coincided with the great American crime decline. The decades of television, transistor radios and rock videos were also decades in which I.Q. scores rose continuously.

*Scientists use email. They are all successful; science is progressing*

4    For a reality check today, take the state of science, which demands high levels of brain-work and is measured by clear benchmarks of discovery. These days scientists are never far from their e-mail, rarely touch paper and cannot lecture without PowerPoint. If electronic media were hazardous to intelligence, the quality of science would be plummeting. Yet discoveries are multiplying like fruit flies, and progress is dizzying. Other activities in the life of the mind, like philosophy, history and cultural criticism, are likewise flourishing, as anyone who has lost a morning of work to the Web site Arts & Letters Daily can attest.

*Key term*

5    Critics of new media sometimes use science itself to press their case, citing research that shows how "experience can change the brain." But cognitive neuroscientists roll their eyes at such talk. Yes, every time we learn a fact or skill the wiring of the brain changes; it's not as if the information is stored in the pancreas. But the existence of neural plasticity does not mean the brain is a blob of clay pounded into shape by experience.

*New media do change brain wiring, but brain is not "blob of clay"*

*Central processes of brain not changed by experience*

6    Experience does not revamp the basic information-processing capacities of the brain. Speed-reading programs have long claimed to do

just that, but the verdict was rendered by Woody Allen after he read "War and Peace" in one sitting: "It was about Russia." Genuine multitasking, too, has been exposed as a myth, not just by laboratory studies but by the familiar sight of an S.U.V. undulating between lanes as the driver cuts deals on his cellphone.

*Training in one area does not help to another area.*  7

Moreover, as the psychologists Christopher Chabris and Daniel Simons show in their new book "The Invisible Gorilla: And Other Ways Our Intuitions Deceive Us," the effects of experience are highly specific to the experiences themselves. If you train people to do one thing (recognize shapes, solve math puzzles, find hidden words), they get better at doing that thing, but almost nothing else. Music doesn't make you better at math, conjugating Latin doesn't make you more logical, brain-training games don't make you smarter. Accomplished people don't bulk up their brains with intellectual calisthenics; they immerse themselves in their fields. Novelists read lots of novels, scientists read lots of science.

*New media don't make us dumb, we don't become what we consume*  8

The effects of consuming electronic media are also likely to be far more limited than the panic implies. Media critics write as if the brain takes on the qualities of whatever it consumes, the informational equivalent of "you are what you eat." As with primitive peoples who believe that eating fierce animals will make them fierce, they assume that watching quick cuts in rock videos turns your mental life into quick cuts or that reading bullet points and Twitter postings

turns your thoughts into bullet points and
Twitter postings.

9     <u>Yes, the constant arrival of information</u>
<u>packets can be distracting or addictive</u>, especially
to people with attention deficit disorder. But distraction is not a new phenomenon. <u>The solution</u>
<u>is not to bemoan(technology)but to develop strat-</u>
<u>egies of self-control</u>, as we do with every other
temptation in life. Turn off e-mail or Twitter
when you work, put away your Blackberry at dinner time, ask your spouse to call you to bed at a
designated hour.

*New me-*
*dia can be*
*distract-*
*ing, but*
*we can*
*just turn*
*them off*

*The*
*problem*
*isn't Power-*
*Point. We*
*simply need*
*to learn to*
*think—like*
*colleges and*
*universities.*

10     And to encourage intellectual depth, don't
rail at PowerPoint or Google. It's not as if <u>habits</u>
<u>of deep reflection</u>, <u>thorough research and rigor-</u>
<u>ous reasoning</u> ever came naturally to people.
They <u>must be acquired in special institutions,</u>
<u>which we call universities, and maintained with</u>
<u>constant upkeep, which we call analysis, criti-</u>
<u>cism and debate</u>. They are not granted by prop-
ping a heavy encyclopedia on your lap, nor are
they taken away by efficient access to information on the Internet.

11     The new media have caught on for a
reason. Knowledge is increasing exponentially;
human brainpower and waking hours are not.
Fortunately, the Internet and information
technologies are helping us manage, search
and retrieve our collective intellectual output
at different scales, from Twitter and previews
to e-books and online encyclopedias. <u>Far from</u>
<u>making us stupid, these technologies are the</u>
<u>only things that will keep us smart.</u>

*It's not*
*just that*
*new*
*media do*
*not make*
*us stu-*
*pid—they*
*actually*
*help us.*

The key point of Pinker's essay could be summarized in a sentence:

> Some people believe that new media are diminishing our brainpower; the evidence suggests otherwise.

If a student were to use that summary in a formal summary assignment or in an essay, the point would need to be attributed to the source, Stephen Pinker. The convention is to name the author (both first and last name are given with the first reference; with subsequent references, only the last name is necessary) and the title of the essay and to provide some information about the source's authority on the topic. In this case, Pinker's job title will do:

> In his essay, "Mind over Mass Media," Harvard psychology professor Stephen Pinker says that although some people believe that new media are diminishing our brainpower, evidence suggests otherwise.

To make this point without naming Pinker as its source would be to plagiarize: The idea does not come from the student's experience or observation, and so the source must be named, even though the language is the student's, not Pinker's.

But note that because the sentence is so lacking in detail, a reader would find it hard to evaluate Pinker's argument, and so a fuller summary would likely be more useful:

> In his essay "Mind over Mass Media," Harvard psychology professor Stephen Pinker argues that contrary to the common belief that new electronic media are "making us stupid," we actually need PowerPoint, Google, and email in order to manage the twenty-first century's flood of information and new knowledge. Pinker notes that in the past, people worried about negative moral and intellectual effects of things we now take for granted (the printing press and newspapers), and he presents evidence from neuroscientists that our brains, while "plastic," are too strong to be rewired by the content of our computer screens. He acknowledges that electronic devices can be

distracting, but says that the solution is self-control: We can always turn them off.

A longer summary might include additional information about Pinker's evidence: A writer might note that he cites a source, the book by Chabris and Simons, to support his claim about the brain's resilience, and that he points out that the concept of "you are what you eat" doesn't apply when we're talking about the mind.

What is the right length for a summary? There's no hard-and-fast rule. One way to decide is to imagine how much information your reader needs given the *purpose* of the summary. Another is simply to consult the instructor who asked you to write it.

---

**A RULE FOR WRITERS**

Pay special attention to **conciseness** when writing summaries.

Write this:

> In "Mind over Mass Media," Harvard psychologist Stephen Pinker argues that . . .

Don't write this:

> In "Mind over Mass Media," an essay by Stephen Pinker, a psychologist at Harvard University, Pinker says . . .

Or this:

> Stephen Pinker, who teaches psychology at Harvard, wrote an article named "Mind over Mass Media" in which he says . . .

---

# Paraphrasing Sources

Briefly, a paraphrase has two key features:

- It is as long as the original, and usually longer.
- It is generally designed to help a reader—or writer—understand a difficult or complicated text.

Like a summary, a **paraphrase** is written **in your own words**. Unlike a summary, which is always shorter than the original, a paraphrase can be as long—even longer. The word *paraphrase* comes from a Greek work meaning "to speak in addition, to amplify," and writers generally paraphrase to make a difficult text more clear, to themselves, or to their readers. A paraphrase is a restatement, a sort of translation, but into the same language.

Let's take, for example, the famous first sentence of Abraham Lincoln's 1863 Gettysburg Address:

> Four score and seven years ago our fathers brought forth on this continent a new nation, conceived in liberty and dedicated to the proposition that all men are created equal.

Here is a student's paraphrase:

```
        Eighty-seven years ago (that is, in 1776, the
year of the American Revolution) our ancestors in-
troduced to North America a new country; this coun-
try was brought into existence ("conceived") by the
male framers of the Constitution who saw liberty as
the mother of the new nation, and it was set apart
or specially marked ("dedicated") as a nation in
which all men are regarded as equal.
```

Note that the student has translated words that readers might misunderstand: "score," "conceived," "dedicated." Note also that the paraphrase is more than twice the length of the original, and that the paraphrase amplifies (literally, makes louder or stronger) the metaphor of fatherhood and birth that was buried in the original. Unlike a summary, which gives the gist of the original, a paraphrase presents all of the original but in different words.

## A RULE FOR WRITERS

In your own essays, do not paraphrase a source simply to avoid summarizing it or quoting it directly. If you merely restate a lucid source, changing words but in essence proceeding phrase by phrase, offering synonyms, you are **plagiarizing**, even if you begin saying something like "Jiménez has pointed out that . . ." Why is such material plagiarism? Because all of the ideas and all of the structure of the thought, as well as some of the words, are someone else's. True, by acknowledging Jiménez ("Jiménez has pointed out,") you are informing the reader that the ideas are not yours, but this acknowledgment does not tell the reader that you are using Jiménez's sentences, substituting some words. For additional information on plagiarism, see "Acknowledging Sources" (pp. 122–29).

" WOOF, WOOF, WOOF — BUT I'M PARAPHRASING. "

Copyright in this image is owned by the original artist, rights to reproduce or use the image may be obtained from www.CartoonStock.com.

In your essays, paraphrases will probably be rare, and offered only when you think your readers may need some help grasping the meaning of the text. If you simply want to remind your readers of the gist of a text you are responding to, it is better to summarize it rather than to paraphrase it. If you want them to see the text that you are discussing, to experience it directly, quote the passage word for word, in quotation marks if it is shorter than four lines of your text, or set off and indented in block-quotation format if it is longer than four lines.

### A RULE FOR WRITERS

Use a **summary** when your purpose is to set out the main points of a text. Use a paraphrase when you need to explain a particularly dense or difficult text, for example, a highly metaphoric or technical text.

# Quoting Sources

When you are writing about a text, quotations from it are indispensable. They provide evidence to support your claims, and information about the context of your discussion. They not only let your readers know what you are talking about, but they also give your readers the material you are responding to, thus letting them share your responses. But quote sparingly. Don't use quotations as padding. If the exact wording of the original is crucial, or especially effective, quote it directly, but if it is not, don't tire your readers with material that can be effectively reduced. As Mary-Claire Van Leunen said in *A Handbook for Scholars*: "Quote for color, quote for evidence. Otherwise, don't quote."

Here are some principles to keep in mind as you incorporate quoted material into your own writing.

1. **Identify the speaker or writer of the quotation.** Usually this identification precedes the quoted material (e.g., "Smith argues") in accordance with the principle of letting readers know where they are going.

2. **When you introduce a quotation, consider using verbs other than "says."** It is almost always more accurate and helpful to your reader to say Smith "argues," "adds," "contends," "points out," "admits," or "comments." The verbs you use help to make clear what you, as the writer, think of the quotation you're presenting. Compare "Smith says" with "Smith admits" and "Smith rightly points out." The "says" doesn't tell us much. "Admits" implies that Smith made his statement with some reluctance. "Rightly points out" tells us that you, as the writer, agree with what Smith has to say. (A verb often used *inaccurately* is "feels." Ralph Smith does not "feel" that "the term *primitive art* has come to be used with at least three distinct meanings." He "points out," "writes," "observes," or "notes.")

3. **Cite the source.** If you're using a print text and the MLA system of parenthetic citation, which we discuss in detail on pages 295–323, you'll likely need only to enclose in parentheses the page number on which the quotation appeared.

```
Christina Thompson notes that "the far north
of Australia occupies roughly the same position,
culturally and semantically, as that of the Deep
South in the United States" (185).
```

4. **Distinguish between short and long quotations and treat each appropriately.** Enclose *short quotations*, four (or fewer) lines of typing, within quotation marks. (And note that the period and comma go inside the quotation marks unless a page citation immediately follows the quotation, in which case, the period follows the closing quotation mark.)

> Anne Lindbergh calls the harrowing period of the kidnapping and murder of her first child the "hour of lead." "Flying," she writes, "was freedom and beauty and escape from crowds" (127).

Set off *long quotations* (more than four lines of typing). Do not enclose them within quotation marks. To set off a quotation, begin a new line, indent one inch from the left margin, and type the quotation double-spaced:

> The last paragraphs of *Five Years of My Life* contain Dreyfus's words when he was finally freed:
>
>> The Government of the Republic gives me back my liberty. It is nothing to me without honor. Beginning with today, I shall unremittingly strive for the reparation of the frightful judicial error of which I am still the victim. I want all France to know by a final judgment that I am innocent. (343)
>
> But he was never to receive that judgment.

Note that long quotations are usually introduced by a sentence ending with a colon (as in the above example) or by an introductory phrase, such as "Dreyfus wrote." Note also that block quotations require the page citation in parentheses *after* the final period of the quotation.

5. **Don't try to introduce a long quotation into the middle of one of your own sentences.** It is too difficult for the reader to come out of the quotation and to pick up your thread. Instead, introduce the quotation, as we did above, set the quotation off, and then begin a new sentence of your own.

6. **An embedded quotation (that is, a quotation embedded into a sentence of your own) must fit grammatically into the sentence**

**of which it is a part.** For example, suppose you want to use Othello's line "I have done the state some service."

### Incorrect

> Near the end of the play Othello says that he "have done the state some service."

### Correct

> Near the end of the play Othello says that he has "done the state some service."

### Correct

> Near the end of the play, Othello says, "I have done the state some service."

7. **Quote exactly.** Check your quotation for accuracy at least twice. If you need to edit a quotation—for example, in order to embed it grammatically, or to inform your reader of a relevant point—observe the following rules:

- Enclose any words that you add or substitute in square brackets—not parentheses.

  > "In the summer of 1816 we [Mary Wollstonecraft and Percy Bysshe Shelley] visited Switzerland and became the neighbors of Lord Byron" (6).

  > Trotsky became aware that "Stalin would not hesitate a moment to organize an attempt on [his] life" (67)

- Indicate the omission of material with ellipses (three periods, with a space before and after each period).

  > As Lisa Laskin notes, "Whereas women on the home front were generally viewed sympathetically ... men who stayed out of the fight were harshly criticized by soldiers" (103).

- If your sentence ends with the omission of the last part of the original sentence, indicate the omission with an ellipsis followed by a period, the sentence period.

  > The textbook says, "If your sentence ends with the omission of the last part of the original

sentence, indicate the omission with an ellipsis
followed by a period....”

- If a page reference follows a quotation that ends with the omission of the last part of original sentence, the fourth period (the sentence period) goes after the parenthetic citation instead of inside the closing quotation mark.

The textbook says, “If a page reference follows
a quotation that ends with the omission of the
last part of original sentence, the fourth
period (the sentence period) goes after the
parenthetic citation...” (121).

Notice that if you begin the quotation with the beginning of a sentence (in the example we have just given, “If a page” is the beginning of a quoted sentence), you do not indicate that material preceded the words you are quoting. Similarly, if you end your quotation with the end of the quoted sentence, you give only a single period, not an ellipsis, although, of course, the material from which you are quoting may have gone on for many more sentences. But if you begin quoting from the middle of a sentence, or end quoting before you reach the end of a sentence in your source, it is customary to indicate the omissions. But even such omissions need not be indicated when the quoted material is obviously incomplete—when, for instance, it is a word or phrase.

8. **Use punctuation accurately.** There are three important rules to observe:

- Commas and periods go inside the quotation marks unless the quotation is followed by a page reference:

“The land,” Nick Thompson observes, “looks after
us.”

“The land,” Nick Thompson observes, “looks after
us” (212).

- Semicolons and colons go outside quotation marks:

He turned and said, “Learn the names of all
these places”; it sounded like an order.

■ Question marks, exclamation points, and dashes go inside if they are part of the quotation, outside if they are your own.

> Amanda ironically says to her daughter, "How old are you, Laura?"

(The question mark is part of the quotation and therefore goes inside the quotation marks.)

> Did you really tell your brother "no"?

9. **Use single quotation marks for a quotation within a quotation.**

> The student told the interviewer, "I ran back to the dorm and I called my boyfriend and I said, 'Listen, this is just incredible,' and I told him all about it."

10. **Do not use quotation marks to enclose slang or a term that you fear is too casual.** Use the term or don't use it, but don't apologize by putting it in quotation marks, as in these examples.

**Incorrect**

> Because of "red tape" it took three years.

**Incorrect**

> At last I was able to "put in my two cents."

---

### A RULE FOR WRITERS

Quote directly only those passages that are particularly effective, or crucial, or memorable. In your finished essay these quotations will provide authority and emphasis.

---

## Acknowledging Sources
### *Using Sources Without Plagiarizing*

Your purpose as an academic writer is to develop *your own ideas* about the topics you are writing about. Secondary sources will help you shape and develop your thoughts about your topic, but your purpose is to develop arguments and analyses that are your own. It is crucial, then, to be clear about the distinction between your words and ideas, and those of your sources. Not to do so is to risk charges of **plagiarism**.

To plagiarize is to use someone else's words or ideas without attributing them to the source; it is to pass off someone else's work as your own. It is, in short, theft. The institutional consequences of plagiarism vary from school to school, and from case to case. In the university where one of us teaches, students who are found guilty of plagiarism are, among other things, banned from the campus for a year. At other schools, students can be expelled permanently; at still others, they simply receive a failing grade for the course and are put on academic probation.

---

### A RULE FOR WRITERS

Respect for your readers and for your sources requires that you acknowledge your indebtedness for material when

- you quote directly from a work, or
- you paraphrase or summarize someone's words (the words of your paraphrase or summary are your own, but the ideas are not), or
- you use an idea that is not common knowledge.

Most commonly, the words, ideas, and information you'll cite in a research essay will come from printed and electronic sources. But you must also acknowledge the advice of peer editors and ideas that come from lectures and class discussions, unless your instructor tells you not to do so. (We explain how to format the citations for all these sources in Chapter 13.)

---

Let's suppose you are going to make use of William Bascom's comment on the earliest responses of Europeans to African art:

> The first examples of African art to gain public attention were the bronzes and ivories which were brought back to Europe after the sack of Benin by a British military expedition in 1897. The superb technology of the Benin bronzes won the praise of experts like Felix von Luschan who wrote in 1899, "Cellini himself could not have made better casts, nor anyone else before or since to the present day." Moreover, their relatively realistic treatment of human features conformed to the prevailing European aesthetic standards. Because of their naturalism and technical excellence, it was at first maintained that they had been produced by Europeans—a view that was still current when the even more realistic bronze heads were

discovered at Ife in 1912. The subsequent discovery of new evidence has caused the complete abandonment of this theory of European origins of the bronzes of Benin and Ife, both of which are cities in Nigeria.

—William Bascom, *African Art in Cultural Perspective* (New York: Norton, 1973), p. 4

## Acknowledging a Direct Quotation

A student wanting to use some or all of Bascom's words might write something like this:

> According to William Bascom, when Europeans first encountered Benin and Ife works of art in the late nineteenth century, they thought that Europeans had produced them, but the discovery of new evidence "caused the complete abandonment of this theory of European origins of the bronzes of Benin and Ife, both of which are cities in Nigeria" (4).

In this example, the writer introduces Bascom with a signal phrase ("According to William Bascom"); then she summarizes several sentences from Bascom; then she uses quotation marks to indicate the passage that comes directly from Bascom's book. Note that the summary does *not* borrow Bascom's language and it does *not* borrow his sentence structure; the words and their arrangement are all the writer's own. Note also that what appears inside the quotation marks is an exact transcription of Bascom's words: Within the quotation marks the writer has not changed any word endings, or omitted any words, or inserted any punctuation of her own. (The "4" inside parentheses at the end of the passage is the page reference. Again, we explain the MLA system of parenthetic citation in detail in Chapter 13.)

## Acknowledging a Paraphrase or Summary

As we noted earlier in this chapter, when you are using secondary sources, you will, for the most part, be writing summaries, not paraphrases—unless the language of the source is especially complex. If Bascom's sentences had been obscure—for instance, if they used highly technical language—there would have been a reason to paraphrase them. In that case, the writer of the essay would explicitly have said she was paraphrasing Bascom, and she would have explained why.

Occasionally you may find that you cannot summarize a passage in your source and yet you don't want to quote it word for word—perhaps because it is too technical or because it is poorly written. In that case, you need to paraphrase the passage—that is, you need to put it into your own words. Even though you have put the idea into your own words, you must give credit to the source because the idea is not yours. *Both summaries and paraphrases must be acknowledged.* In both cases, the author must be identified by name, and the location of the source—a page reference if you are using a print source—must be given.

Here is an example of an **acceptable summary:**

> William Bascom, in *African Art*, points out that the first examples of African art brought to Europe—Benin bronzes and ivories—were thought by Europeans to be of European origin because they were realistic and well made, but evidence was later discovered that caused this theory to be abandoned (4).

The summary is adequate, and the page reference indicates where the source is to be found. But if the writer had omitted the signal phrase "William Bascom, in *African Art*, points out that," the result would have been plagiarism. Not to give Bascom credit would be to plagiarize, even if the words are the writer's own. The offense is just as serious as not acknowledging a direct quotation.

The following paragraph is an example of an **unacceptable summary**. The writer uses too much of Bascom's language, and she follows his organization of the material: She has not turned the material into her own writing. And she gives Bascom no credit for his ideas.

> The earliest examples of African art to become widely known in Europe were bronzes and ivories that were brought to Europe in 1897. These works were thought to be of European origin, and one expert said that Cellini could not have done better work. Their technical excellence, as well as their realism, fulfilled the European standards of the day. The later discovery of new evidence at Benin and Ife, both in Nigeria, refuted this belief.

Again, one problem here is that all the *ideas* are Bascom's—and his name appears neither in a signal phrase nor in a citation. Another problem is that the writer doesn't put the passage entirely into her own words. Rather, she simply substitutes one phrase for another, maintaining much of the structure and organization of Bascom's sentences. The writing is Bascom's, in a thin disguise. She substitutes

"The earliest examples of African art"

for Bascom's

*"The first examples of African art"*

she substitutes

"to become widely known"

for

*"to gain public attention";*

she substitutes

"Their technical excellence, as well as their realism"

for

*"their naturalism and technical excellence."*

*The writer here is plagiarizing*—perhaps without even knowing it. This form of plagiarism, where a writer simply substitutes his or her own phrases here and there but retains the form and content of the original passage, is one of the most common forms of plagiarism that writing instructors see. Much of it occurs, we believe, because students don't know it's wrong—and because they don't see their job as developing their *own* ideas in relation to their sources.

As we have noted, it is unlikely that a writer would paraphrase a passage that is as straightforward and as free of technical language as Bascom's: The main reason for paraphrasing is to clarify a text that might be confusing to a reader—a literary text, for example, or a particularly complex or technical piece of writing. In the following example, a passage that contains an **acceptable paraphrase** of a sentence from Darwin's *Origin of Species*, the student clarifies a key point in Darwin's argument:

Before discussing the relationship between Darwin's observations of animal life and his views of the nature of human society, it may be helpful to clarify the meaning of a key sentence in *The Origin of Species*. Darwin says, in Chapter 3,

> I should premise that I use the term Struggle for Existence in a large and metaphorical sense, including dependence of one being on another, and including (which is more important) not only the life of the individual, but success in leaving progeny.

In other words, Darwin notes that he wishes to say in advance that his phrase "Struggle for Existence" is to be understood in a figurative way to indicate not only how the survival of a creature is dependent on other creatures but also to refer to the importance of producing offspring.

The paraphrase clarifies the terms that might have been obscure in the original ("premise" means "say in advance"; "progeny" means "offspring"), and it is entirely in the student's own language. If the student had borrowed any of Darwin's phrases or significant words, the paraphrase would have been inadequate. Here is an example of an **unacceptable paraphrase** of Darwin's sentence:

> In other words, Darwin says that he wants to posit that he will use the term Struggle for Existence in a grand and poetical way, to mean dependence of one being on another, as well as—more significantly— its success in leaving offspring.

Note that several phrases are lifted directly from the source (for example, "use the term Struggle for Existence" and "dependence of one being on another"); note also the cheesy substitution of "posit" for "premise" and "grand and poetical" for "large and metaphorical." The source (Darwin) is identified, and in a way, the problems *seem* minor: It's just a sentence, after all. But if there were a pattern of such problems in a student essay, if there were several such sentences, the student would be open to charges of plagiarism.

## Acknowledging an Idea

Let's say you have read an essay in which Irving Kristol argues that journalists who pride themselves on being tireless critics of national policy are in fact irresponsible critics because they have no policy they prefer. If this strikes you as a new idea and you adopt it in an essay—even though you set it forth entirely in your own words and with examples not offered by Kristol—you must acknowledge your debt to Kristol. *Not to acknowledge such borrowing is plagiarism.* Your readers will not think less of you for naming your source; rather, they will be grateful to you for telling them about an interesting writer.

## Fair Use of Common Knowledge

If in doubt as to whether or not to give credit (either with formal documentation or merely in a phrase such as "Carol Gilligan says . . ."), give credit. If you over-cite, you'll look like you don't really know what you're doing, and that's not good, but it's better than risking a plagiarism charge. But as you begin to read widely in your field or subject, you will develop a sense of what is considered common knowledge.

Unsurprising definitions in a dictionary can be considered common knowledge, and so there is no need to say "According to Webster, a novel is a long narrative in prose." (That's weak in three ways: It's unnecessary, it's uninteresting, and it's inexact since "Webster" appears in the titles of several dictionaries, some good and some bad.)

Similarly, the date of Freud's death can be considered common knowledge. Few can give it when asked, but it can be found out from innumerable sources, and no one need get the credit for providing you with the date. Again, if you simply *know,* from your reading of Freud, that Freud was interested in literature, you need not cite a specific source for an assertion to that effect, but if you know only because some commentator on Freud said so, and you have no idea whether the fact is well known or not, you should give credit to the source that gave you the information. Not to give credit—for ideas as well as for quoted words—is to plagiarize.

---

### A RULE FOR WRITERS

Material that is regarded as common knowledge, such as the date of Freud's death, is not cited because all sources can be expected to give the same information—*but if you are in doubt about whether something is or is not common knowledge, cite your source.*

---

## "But How Else Can I Put It?"

If you have just learned—say from an encyclopedia—something that you sense is common knowledge, you may wonder how to change into your own words the simple, clear words that this source uses in setting forth this simple fact. For example, if before writing an analysis of a photograph of

Buffalo Bill and Sitting Bull you look up these names in the *Encyclopaedia Britannica*, you will find this statement about Buffalo Bill (William F. Cody): "In 1883 Cody organized his first Wild West exhibition." You could not use this statement as your own, word for word, without feeling uneasy. But to put in quotation marks such a routine statement of what can be considered common knowledge, and to cite a source for it, seems pretentious. After all, the *Encyclopedia Americana* says much the same thing in the same routine way: "In 1883 . . . Cody organized Buffalo Bill's Wild West." It may be that the word "organized" is simply the most obvious and the best word, and perhaps you will end up using it. Certainly, to change "Cody organized" into "Cody presided over the organization of" or "Cody assembled" or some such thing in an effort to avoid plagiarizing would be to make a change for the worse and still to be guilty of plagiarism. What, then, can you do? You won't get yourself into this mess of wondering whether to change clear, simple wording into awkward wording if in the first place, when you take notes, you *summarize* your sources, thus: "1883: organized Wild West," or "first Wild West: 1883." Later (even if only thirty minutes later), when drafting your paper, if you turn this nugget—probably combined with others—into the best sentence you can, you will not be in danger of plagiarizing, even if the word "organized" turns up in your sentence.

Of course, even when dealing with material that can be considered common knowledge—and even when you have put it into your own words—you probably *will* cite your source if you are drawing more than just an occasional fact from a source. For instance, if your paragraph on Buffalo Bill uses half a dozen facts from a source, cite the source. You do this both to avoid charges of plagiarism and to protect yourself in case your source contains errors of fact.

CHECKLIST for Avoiding Plagiarism

☐ In taking notes, did you indicate clearly when you were quoting directly, when you were paraphrasing, and when you were summarizing? Did you record the sources of all online material that you cut and pasted into your notes? (See pp. 109–22.)

☐ Are all quotations enclosed within quotation marks and acknowledged? (See pp. 118–22.)

☐ Are all changes within quotations indicated by square brackets for additional words or punctuation and ellipses (. . .) for omissions? Are quotations otherwise exact? Have you transcribed quoted passages *precisely* as they appear in the source? (See pp. 120–21.)

- ☐ Are the sources for all ideas that are not your own acknowledged, and are these ideas set forth in your own words and with your own sentence structure? (See pp. 122–28.)
- ☐ Does the list of sources include all the sources (online as well as print) that you have used? (See pp. 109–22.)

## A Plagiarism Self-test

Students sometimes download into their essays large chunks of material from Wikipedia, or buy essays from Internet sources. We suspect they know that doing these things is wrong. (We're still puzzling, though, over a student charged with plagiarism because her essay was composed mostly of material downloaded from an online encyclopedia. Her bewildered response to the charges: "I didn't do it! My *mother* wrote that essay!")

We also know that students sometimes plagiarize inadvertently. Sometimes they just don't know the rules. Or perhaps they sort-of learned the rules. But then a busy teacher or overworked TA doesn't notice an absence of quotation marks around material that should have been cited, and gives a sloppily documented essay a decent grade. The student is rewarded for the plagiarism; the bad practice becomes habit—until someone catches on, and the student winds up in a room with a disciplinary committee that's deciding whether he or she should be expelled.

You need to know if you know the rules. If you do, great: You've got a solid foundation for the kind of writing we'll discuss in the next chapters of this book. If you don't, learn them: Reread this chapter; make an appointment with your instructor; go to your college or university writing center.

To determine if you know the rules, take this self-test. An answer key appears on page 135.

## Quiz Yourself: How Much Do You Know About Citing Sources?

### Section 1: Plagiarism and Academic Dishonesty

Place a check mark next to each violation of academic integrity.

\_\_\_\_\_ 1. Your history professor and your political science professor both assign a term paper. To save time, you write one paper that meets both requirements and hand it in to both professors.

Carmen Lowe: "Quiz Yourself: How Much Do You Know About Citing Sources?" Reprinted by permission of Carmen Lowe, Tufts University Academic Resource Center.

_____ 2. You don't want to have too many quotations in your paper, so you do not put quotation marks around some sentences you copied from a source. You cite the source correctly at the end of the paragraph and in your bibliography.

_____ 3. You have copied a long passage from a book into your paper, and you changed some of the wording. You cite the source at the end of the passage and again in the bibliography.

_____ 4. While writing a long research paper, you come across an interesting hypothesis mentioned in a book, and you incorporate this hypothesis into your main argument. After you finish writing the paper, you can't remember where you initially found the hypothesis, so you don't bother to cite the source of your idea.

## Section 2: Common Knowledge

Common knowledge is information that is widely known within a society or an intellectual community; therefore, if you include common knowledge in your paper, you do not need to cite where you found that information.

**Answer** *Yes* or *No* to the following questions:

_____ 1. In a high school class on American government, you learned about the checks-and-balances system of government that separates power into the judicial, executive, and legislative branches. Now you are writing a paper for an introductory political science class, and you mention the concept of checks-and-balances you learned in high school. Should you cite your old high school textbook?

_____ 2. In writing a paper about pop culture in the 1980s, you want to include the year that Reagan was shot, but you cannot remember if it was 1980 or 1981, so you look up the correct date in an encyclopedia. Do you have to include that encyclopedia as a source for the date on which Reagan was shot?

_____ 3. You do most of your research online and find lots of interesting Web sites from which you quote several passages. After you write the first draft, you ask an older and more experienced classmate if he knows how to cite Web sites. He says that Web sites are in the public domain and constitute common knowledge, and they therefore do not need to be cited. Is this true?

_____ 4. In writing a research paper on astrophysics, you come across something called the Eridanus Effect several times. You have never heard of this effect nor discussed it in your class, but after reading about it in six different astrophysics journal articles, you have a pretty clear idea of what it is and its most common characteristics. Is the Eridanus Effect common knowledge within astrophysics?

_____ 5. You are writing a paper on Shakespeare's _Hamlet_. A footnote in your textbook mentions that some literary historians now believe that Shakespeare himself played the ghost when the play was first performed. If you mention Shakespeare playing the ghost, do you need to cite this footnote in your textbook?

_____ 6. You are writing a paper on the assassination of Robert F. Kennedy. The most influential biography on him mentions a controversial conspiracy theory first put forward in the early 1970s by a journalist for the _Washington Post_. When you mention this conspiracy theory, should you cite the biography?

## Section 3: Quoting, Paraphrasing, and Summarizing Texts

Read the following passage excerpted from an online edition of a foreign policy magazine. Determine whether any of the sample sentences that follow are improperly cited within the sentence or plagiarized.

> _The illegal trade in drugs, arms, intellectual property, people, and money is booming. Like the war on terrorism, the fight to control these illicit markets pits governments against agile, stateless, and resourceful networks empowered by globalization. Governments will continue to lose these wars until they adopt new strategies to deal with a larger, unprecedented struggle that now shapes the world as much as confrontations between nation-states once did._
>
> —from Moisés Naím, "The Five Wars of Globalization."
> Foreign Policy Jan.-Feb. 2003: Web. 13 January 2003.

Read the following passages and then mark _OK_ if the passage is fine. If the passage is plagiarized, improperly paraphrased, or otherwise cited inadequately, mark it with _X_.

_____ 1. In his essay on "The Five Wars of Globalization," Moisés Naím argues that governments need to find new ways to handle the kinds of borderless illegal activity increasing under globalization.

_____ 2. In describing the "illegal trade in drugs, arms, intellectual property, people, and money" as "booming," Moisés Naím asserts that governments need to adopt new strategies to deal with this unprecedented struggle that now shapes the world (http://www.foreignpolicy.com).

_____ 3. Like the war on terror, the struggle to control illegal trade in drugs, arms, money, etc., pits governments against cunning, stateless, and enterprising networks empowered by globalization (Moises 2003).

_____ 4. Many experts believe that globalization is changing the face of foreign policy.

Read the following passage from a book on romance novels and soap operas and then read the citations of it that follow to determine whether any are plagiarized or improperly cited within the sentence.

> *The complexity of women's responses to romances has not been sufficiently acknowledged. Instead of exploring the possibility that romances, while serving to keep women in their place, may at the same time be concerned with real female problems, analysts of women's romances have generally seen the fantasy embodied in romantic fiction either as evidence of female "masochism" or as a simple reflection of the dominant masculine ideology. For instance, Germaine Greer, referring to the idealized males of women's popular novels, says, "This is the hero that women have chosen for themselves. The traits invented for him have been invented by women cherishing the chains of their bondage." But this places too much blame on women, and assumes a freedom of choice which is not often in evidence—not in their lives and therefore certainly not in their popular arts.*

> *—from Tania Modleski,* Loving with a Vengeance: Mass-Produced Fantasies for Women *(New York and London Methuen, 1982), 37–38. Print.*

Read the following passages and then mark *OK* if the passage is fine. If the passage is plagiarized in part or whole or is otherwise cited improperly, mark it with *X*.

_____ 1. Tania Modleski claims that Germaine Greer oversimplifies why women read romance novels (38).

_____ 2. Modleski states that although romance novels may keep women in their place, they also address real female problems (37).

_____ 3. Feminist critics see the fantasy embodied in romance novels either as evidence of female "masochism" or as a simple reflection of male chauvinism (Modleski 37–38).

_____ 4. One feminist writer, Germaine Greer, says that the idealized male featured in women's popular romance novels "is the hero that women have chosen for themselves. The traits invented for him have been invented by women cherishing the chains of their bondage"(38).

_____ 5. Tania Modleski rejects the idea that the fantasies expressed in romance novels are merely a reflection of some innate masochism in women who, in the words of Germaine Greer, "cherish[. . .] the chains of their bondage" (37; Greer qtd. in Modleski, 38).

# Answer Key to Plagiarism Quiz

## Section 1: *Plagiarism and Academic Dishonesty*

All four incidents are forms of plagiarism or academic dishonesty.

## Section 2: *Common Knowledge*

1. No; the basic facts about the checks-and-balances system are common knowledge and do not need to be cited.

2. No; even if you cannot remember the exact date of the assassination attempt on Reagan, it is common knowledge because the date is undisputed and can be found in a variety of sources.

3. No; writing on the Web is protected by copyright and must be cited even if no author is listed.

4. Yes; it's common knowledge if it appears *undocumented* in five or more sources.

5. Hmmm. This is a tricky situation. Because *some* but not all literary historians believe Shakespeare himself played the ghost, this is probably common knowledge among Shakespeare experts. However, you're not a Shakespeare expert, so it would be wise to cite the footnote just to be safe. So, the answer is, Yes—cite it.

6. Yes; conspiracy theories are controversial, and the details of such controversies need to be cited. If you were only to cite the journalist directly, you'd be failing to give the biographer sufficient credit.

# Section 3: Quoting, Paraphrasing, and Summarizing Texts

## Illegal Trade Passage:

1. OK; an example of summary. The sentence gives the author and the title. (Remember, the bibliography would provide more publication information.)
2. X; two things are wrong: Some of the language is too similar to the original, and the citation method is incorrect. Do not list the URL in your paper. The phrase "adopt new strategies to deal with this unprecedented struggle that now shapes the world" is too close to the source—in some places, identical to it.
3. X; this paraphrase is too close to the original. The writer used a thesaurus to change key words, but the sentence structure is identical to the original. Plus, the author's last name (not first name) should appear in the parenthetical citation. (Also, using "etc." in the text is annoying!)
4. OK; This is common knowledge. The sentence is so general, it really has nothing to do with the passage from Moisés Naím, so there is no reason to cite him.

## Romance Novel Passage:

1. OK; this summary is correct; the author's name appears in the sentence, so it does not need to appear in the parenthetical citation.
2. X; although the source is documented properly, some of the language is too close to the source, especially the phrases "keep women in their place" and "real female problems." These phrases need to be put into quotation marks or rewritten.
3. X; most of this sentence is copied directly from the source; it needs to be rewritten or partially enclosed in quotes.
4. X; the quote is properly attributed to Greer, but the page number refers to Modleski's book. Also, there's no need to copy the footnote from the original.
5. OK; this example shows how to properly cite one writer quoted within the work of another. Also, note how the ellipses and brackets indicate how the "-ing" part of "cherish" was deleted to make the quote flow better. The ellipses indicate that something was deleted; the brackets indicate that the ellipses were not in the original source.

# Analyzing Texts

## Analyzing an Image

Look at the drawing below by Pieter Brueghel the Elder, titled *The Painter and the Connoisseur* (done about 1565), and then jot down your responses to the questions that follow.

1. One figure is given considerably more space than the other. What may be implied by this fact?
2. What is the painter doing (besides painting)?
3. What is the connoisseur doing?
4. What does the face of each figure tell you about each man's character? The figures are physically close; are they mentally close? How do you know?

Now consider a student's brief discussion of the drawing.

> The painter, standing in front of the connoisseur and given more than two-thirds of the space, dominates this picture. His hand holds the brush with which he creates, while the connoisseur's hand awkwardly fumbles for money in his purse. The connoisseur apparently is pleased with the picture he is looking at, for he is buying it, but his parted lips give him a stupid expression and his eyeglasses imply defective vision. In contrast, the painter looks away from the picture and fixes his eyes on the model (reality) or, more likely, on empty space, his determined expression suggesting that he possesses an imaginative vision beyond his painting and perhaps even beyond earthly reality.

The author of this paragraph uses *analysis* to interpret the drawing, to discover its meaning. The paragraph doesn't simply tell us that the picture shows two people close together—that would be a *description*, not an analysis. This analytic paragraph separates the parts of the picture, pointing out that the two figures form a contrast. The paragraph explains why one figure gets much more space than the other, and it explains what the contrasting gestures and facial expressions imply. The writer of the comment has interpreted the drawing by examining how the parts function—that is, how they relate to the whole.

# Analyzing Advertisements (Visual Rhetoric)

Most print advertisements rely on pictures: A happy family stands by an automobile and a few lines of text tell us to buy the car; an image of a sexy body accompanies an invitation to buy a particular perfume or some exercise equipment; a photograph of a starving child seeks to persuade us to contribute to a charity.

Ads for charities aside, most ads are images not so much of the product—a car, a perfume—as they are images of a desirable condition, a state, for instance, of happiness or sexual attractiveness or health. The ads are first of all selling an idea, such as "You deserve to be happy" (or sexy, or healthy). After the ad has conveyed this point, it then hooks the product to it: If you buy this particular car, you and your family will have fun; if you use this perfume, you will attract a sexual partner. Cleaning the stove too much of a chore? Use X oven cleaner. Are you worried that you won't have enough money for your child's college tuition? Just open a savings plan with Bank Y, and find peace of mind.

Sometimes, no clear relation exists between the picture in an advertisement and the product it promotes. This may seem odd, but it's not. Advertisers want you to remember their products. The picture has served its purpose if it catches your attention and leads you to see and remember the product's name. (You may recall—or view now on YouTube—the television advertisement for Hardee's hamburgers, which featured Paris Hilton, in a bathing suit, washing a car.) Some very successful advertisements don't even mention the product itself. There's just an image—unusual, violent, shocking, amusing, or sexually explicit. The image creates a buzz, and the controversy gets people talking. Who placed the image? Why? Haven't they gone too far? Generally, advertisers are pleased when such questions are debated because the product is being noticed.

Even ads that appeal to reason ("proven," "doctors recommend," "more economical") use pictures as the hook. A solemn doctor in a lab coat, say, promotes a new drug for cholesterol; the text explains how it works and offers up facts and figures to support the drug manufacturer's claims. And ads for charities, which primarily appeal to emotion, even more obviously rely on pictures, using vivid images of suffering to appeal to our sense of pity or fairness or outrage—and sometimes all three at once.

We reprint here a photograph from a 2010 advertising campaign for the Italian fashion house Dolce & Gabbana. We also reprint a brief essay that describes and analyzes the advertisement. The analysis points to several of the ways in which advertisers can catch and hold our attention. Look carefully at the advertisement; read the essay; then reread it considering the following questions:

■ Does the writer effectively describe the advertisement?
■ Do you find her analysis persuasive?

Advertising Archives

Nashida Mansoor
November 7, 2011

Who's That Girl? An Analysis of an
Advertisement for Dolce & Gabbana

The advertisement, which appeared in the
January 2010 issue of *Vogue*, takes up two full
magazine pages and gives no caption other than
the words "Dolce & Gabbana" in 1-1/4" gray capital letters running across the bottom of the pages.
On first impression, the scene is incongruous. The
black and white photograph (which is itself a bit
odd among the color images in the magazine) shows
an attractive blonde woman washing dishes, dressed
in a lacy, low-cut, leopard-print black dress with
a diamond-studded cross hanging from a thin chain
around her neck. Her blonde hair is perfectly
tousled, her face is perfectly smooth, her eyebrows
are penciled, and her lips shine. If we realize
that the woman is the pop star Madonna, our sense
of incongruity increases. Madonna? Washing *dishes*?

The kitchen is not modern. The wall is dark
wood to about shoulder height. The rest of the wall
is white, and a framed picture or mirror—we can't
tell which—hangs on the wall over and to the left

of the sink. An old—fashioned lace curtain filters daylight through the window that frames Madonna's shoulders and head, and on the counter behind her are dirty pots and pans. On the counter to the left is a pan with the remains of what might be tomato sauce. On the right are two more pans and a large pot, also encrusted with sauce, of the sort that one might use to cook pasta. Madonna holds a shallow white bowl (perhaps a pasta bowl) under running water issuing from an old-fashioned stainless steel faucet. White lace, black lace, spaghetti pots, sauce: Elements of the photograph call to mind images of a kitchen after Sunday dinner in the kind of Italian or Italian-American home that we know from old films. But in this picture, it's Madonna, looking like a movie star—not Grandma—washing up.

Madonna appears not to be posing for the camera in this photograph. She leans at a slight angle over the sink, but her head is turned to her right shoulder. Her mouth is open, and she is gazing at something outside the frame of the photograph. Perhaps she was startled by something just behind her and to her right, or perhaps she's simply talking to someone over her shoulder. Either way, something is happening in the kitchen, but we don't know what it is. The intimacy of the image engages our curiosity; so do the questions it raises but doesn't answer. We want to know: What just happened? What does this woman see and hear? To whom is she talking? (And if she turns just a bit further, what will happen to the lacy dress that at this moment just barely provides the necessary coverage?) We might also ask: What product, exactly, is this advertisement promoting?

The answer to this question is also unclear. Dolce & Gabbana is an Italian fashion company, as readers of *Vogue* would likely know. So perhaps the advertisement is promoting the lacy black dress. But if that were the case, surely the photograph would give us a better look at it. More likely, the point of this complex and memorable photograph with its mysterious mini-drama, its striking blend of nostalgia and sex, and its self-conscious references to things Italian, is simply to advertise Dolce & Gabbana itself.

If your instructor asks you to write an analysis of an advertisement, keep in mind that you will need to describe it accurately enough to enable someone who hasn't seen it to envision it. For an example of description and analysis at work in an academic essay, see Dolores Hayden's "Advertisements, Pornography, and Public Space" on pages 144–48. The following checklist may also help you develop ideas for your analysis.

### CHECKLIST for Analyzing Advertisements

☐ What is your first impression of the ad? Excitement, perhaps conveyed by a variety of colors and large type? Dignity, perhaps conveyed by grays, lots of empty space, and smaller type?

☐ Who is the audience for the ad? Affluent young women? College students? Retired persons?

☐ Does the image appeal to an emotion—to your sense of fairness, pity, patriotism, envy, fear?

☐ Is the image intentionally shocking?

☐ Does the text make a logical, rational appeal?

☐ What does the text do? Does it convey information? Entertain?

☐ What is the relation of the image to the text? Does the image do most of the work, or is its job mostly to get you to read the text?

☐ Does the ad strike you as deceptive? Does it seem honest?

☐ How effective is it? Would you buy the product it promotes?

# Analyzing Texts

Much of academic reading and writing is analytical. You read of the causes of a revolution, of the effects of inflation, or of the relative importance of heredity and environment; you write about the meaning of a short story, the causes and effects of poverty, the strengths and weaknesses of some proposed legislative action. And much of this reading and writing is based on the analysis of *texts*. The word "text" derives from the Latin for "woven" (as in textile), and it has come to refer not only to words stitched together into sentences (whether novels or letters or advertisements) but also to all kinds of objects of interpretation: films, paintings, music videos, Facebook pages, even food on a plate.

For that reason, much of our discussion in this chapter focuses on textual analysis. Of course writing an analysis of a drawing differs from writing an analysis of a poem (or, for that matter, from an analysis of a legislative proposal or an argument about the causes of inflation). Nevertheless, we believe that there are important similarities between these processes. In all cases,

- the writer must precisely summarize or describe the object under scrutiny, so that the reader is able to envision it;
- the writer must pay close attention to the details, what they imply, and how they relate to each other and to the whole; and
- the writer must be able to explain what the text *means*.

Keep in mind, too, that when academic writers write analytically, their purpose is to persuade the reader to see things *their* way: to understand the poem the way they do; to reach their conclusion about the causes of poverty; to adopt their position on the proposed legislative action. The analysis helps the writer to make a larger point: It provides the evidence for the argument. In Chapter 9, "Persuading Readers," we discuss argument in more detail.

## Classifying and Thinking

Analysis (literally a separating into parts) is not only the source of much writing that seeks to explain but also a way of thinking, a way of arriving at conclusions (generalizations), a way of discovering meaning. Much of what we normally mean by analysis requires classifying ideas or things into categories and thinking about how the categories relate to each other.

When you think about choosing courses, for example, you classify the courses by subject matter, or by degree of difficulty ("Since I'm taking two hard courses, I ought to look for an easy one"), or by the hour at which they are offered, or by the degree to which they interest you, or by their merit as determined through the grapevine. In this case, you establish categories by breaking down the curriculum into parts, and by then putting into each category courses that significantly resemble each other but that are not identical. We need categories: We simply cannot get through life treating every object as unique.

### Examples of Classifying

Suppose you were asked to write an essay putting forth your ideas about punishment for killers. You would need to distinguish between those killers whose actions are premeditated and those killers whose actions are not. And in the first category you might make further distinctions:

1. Professional killers who carefully contrive a death.
2. Killers who are irrational except in their ability to contrive a death.
3. Robbers who contrive a property crime and who kill only when they believe that killing is necessary in order to commit that crime.

You can hardly talk usefully about capital punishment or imprisonment without making some such analysis of killers. You have, then, taken killers and *classified* them, for the sake of educating yourself and those persons with whom you discuss the topic. You have engaged in critical thinking. Unless you agree with the "Off with their heads" attitude of the mad Queen of Hearts, you will be satisfied with your conclusion only after you have tested it by dividing your topic into parts, each clearly distinguished from the others, and then showed how they are related.

Often the keenest analytical thinking considers not only what parts are in the whole but also what is *not* there—what is missing in relation to a larger context that we can imagine. For example, if we analyze the female characters in the best-known fairy tales, we will find that most are either sleeping beauties or wicked stepmothers. These categories are general: "Sleeping beauties" includes all passive women valued only for their appearance, and "wicked stepmothers" includes Cinderella's cruel older sisters. (Fairy godmothers form another category, because they are not human beings.) Analysis helps us to discover the almost total absence of resourceful, productive women in the typical fairy tale. You might begin a thoughtful essay with a general statement to this effect and then support the statement—your thesis—with an analysis of "Cinderella," "Little Red Riding Hood," and "Snow White."

# Cause and Effect

Analytical reasoning moving from cause to effect is also often expected in academic discussions, especially, but not exclusively, in the social sciences. These discussions are given to questions such as the following:

What part, if any, did oil play in our invasion of Iraq in 2003?
How does the death penalty affect jury verdicts?

Why do people enjoy horror movies?

What are the effects of billboard advertising?

Let's look at the first eight paragraphs of an essay, by the architect and scholar Dolores Hayden, which addresses the last question on the list, arguing from cause to effect.

**DOLORES HAYDEN**

# Advertisements, Pornography, and Public Space

1    Americans need to look more consciously at the ways in which the public domain is misused for spatial displays of gender stereotypes. These appear in outdoor advertising, and to a lesser extent in commercial displays, architectural decoration, and public sculpture. While the commercial tone and violence of the American city is often criticized, crude stereotypes still appear in public, urban spaces as the staple themes of advertising. Most Americans have long been accustomed to seeing giant females in various states of undress, smiling and caressing products such as whiskey, food, and records.

2    Male models also sell goods, but are usually active and clothed. Ad campaigns of the 1980s aimed at gay men were the first major exception. Several geographers have suggested that men are most often shown playing sports or posed in the great outdoors; women are shown in reflective postures responding to male demands in interior spaces. As the nineteenth-century sexual double standard is preserved by the urban advertising, many twentieth-century urban men behave as if good women are at home while bad ones adorn the billboards and travel on their own in urban space. At the same time, urban women are encouraged to think of emotionlessness as natural to the Marlboro cowboy and every other male adult.

3    This double standard is the result of advertising practices, graphic design, and urban design. Sanctioned by the zoning laws, billboards are approved by the same urban planning boards who will not permit child-care centers or mother-in-law apartments in many residential districts. But the problem with billboards is not only aesthetic degradation. By presenting gender stereotypes in the form of nonverbal body language, fifty-feet long and thirty-feet

high, billboards turn the public space of the city into a stage set for a drama starring enticing women and stern men.

4      Imagine two women on an urban commuting trip along the Sunset Strip in Los Angeles. Standing on a street corner, the two women are waiting for a bus to go to work. The bus arrives, bearing a placard on the side advertising a local night club. It shows strippers doing their act, their headless bodies naked from neck to crotch except for a few blue sequins. The two women get on the bus and find seats for the ride along Sunset Boulevard. They look out the windows. As the bus pulls away, their heads appear incongruously above the voluptuous cardboard female bodies displayed on the side. They ride through a district of record company headquarters and film offices, one of the most prosperous in L.A.

5      Their first views reveal rows of billboards. Silent Marlboro man rides the range; husky, khaki-clad Camel man stares at green hills; gigantic, uniformed professional athletes catch passes and hit home runs on behalf of booze. These are the male images. Then, on a billboard for whiskey, a horizontal blonde in a backless black velvet dress, slit to the thigh, invites men to "Try on a little Black Velvet." Next, a billboard shows a well-known actress, reclining with legs spread, who notes that avocados are only sixteen calories a slice. "Would this body lie to you?" she asks coyly, emphasizing that the body language which communicates blatant sexual availability is only meant to bring attention to her thin figure.

6      Next the bus riders pass a club called the Body Shop that advertises "live, nude girls." Two reclining, realistic nudes, one in blue tones in front of a moonlight cityscape, one in orange sunshine tones, stretch their thirty-foot bodies along the sidewalk. This is the same neighborhood where a billboard advertising a Rolling Stones' record album called *Black and Blue* made news in the 1970s, when a manacled, spread-legged woman with torn clothes proclaimed, "I'm Black and Blue from the Rolling Stones—and I love it!" Members of a group called Women Against Violence Against Women (WAVAW) arrived with cans of spray paint and climbed the scaffolding to make small, uneven letters of protest: "This is a crime against women." Demonstrations and boycotts eventually succeeded in achieving the removal of that image, but not in eliminating the graphic design problem. *Black and Blue* has been replaced by James Bond in a tuxedo, pistol in hand, viewed through the spread legs and buttocks of a giant woman in a bathing suit and improbably high heels, captioned *For Your Eyes Only*.

7       When the two women get off the bus in Hollywood, they experience more gender stereotypes as pedestrians. First, they walk past a department store. In the windows, mannequins suggest the prevailing ideals of sartorial elegance. The male torsos lean forward, as if they are about to clinch a deal. The female torsos, pin-headed, tip backward and sideways, at odd angles, as if they are about to be pushed over onto a bed. Next, the women pass an apartment building. Two neoclassical caryatids support the entablature over the front door. Their breasts are bared, their heads carry the load. They recall the architecture of the Erechtheum on the Acropolis in Athens, dating from the 5th century B.C., where the sculptured stone forms of female slaves were used as support for a porch in place of traditional columns and capitals. This is an ancient image of servitude.

Now let's analyze these paragraphs. In the first paragraph Hayden introduces the question her essay will address: "How do billboards and other outdoor representations of male and female bodies perpetuate gender stereotypes?" (our paraphrase). She points out that "crude stereotypes still appear in public," thus suggesting that her question is worth investigating. In the last sentence of the third paragraph, she states an argument: "billboards turn the public space of the city into a stage set for a drama starring enticing women and stern men." Paragraphs 5 through 7 discuss the "representations of bodies," the *causes* of the stereotypes she is examining. We note Hayden classifies these images fairly methodically: paragraphs 5 and 6 focus on billboards representing women as "available"; paragraph 7 focuses on mannequins that represent women as vulnerable and on architectural elements that represent women as subservient.

In the next (and last) four paragraphs of the essay, Hayden discusses the *effects* of these representations: "women guard themselves," "men assume that ogling is part of normal public life," and the "sexual double standard" is maintained "in a brutal and vulgar way."

8       After the neoclassical apartment house, the commuters approach a construction site. Here they are subject to an activity traditionally called "running the gauntlet," but referred to as "girl watching" by urban sociologist William H. Whyte. Twelve workers stop whatever they are doing, whistle, and yell: "Hey, baby!" The women put their heads down, and walk faster, tense with anger. The construction workers take delight in causing exactly this response: "You're cute when you're mad!" Whyte regards this type of behavior as charming, pedestrian fun in "Street Life," where he even took pleasure

in tracing its historic antecedents. He has never been whistled at, hooted at, and had the dimensions of his body parts analyzed out loud on a public street.[1] Finally, these women get to the office building where they work. Their journey has taken them through an urban landscape filled with images of men as sexual aggressors and women as submissive sexual objects.

9    The transient quality of male and female interaction in public streets makes the behavior provoked by billboards and their public design images particularly difficult to attack. Psychologist Erving Goffman has analyzed both print ads and billboards as *Gender Advertisements*, concluding that art directors use exaggerated body language because consumers buy not products, but images of masculinity or femininity.[2] If passersby are driving at fifty miles per hour, these gender cues cannot be subtle. In *Ways of Seeing*, art historian John Berger describes the cumulative problem that gender stereotypes in advertising create for woman as "split consciousness."[3] While many women guard themselves, some men assume that ogling is part of normal public life. Women are always wary, watching men watch them, and wondering if and when something is going to happen to them.

10   Urban residents also encounter even more explicit sexual images in urban space. Tawdry strip clubs, X-rated films, "adult" bookstores, and sex shops are common sights, as are pornographic magazine and video stores. Pornography is a bigger, more profitable industry in the United States than all legitimate film and record business combined.[4] It spills over into soft-porn, quasi-porn, and tasteless public imagery everywhere. In the midst of this sexploitation, if one sees a real prostitute, there is mild surprise. Yet soliciting is still a crime. Of course, the male customer of an adult prostitute is almost never arrested. The graphic designer, the urban designer,

---

[1]William H. Whyte, "Street Life," *Urban Open Spaces* (Summer 1980); for a more detailed critique of hassling: Lindsy Van Gelder, "The International Language of Street Hassling," *Ms.* 9 (May 1981), 15–20, and letters about this article, *Ms.* (September 1981); and Cheryl Benard and Edith Schlaffer, "The Man in the Street: Why He Harasses," *Ms.* 9 (May 1981), 18–19.

[2]Erving Coffman, *Gender Advertisements* (New York: Harper Colphon, 1976), pp. 24–27; Nancy Henley, *Body Politics: Power, Sex, and Nonverbal Communication* (Englewood Cliffs, NJ: Prentice-Hall, 1977), p. 30; Marianne Wex, *Let's Take Back Our Space* (Berlin: Movimento Druck, 1979).

[3]John Berger et al., *Ways of Seeing* (Harmondsworth, England: BBC and Penguin, 1972), pp. 45–64.

[4]Tom Hayden, *The American Future: New Visions Beyond Old Frontiers* (Boston: South End Press, 1980), p. 15.

and the urban planner never come under suspicion for their contributions to a commercial public landscape that preserves the sexual double standard in a brutal and vulgar way.

11     Feminist Laura Shapiro calls the U.S. a "rape culture."[5] Surely most Americans do not consciously, deliberately accept public space given over to commercial exploitation, violence, and harassment of women. The success of campaigns against obscenity in films or music lyrics suggests how few activists have been able to tap public concern about commercialized sexuality, albeit in a narrow, antihumanist way. In contrast, the example of the Women's Christian Temperance Union under Frances Willard's leadership, and the parks movement under Olmsted's, show religious idealism, love of nature, and concern for female safety were activated into Progressive-era urban reform movements that enlarged domestic values into urban values, instead of diminishing them into domestic pieties.

## Analysis and Description

Analysis differs from description, as we note on page 137, but passages of description are commonly used in essays to support analysis of visual texts. In the essay "Advertisements, Pornography, and Public Space," for example, Dolores Hayden asks and answers the question "What are the effects of representations of women in public space?"; as she answers this question, she presents us with brief but vivid descriptions of billboards, mannequins, and architectural elements. Although Hayden's essay includes some description, it is nevertheless primarily analytical. Reading it, we share the writer's thoughts, but these thoughts are not the random and fleeting notions of reverie. The thoughts have been organized for us; the effects of billboards and other images on both women and men have been classified and presented to us in an orderly and coherent account made vivid by passages of description. Even if we have never seen the advertisement for the James Bond film or the Rolling Stones album, we can visualize these images because Hayden has made them present to us. Through these passages, we share at least imaginatively in the experiences that gave rise to her thinking. And through description, if the communication between writer and reader has been successful, we are persuaded to share the writer's opinions.

[5]Laura Shapiro, "Violence: The Most Obscene Fantasy," in Jo Freeman, ed., *Women: A Feminist Perspective*, 2nd ed. (Palo Alto, CA: Mayfield, 1979), pp. 469–73.

# Description at Work in the Analytic Essay

Hayden uses description in her essay to support her analysis of the effects of certain kinds of representations of women—the kind of analysis that might be written for a course in sociology or popular culture.

But because description is not analysis, if you are asked to analyze a painting for your art history class or an advertisement for your media studies class, it won't be enough simply to describe the thing in detail. It may be useful, then, to make some distinctions between the two processes, *description* and *analysis*. Hayden *describes* a billboard when she says, "a horizontal blonde in a backless black velvet dress, slit to the thigh, invites men to 'Try on a little Black Velvet'"; she *describes* mannequins in a department store window: "The female torsos, pin-headed, tip backward and sideways, at odd angles." She reports what any viewer might see if he or she looked closely enough. These statements don't offer evaluations, although Hayden's diction and tone—the words "slit" and "pin-headed," for example—do begin to shape our responses to these images. But when Hayden goes on to say that those mannequins look "as if they are about to be pushed over onto a bed" she is making an *inference*, she's telling her readers what the image *implies* or *suggests*; she is thinking critically about the image, *analyzing* it. Likewise, she *describes* the caryatids (columns in the shape of females) on the front door of an apartment building when she says,

> Their breasts are bared, their heads carry the load.

But she's *analyzing* when she says,

> They recall the architecture of the Erechtheum on the
> Acropolis in Athens, dating from the 5th century B.C., where the
> sculptured stone forms of female slaves were used as support for
> a porch in place of traditional columns and capitals. This is an
> ancient image of servitude.

She's comparing (a common analytic procedure) the modern caryatids to those on the Acropolis, and she's offering an evaluation, a judgment: The caryatids at the entrance of the modern building present an "image of servitude." In another sense, she's explaining how the caryatids function. She not only answers the question, "What do these images mean?", she explains *how* they mean.

# Comparing

> If you want to really see something,
> look at something else.
>
> —*Howard Nemerov*

We began this chapter with a brief analysis of a Brueghel drawing. We *compared* Brueghel's handling of the two figures: the amount of space each figure occupied, their activities, their facial expressions, the directions of their gaze; we thereby arrived at an interpretation of the *meaning* of Brueghel's drawing. We might say that the drawing invites the comparison, and in so doing communicates Brueghel's understanding of the artist's vision, or of the value of art.

Writers, too, often use comparisons to explain a concept or idea or to arrive at a judgment or conclusion. As in drawing or painting, the point of a comparison in writing is not simply to list similarities or differences, but to explain something, to illuminate what the similarities and differences add up to. What the comparison—or analysis—adds up to is sometimes referred to as a *synthesis*—literally, a combining of separate elements to form a coherent whole.

Notice George Orwell's technique in the following paragraph, from an essay titled "England, Your England," written during World War II. Orwell clarifies our understanding of one kind of military march, the Nazi goosestep, by calling attention to how it differs from the march used by English soldiers. Notice, too, the point of his comparison, which he makes clear in his second sentence, and which resonates throughout the comparison.

> One rapid but fairly sure guide to the social atmosphere of a country is the parade-step of its army. A military parade is really a kind of ritual dance, something like a ballet, expressing a certain philosophy of life. The goose-step, for instance, is one of the most horrible sights in the world, far more terrifying than a dive-bomber. It is simply an affirmation of naked power; contained in it, quite consciously and intentionally, is the vision of a boot crashing down on a face. Its ugliness is part of its essence, for what it is saying is "Yes, I *am* ugly, and you daren't laugh at me," like the bully who makes faces at his victim. Why is the goose-step not used in England? There are, heaven knows, plenty of army officers who would be only too glad to introduce some such thing. It is not used because the people in the street would laugh. Beyond a

certain point, military display is only possible in countries wh
the common people dare not laugh at the army. The Italians
adopted the goose-step at about the time when Italy passed de
nitely under German control, and, as one would expect, they
less well than the Germans. The Vichy government, if it survives,
is bound to introduce a stiffer parade-ground discipline into what
is left of the French army. In the British army the drill is rigid
and complicated, full of memories of the eighteenth century, but
without definite swagger; the march is merely a formalised walk.
It belongs to a society which is ruled by the sword, no doubt, but a
sword which must never be taken out of the scabbard.

—*George Orwell*

## Organizing Short Comparisons

An essay may be devoted entirely to a comparison, say of two kinds of
tribal organization. But such essays are relatively rare. More often, an essay
includes only a paragraph or two of comparison—for example, explaining
something unfamiliar by comparing it to something familiar. Let's spend a
moment discussing how to organize a paragraph that makes a comparison—
though the same principles can be applied to entire essays.

The first part may announce the topic, the next part may discuss
one of the two items being compared, and the last part may discuss the
other. We can call this method *lumping*, because it presents one item in
a lump, and then the other in another lump. Thus, Orwell says all that
he wishes to say about the goose-step in one lump, and then says what
he wishes to say about the British parade-step in another lump. But in
making a comparison a writer may use a different method, which we'll
call *splitting*. The discussion of the two items may run throughout the
paragraph, the writer perhaps devoting alternate sentences to each.

Because almost all writing is designed to help the reader see what
the writer has in mind, it may be especially useful here to illustrate
these two structures, lumping and splitting, with two paragraphs that
compare two sculptures. The first comparison of a Japanese statue of a
Buddha with a Chinese statue of a bodhisattva (a slightly lower spiritual being, dedicated to saving humankind) treats the Buddha first,
and then the bodhisattva. As you will see, it is an example of lumping.

The Buddha, recognizable by a cranial bump that indicates
a sort of supermind, sits erect and austere in the lotus position
(legs crossed, each foot with the sole upward on the opposing

thigh), in full control of his body. The carved folds of his garments, in keeping with the erect posture, are severe, forming a highly disciplined pattern that is an outward expression of his remote, constrained, austere inner nature. The bodhisattva, on the other hand, sits in a languid, sensuous posture known as "royal ease," the head pensively tilted downward, one knee elevated, one leg hanging down. He is accessible, relaxed, and compassionate.

The structure is, simply this:

The Buddha (posture, folds of garments, inner nature)
The bodhisattva (posture, folds of garments, inner nature)

If, however, the writer had wished to split rather than to lump, she would have compared an aspect of the Buddha with an aspect of the bodhisattva, then another aspect of the Buddha with another aspect of the bodhisattva, and so on, perhaps ending with a synthesis to clarify the point of the comparison. The paragraph might have read like this:

The Buddha, recognizable by a cranial bump that indicates a sort of supermind, sits erect and austere, in the lotus position (legs crossed, each foot with the sole upward on the opposing thigh), in full control of his body. In contrast, the bodhisattva sits in a languid, sensuous posture known as "royal ease," the head pensively tilted downward, one knee elevated, one leg hanging down. The carved folds of the Buddha's garments, in keeping with his erect posture, are severe, forming a highly disciplined pattern, whereas the bodhisattva's garments hang naturalistically. Both figures are spiritual but the Buddha is remote, constrained, and austere; the bodhisattva is accessible, relaxed, and compassionate.

In effect the structure is this:

The Buddha (posture)
The bodhisattva (posture)
The Buddha (garments)
The bodhisattva (garments)
The Buddha and the bodhisattva (synthesis)

Whether in any given piece of writing you should compare by lumping or by splitting will depend largely on your purpose and on the complexity of the material. We can't even offer the rule that splitting is good for brief,

*Shaka, the Historical Buddha*, Japan, Heian period, late tenth–early eleventh century; cherry with polychrome and gold; single woodblock construction; 83 cm (height of figure); 72.5 cm (height of hairline).

*Guanyin*, China, Jin Dynasty, twelfth century; wood with traces of polychrome and gold, 141 × 88 × 88 cm.

relatively obvious comparisons, lumping for longer, more complex ones, although such a rule usually works. We can, however, give some advice:

1. If you split, reread your draft with two points in mind:
   - *Imagine your reader*, and ask yourself if it is likely that this reader can keep up with the back-and-forth movement. Make sure (perhaps by a summary sentence at the end) that the larger picture is not obscured by the zigzagging.
   - *Don't leave any loose ends*. Make sure that if you call attention to points 1, 2, and 3 in X, you mention all of them (not just 1 and 2) in Y.

2. If you lump, do not simply comment first on X and then on Y.
   - *Let your reader know where you are going*, probably by means of an introductory sentence.
   - *Don't be afraid in the second half to remind your reader of the first half*. It is legitimate, and even desirable, to relate the second half of the comparison to the first half. A comparison organized by lumping will not break into two separate halves if the second half develops by reminding the reader how it differs from the first half.

## Longer Comparisons

Now let's think about a comparison that extends through two or three paragraphs. If you are comparing the indoor play (for instance, board games or play with toys) and the sports of girls with those of boys, you can, for example, devote one paragraph to the indoor play of girls, a second paragraph to the sports of girls, a third to the indoor play of boys, and a fourth to the sports of boys. If you are thinking in terms of comparing girls and boys, such an organization uses lumps, girls first and then boys (with a transition such as "Boys on the other hand . . ."). But you might split, writing four paragraphs along these lines:

> Indoor play of girls
> Indoor play of boys
> Sports of girls
> Sports of boys

Or you might organize the material into two paragraphs:

> Play and sports of girls
> Play and sports of boys

There is no rule, except that the organization and the point of the comparison be clear.

Consider these paragraphs from an essay by Sheila Tobias on the fear of mathematics. The writer's thesis in the essay is that although this fear is more commonly found in females than in males, biology seems not to be the cause. After discussing some findings (for example, that girls compute better than boys in elementary school, and that many girls tend to lose interest in mathematics in junior high school), the writer turns her attention away from the schoolhouse. Notice that whether a paragraph is chiefly about boys or chiefly about girls, the writer keeps us in mind of the overall point: reasons that more females than males fear math.

1    Not all the skills that are necessary for learning mathematics are learned in school. Measuring, computing, and manipulating objects that have dimensions and dynamic properties of their own are part of the everyday life of children. Children who miss out on these experiences may not be well primed for math in school.

2    Feminists have complained for a long time that playing with dolls is one way of convincing impressionable little girls that they may only be mothers or housewives—or, as in the case of the Barbie doll, "pinup girls"—when they grow up. But doll-playing may have

even more serious consequences for little girls than that. Do girls find out about gravity and distance and shapes and sizes playing with dolls? Probably not.

3     A curious boy, if his parents are tolerant, will have taken apart a number of household and play objects by the time he is ten, and, if his parents are lucky, he may even have put them back together again. In all of this he is learning things that will be useful in physics and math. Taking parts out that have to go back in requires some examination of form. Building something that stays up or at least stays put for some time involves working with structure.

4     Sports is another source of math-related concepts for children which tends to favor boys. Getting to first base on a not very well hit grounder is a lesson in time, speed, and distance. Intercepting a football thrown through the air requires some rapid intuitive eye calculations based on the ball's direction, speed, and trajectory. Since physics is partly concerned with velocities, trajectories, and collisions of objects, much of the math taught to prepare a student for physics deals with relationships and formulas that can be used to express motion and acceleration.

A few points about the organization of these paragraphs:

- Paragraph 1 offers a generalization about "children"—that is, about boys and girls.
- Paragraph 2 discusses the play of girls with dolls in the context of its relevance—irrelevance, really—to mathematics.
- Paragraph 3 discusses the household play of boys, again in the context of mathematics.
- Paragraph 4 discusses the outdoor sports of boys, but notice that girls are not forgotten, for its first sentence is "Sports is another source of math-related concepts for children which tends to favor boys."

In short, even when there is a sort of seesaw structure, boys on one end and girls on the other, we never lose sight of the thesis that comprises both halves of the comparison.

## Ways of Organizing an Essay Devoted to a Comparison

What happens if you want to organize a comparison or contrast that runs through an entire essay, say a comparison between two political campaigns, or between the characters in two novels? Remember that you are writing a comparison not merely as an exercise but in order to make a significant point—let's say, to demonstrate the superiority of X to Y.

Probably your first thought, after making some jottings in which you perhaps draw up two lists, will be to lump rather than to split— that is, to discuss one half of the comparison and then to go on to the second half. We'll discuss this useful method of organization in a moment, but here we want to point out that many instructors and textbooks disapprove of such an organization, arguing that the essay too often breaks into two parts and that the second part involves a good deal of repetition of categories set up in the first part. They prefer splitting. Let's say you are comparing the narrator of *Huckleberry Finn* with the narrator of *The Catcher in the Rye*, in order to show that despite superficial similarities, they are very different, and that the difference is partly the difference between the nineteenth century and the twentieth. An organization often recommended is something like this:

1. First similarity (the narrator and his quest)
   a. Huck
   b. Holden
2. Second similarity (the corrupt world surrounding the narrator)
   a. Society in *Huckleberry Finn*
   b. Society in *The Catcher in the Rye*
3. First difference (degree to which the narrator fulfills his quest and escapes from society)
   a. Huck's plan to "light out" to the frontier
   b. Holden's breakdown

And so on, for as many additional differences as seem relevant. Here is another way of splitting and organizing a comparison:

1. First point: the narrator and his quest
   a. Similarities between Huck and Holden
   b. Differences between Huck and Holden
2. Second point: the corrupt world
   a. Similarities between the worlds in *Huck* and *The Catcher*
   b. Differences between the worlds in *Huck* and *The Catcher*
3. Third point: degree of success
   a. Similarities between Huck and Holden
   b. Differences between Huck and Holden

But a comparison need not employ either of these methods of splitting. There is even the danger that an essay employing either of them may not come into focus until the essayist stands back from the seven-layer cake and announces, in the concluding paragraph, that the odd layers taste better. In your preparatory thinking you may want to make comparisons in pairs, but you must come to some conclusions about what these add up to before writing the final version. The final version should not duplicate the thought processes; rather, it should be organized so as to make the point clearly and effectively.

## A RULE FOR WRITERS

The point of comparison is not to list pairs of similarities or differences, but to illuminate a topic.

Although in a long essay you cannot postpone until page 30 a discussion of the second half of the comparison, in an essay of, say, fewer than ten pages, nothing is wrong with setting forth half of the comparison and then, in the light of what you've already said, discussing the second half. True, an essay that uses lumping will break into two unrelated parts if the second half makes no use of the first or fails to modify it; but the essay will hang together if the second half looks back to the first half and calls attention to differences that the new material reveals.

The danger of organizing the essay into two unrelated lumps can be avoided if in formulating your thesis you remember that your aim is to call attention to the unique features of something by holding it up against something similar but significantly different. If the differences are great and apparent, a comparison is a waste of effort. ("Blueberries are different from elephants. Blueberries do not have trunks. And elephants do not grow on bushes.") Indeed, a comparison between essentially and evidently unlike things can only obscure, for by making the comparison the writer implies there are significant similarities, and readers can only wonder why they do not see them. The essays that do break into two halves are essays that make *uninstructive comparisons*: The first half tells the reader five things about baseball, the second half tells the reader five unrelated things about football.

- ☐ Is the point of the comparison—your reason for making it—clear? (See pp. 150–57.)
- ☐ Do you cover all significant similarities and differences? (See pp. 150, 155–57.)
- ☐ Is the comparison readable—that is, is it clear and yet not mechanical? (See pp. 150–57.)
- ☐ Is lumping or splitting the best way to make this comparison? (See pp. 151–53, 157.)
- ☐ If you are offering a value judgment, is it fair? Have you overlooked weaknesses in your preferred subject and strengths in your less preferred subject?

## Process Analysis

Popular writing offers many examples of the form known as **process analysis**. Newspaper articles explain how to acquire a home aquarium or how to "detail" your car to improve its resale value; magazine articles explain how to begin a program of weight training or how to make a safe exit in an airplane emergency. The requirements a writer must follow when preparing such an article, sometimes called a **directive process analysis**, can be simply stated:

- ■ Know the material thoroughly.
- ■ Keep your audience in mind.
- ■ Set forth the steps clearly, usually in chronological order.
- ■ Define unfamiliar terms.

Explaining a process is common in academic writing too, though usually the explanation is of how something happens or has happened, and it is thus sometimes called an **informative process analysis**. The writer's purpose is for the reader to understand the process, not to perform it. You may find yourself reading or writing about a successful election strategy or a botched military campaign. In an exam you may be explaining your plan to solve a mathematical problem, or you may be explaining how the imagery works in a Shakespearean sonnet. You might write an essay on the camera techniques Hitchcock used in a sequence, or a term paper based on your research in marine biology. Once again, you will need to keep your reader in mind, to organize your explanation clearly and logically, and, of course, to write with expert knowledge of your subject.

The essay below reports on a lecture that was, from the evidence, an entertaining example of an *informative process analysis*.

ANNE HEBALD MANDELBAUM

# It's the Portly Penguin That Gets the Girl, French Biologist Claims

1   The penguin is a feathered and flippered bird who looks as if he's on his way to a formal banquet. With his stiff, kneeless strut and natural dinner jacket, he moves like Charlie Chaplin in his heyday dressed like Cary Grant in his.

2   But beneath the surface of his tuxedo is a gallant bird indeed. Not only does he fast for 65 days at a time, sleep standing up, and forsake all others in a lifetime of monogamy, but the male penguin also guards, watches over, and even hatches the egg.

3   We owe much of our current knowledge of the life and loves of the king and emperor penguins to—*bien sûr*—a Frenchman. Twenty-eight-year-old Yvon Le Maho is a biophysiologist from Lyons who visited the University last week to discuss his discoveries and to praise the penguin. He had just returned from 14 months in Antarctica, where he went to measure, to photograph, to weigh, to take blood and urine samples of, to perform autopsies on—in short, to study the penguin.

4   Although his original intent had been to investigate the penguin's long fasts, Monsieur Le Maho was soon fascinated by the amatory aspect of the penguin. Copulating in April, the female produces the egg in May and then heads out to sea, leaving her mate behind to incubate the egg. The males huddle together, standing upright and protecting the 500-gram (or 1.1-pound) egg with their feet for 65 days. During this time, they neither eat nor stray: each steadfastly stands guard over his egg, protecting it from the temperatures which dip as low as −40 degrees and from the winds which whip the Antarctic wilds with gusts of 200 miles an hour.

5   For 65 days and 65 nights, the males patiently huddle over the eggs, never lying down, never letting up. Then, every year on July 14th—Bastille Day, the national holiday of France—the eggs hatch and thousands of penguin chicks are born, M. Le Maho told his amused and enthusiastic audience at the Biological Laboratories.

6   The very day the chicks are born—or, at the latest, the following day—the female penguins return to land from their two-and-a-half month fishing expedition. They clamber out of the water and toboggan along the snow-covered beaches toward the rookery and their mates.

At this moment, the males begin to emit the penguin equivalent of wild, welcoming cheers—"*comme le cri de trompette*," M. Le Maho later told the *Gazette* in an interview—"like the clarion call of the trumpet."

7     And, amid the clamorous thundering of 12,000 penguins, the female recognizes the individual cry of her mate. When she does, she begins to cry to him. The male then recognizes *her* song, lifts the newborn chick into his feathered arms, and makes a beeline for the female. Each singing, each crying, the males and females rush toward each other, slipping and sliding on the ice as they go, guided all the while by the single voice each instinctively knows.

8     The excitement soon wears thin for the male, however, who hasn't had a bite to eat in more than two months. He has done his duty and done it unflaggingly, but even penguins cannot live by duty alone. He must have food, and quickly.

9     Having presented his mate with their newborn, the male abruptly departs, heading out to sea in search of fish. The female, who has just returned from her sea-going sabbatical, has swallowed vast quantities of fish for herself and her chick. Much of what she has eaten she has not digested. Instead, this undigested food becomes penguin baby food. She regurgitates it, all soft and paplike, from her storage throat right into her chick's mouth. The chicks feed in this manner until December, when they first learn to find food on their own.

10    The penguins' reproductive life begins at age five, and the birds live about 25 years. Their fasting interests M. Le Maho because of its close similarities with fasting in human beings. And although many migratory birds also fast, their small size and indeed their flight make it almost impossible to study them closely. With the less-mobile and non-flying penguin, however, the scientist has a relatively accessible population to study. With no damage to the health of the penguin, M. Le Maho told the *Gazette*, a physiobiologist can extract blood from the flipper and sample the urine.

11    "All fasting problems are the same between man and the penguin," M. Le Maho said. "The penguin uses glucose in the brain, experiences ketosis as does man, and accomplishes gluconeogenesis, too." Ketosis is the build-up of partially burned fatty acids in the blood, usually as a result of starvation; gluconeogenesis is the making of sugar from non-sugar chemicals, such as amino acids. "The penguin can tell us a great deal about how our own bodies react to fasting conditions," M. Le Maho said.

12    He will return to Antarctica, M. Le Maho said, with the French government-sponsored *Expéditions Polaires Françaises* next December.

There he will study the growth of the penguin chick, both inside the egg and after birth; will continue to study their mating, and to examine the penguin's blood sugar during fasting.

13      During the question-and-answer period following his talk, M. Le Maho was asked what the female penguin looks for in a mate. Responding, M. Le Maho drew himself up to his full five-foot-nine and said, "*La grandeur.*"

# Explaining an Analysis

As we have suggested, the writer of an analytical essay arrives at a thesis by asking questions and answering them, by separating the topic into parts, and by seeing—often through the use of lists and scratch outlines—how those parts relate. Or, we might say, analytic writing presupposes detective work: The writer looks over the evidence, finds some clues, pursues the trail from one place to the next, and makes the arrest. Elementary? Perhaps.

You may recall that Sherlock Holmes customarily searches for evidence, finds it, and then—and this is important—explains it to his listener, usually Dr. Watson. When you write an analytic essay, you are Holmes, and your reader is Watson. Even when as a writer, after preliminary thinking you have solved a problem—that is, focused on a topic and formulated a thesis—you are, as we have said before, not yet done. It is, alas, not enough simply to present the results of your analytical thinking to a reader who, like Dr. Watson, will surely want to know "How in the world did you deduce that?" And like Holmes, writers are often impatient; we long to say with him "I have no time for trifles." But the real reason for our impatience is, as Holmes is quick to acknowledge, that "It was easier to know it than to explain why I know it." But explaining to readers why or how, presenting both the reasoning that led to a thesis and the evidence that supports the reasoning, is the writer's job.

In your preliminary detective work (that is, in reading, taking notes, musing, jotting down some thoughts, and writing rough drafts) some insights (perhaps including your thesis) may come swiftly, apparently spontaneously, and in random order. You may be unaware that you have been thinking analytically at all. In preparing your essay for your reader, however, you become aware, in part because *you must become aware*. To replace your reader's natural suspicion with respect for your analysis, you must explain your reasoning in an orderly and interesting fashion, and you must present your evidence.

# Persuading Readers

The difficult part in an argument is not to defend one's opinion, but rather to know it.

—André Maurois

To PERSUADE READERS IS TO CONVINCE THEM OF THE MERIT OF your point of view, whether you're arguing against censorship, or for state-sponsored lotteries, or in favor of a particular interpretation of a short story. To be persuasive, you must present *reasonable arguments*, supported with *evidence*. In academic essays, the distinction between argument and analysis is often blurry. In the preceding chapter, for example, Dolores Hayden's analytic essay ("Advertisements, Pornography, and Public Space") does more than assert that certain kinds of images appear in certain places. It sets forth an **argument**: We ought not to allow public space to be given over to the harassment of women. The writer supports that argument with **evidence**, a report of images that she has observed, images that she subjects to careful **analysis**. In Chapter 10, "Writing the Research Essay," we'll examine an essay in which the writer uses **analysis** and **argument** in roughly equal proportion. In this chapter, after a brief comment on persuasion by emotional appeal, we'll focus on the elements of argument: on the distinction between claims and evidence, on the importance of defining terms and of avoiding fallacies, and on the use of wit in persuasive writing.

## Emotional Appeals

It is often said that good argumentative writing appeals only to reason and logic (Greek: *logos*), never to emotion (*pathos*), and that any sort of emotional appeal is illegitimate, irrelevant, fallacious. Logic textbooks may even stigmatize with Latin labels the various sorts of emotional appeal—for instance, *argumentum ad populam* (appeal to the prejudices of the mob, as in "Come on, we all know that schools don't teach anything anymore") and *argumentum ad misericoridam* (appeal to pity, as in "No one can blame this poor kid for stabbing a classmate because his mother was often institutionalized and his father beat him").

True, appeals to emotion may get in the way of the facts of the case; they may blind the audience by stimulating anger or tears. When an emotional argument confuses the issue or shifts attention away from the facts, we can reasonably speak of the fallacy of emotional appeal. But no fallacy is involved when an emotional appeal heightens the facts, bringing them home to the audience rather than masking them. If we are talking about legislation that would govern police actions, it is legitimate to show a photograph of the battered, bloodied face of a victim of alleged police brutality. Of course such a photograph cannot tell if the subject threatened the officer with a gun or repeatedly resisted an order to surrender. But it can tell us that the victim was severely beaten and (like a comparable description in words) evoke in us emotions that may properly enter into our decision about what sorts of limitations on police actions are appropriate.

In appealing to emotions, then:

- Do not falsify (especially by oversimplifying) the issue.
- Do not distract attention from the facts of the case.

For the most part, you should focus on the facts and concentrate on offering reasons (essentially, statements linked with "because"), but you may also legitimately bring the facts home to your readers by seeking to induce in them the appropriate emotions.

## Making Reasonable Arguments

Persuasive writing that offers evidence and relies chiefly on reasoning rather than on appeals to the emotions is usually called *argument*. What distinguishes argument from exposition is this: Whereas both consist of statements, in argument some statements are offered as *reasons* for other statements. Another way of characterizing argument is that argument assumes there is or may be substantial disagreement between informed readers. To overcome this disagreement, the writer of an argument offers reasons that seek to convince by their validity. Here, for example, is C. S. Lewis arguing against vivisection, the experimentation on live animals for scientific research:

> A rational discussion of this subject begins by inquiring whether pain is, or is not, an evil. If it is not, then the case against vivisection

falls. But then so does the case for vivisection. If it is not defended on the ground that it reduces human suffering, on what ground can it be defended? And if pain is not an evil, why should human suffering be reduced? We must therefore assume as a basis for the whole discussion that pain is an evil, otherwise there is nothing to be discussed.

Now if pain is an evil then the infliction of pain, considered in itself, must clearly be an evil act. But there are such things as necessary evils. Some acts which would be bad, simply in themselves, may be excusable and even laudable when they are necessary means to a greater good. In saying that the infliction of pain, simply in itself, is bad, we are not saying that pain ought never to be inflicted. Most of us think that it can rightly be inflicted for a good purpose—as in dentistry or just and reformatory punishment. The point is that it always requires justification. On the man whom we find inflicting pain rests the burden of showing why an act which in itself would be simply bad is, in those particular circumstances, good. If we find a man giving pleasure, it is for us to prove (if we criticize him) that his action is wrong. But if we find a man inflicting pain, it is for him to prove that his action is right. If he cannot, he is a wicked man.

And here is Supreme Court Justice Louis Brandeis, concluding his justly famous argument that government may not use evidence illegally obtained by wiretapping:

Decency, security and liberty alike demand that government officials shall be subjected to the same rules of conduct that are commands to the citizen. In a government of laws, existence of the government will be imperiled if it fails to observe the law scrupulously. Our Government is the potent, the omnipresent teacher. For good or for ill, it teaches the whole people by its example. Crime is contagious. If the Government becomes a lawbreaker, it breeds contempt for law; it invites every man to become a law unto himself; it invites anarchy. To declare that in the administration of the criminal law the end justifies the means—to declare that the Government may commit crimes in order to secure the conviction of a private criminal—would bring terrible retribution. Against that pernicious doctrine this Court should resolutely set its face.

Notice here that Brandeis's reasoning is highlighted by his forceful style. Note the resonant use of parallel constructions ("Decency, security and liberty," "For good or for ill," "it breeds . . . it invites," "To declare . . . to declare") and the variation between long and short sentences. Note too the wit in his comparisons: Government is a teacher, crime is like a disease.

# Claims and Evidence

**Evidence** is what a writer offers in support of a **claim**—an assertion, usually that something is true, or right, or good. Evidence usually comes in the form of examples, testimony, and statistics.

# Three Kinds of Claims: Claims of Fact, Value, and Policy

We can usually distinguish between two kinds of claims, claims of fact and claims of value, and we can sometimes distinguish these from a third kind of claim, claims of policy.

## *Claims of Fact*

**Claims of fact** assert that something is or was or will be. (Note that claims of fact are not themselves facts.) They include, for instance, arguments about cause and effect, correlation, probability, and states of affairs. The following examples can be considered claims of fact:

Pornography stimulates violence against women.

Pornography serves a useful social purpose because it offers a harmless release of impulses that might otherwise be released in such activities as molestation or rape.

Capital punishment reduces crime.

Capital punishment does not reduce crime.

To support a claim of this sort, you must provide evidence. Such evidence might be testimony (for instance, your own experience, or statements by men who have said that pornography stimulated them to violence), or it might be statistics (gathered from a report in a scholarly journal). Even if the claim has to do with the future—let's say the claim that gun control will not reduce crime—you try to offer evidence. For example, you might gather information about the experiences of other countries, or even of certain states, that have adopted strict regulations concerning the sale of guns. The implication is that if a policy had a particular effect in one place, it will have the same effect in another. Opponents may point out that results in, say, Miami, are no guarantee of the same results in, say, Chicago, but our point is that even claims for future facts must offer evidence.

# Claims of Value

**Claims of value** concern what is right or wrong, good or bad, better or worse than something else:

> Country music deserves to be taken seriously.
> Capital punishment is barbaric.
> Euthanasia is immoral.

Some claims of value may be mere expressions of taste: "Vanilla is better than chocolate." It is hard to imagine how one could go about supporting such a claim—or refuting it. One probably can do no better than reply with the Latin proverb, "*De gustibus non est disputandum*," (There is no disputing about tastes). Notice, however, that the claim that vanilla is better than chocolate is quite different from the claim that most Americans prefer vanilla to chocolate. The last statement is a claim of fact, not of value, and it can be proved or disproved with evidence—for example, with information provided by the makers of ice cream.

Claims of value that go beyond the mere expression of taste—for instance, claims of morality or claims of artistic value—are usually supported by appeals to standards. ("The Patriot Act is bad *because* governments should not restrict the rights of individuals," or "Hip-hop music is good *because* it is complex.") In supporting claims of value, writers usually appeal to standards that they believe are acceptable to their readers. Here are some examples:

> Sex-education programs in schools are inappropriate *because* aspects of moral education should properly be given only by parents.

> Sex-education programs in schools are appropriate *because* society has a duty to provide what most parents obviously are reluctant to provide.

> Doctors should be permitted to end a patient's life if the patient makes such a request, *because* each of us should be free to make the decisions that most concern us.

> Euthanasia is unacceptable *because* only God can give or take life.

In arguing a claim of value, be sure you have clearly in mind the standards that you believe support the claim. You may find it appropriate to explain *why* you hold these standards, and *how* adherence to these standards will be of benefit.

## Claims of Policy

**Claims of policy** assert that a policy, law, or custom should be initiated or altered or dropped. Such claims usually are characterized by words like "should," "must," and "ought."

Children should be allowed to vote, if they wish to.

A course in minority cultures ought to be required.

The federal tax on gasoline must be raised.

In defending an unfamiliar claim of policy, you may begin by pointing out that there is a problem that is usually overlooked. For instance, if you urgently believe that children should have the right to vote—a view almost never expressed—you'll probably first have to convince your audience that there really is an arguable issue here, an issue concerning children's rights, an issue that deserves serious thought.

In defending a claim of policy, you will probably find yourself providing information, just as you would do in support of a claim of fact. For instance, if your topic is children and the vote, you might point out that until 1920 women could not vote in the United States, the usual arguments being that they were mentally unfit and that they would vote the way their men told them to vote. Experience has proved that these low estimates of the capabilities of the disenfranchised were absurd.

But in defending a claim of policy, you will probably have to consider values as well as facts. Thus, in arguing for an increase in the gasoline tax, you might want not only to provide factual information about how much money a five-cents-per-gallon tax would raise but also to argue that such an increase is *fairer* than an alternative such as reducing Social Security benefits.

# Three Kinds of Evidence: Examples, Testimony, Statistics

Writers of arguments seek to persuade by offering evidence. There are three chief forms of evidence used in argument:

- Examples
- Testimony, the citation of authorities
- Statistics

We'll briefly consider each of these.

## Examples

The word *example* is from the Latin *exemplum*, which means "something taken out." An example is the sort of thing, taken from among many similar things, that one selects and holds up for view, perhaps after saying "for example," or "for instance."

Three categories of examples are especially common in written arguments:

- Real examples
- Invented instances
- Analogies

**Real examples** are actual instances that have occurred. If, say, we are arguing that gun control won't work, we point to those states that have adopted gun control laws and that nevertheless have had no reduction in crimes using guns. Or, if we want to support the assertion that a woman can be a capable head of state, we may find ourselves pointing to women who actually served as heads of state, such as Golda Meir and Indira Gandhi (prime ministers of Israel and India) or to Angela Merkel (Chancellor of Germany) and Mary McAleese (President of Ireland).

The advantage of using real examples is, clearly, that they are real. Of course, an opponent might stubbornly respond that Golda Meir and Indira Gandhi, for some reason or other, could not function as the head of state in *our* country. Someone might argue, for instance, that the case of Golda Meir proves nothing, since the role of women in Israeli society is different from the role of women in the United States. And another person might argue that much of Mrs. Gandhi's power came from the fact that she was the daughter of Nehru, an immensely popular Indian statesman. Even the most compelling real example inevitably will in some ways be special or particular, and in the eyes of some readers may not seem to be a fair example.

**Invented instances** are exempt from the charge that, because of some detail or other, they are not relevant as evidence. Suppose, for example, you are arguing against capital punishment, on the grounds that if an innocent person is executed, there is no way of even attempting to rectify the injustice. If you point to the real case of X, you may be met with the reply that X was not in fact innocent. Rather than get tangled up in the guilt or innocence of a particular person, it may be better to argue that we can suppose—we can imagine—an innocent person convicted and executed, and we can imagine that evidence later proves the person's innocence.

Invented instances have the advantage of presenting an issue clearly, free from all of the distracting particularities and irrelevancies that are bound up with any real instance. But invented instances have the disadvantage of being invented, and they may seem remote from the real issues being argued.

**Analogies** are comparisons pointing out several resemblances between two rather different things. For instance, one might assert that a government is like a ship, and in times of stress—if the ship is to weather the storm—the authority of the captain must not be questioned.

But don't confuse an analogy with proof. An analogy is an extended comparison between two things; it can be useful in exposition, for it explains the unfamiliar by means of the familiar: "A government is like a ship, and just as a ship has a captain and a crew, so a government has . . ."; "Writing an essay is like building a house; just as an architect must begin with a plan, so the writer must . . ." Such comparisons can be useful, helping to clarify what otherwise might be obscure, but their usefulness goes only so far. Everything is what it is, and not another thing. A government is not a ship, and what is true of a captain's power need not be true of a president's power; and a writer is not an architect. Some of what is true about ships may be roughly true of governments, and some of what is true about architects may be true of writers, but there are differences too. Consider the following analogy between a lighthouse and the death penalty:

> The death penalty is a warning, just like a lighthouse throwing its beams out to sea. We hear about shipwrecks, but we do not hear about the ships the lighthouse guides safely on their way. We do not have proof of the number of ships it saves, but we do not tear the lighthouse down.

> —*J. Edgar Hoover*

How convincing is Hoover's analogy as an argument—that is, as a reason for retaining the death penalty?

## Testimony

**Testimony**, or the citation of authorities, is rooted in our awareness that some people are recognized as experts. In our daily lives we constantly turn to experts for guidance: We look up the spelling of a word in the dictionary, we watch weather forecasts on television, we take an ailing cat to the vet for a checkup. Similarly, when we want to become informed about controversial matters, we often turn to experts, first to help educate ourselves, and then to help convince others.

Don't forget that *you* are an authority on many things. For example, today's newspaper includes an article about the cutback in funding for the teaching of the arts in elementary and secondary schools. Art educators are responding that the arts are not a frill, and that in fact the arts provide the analytical thinking, teamwork, motivation, and self-discipline that most people agree are needed to reinvigorate American schools. If you have been involved in the arts in school—for instance, if you studied painting or learned to play a musical instrument—you are in a position to evaluate these claims.

There are at least two reasons for offering testimony in an argument. The obvious one is that expert opinion carries some weight with any audience; the less obvious one is that a change of voice (if the testimony is not your own) in an essay may afford the reader a bit of pleasure. No matter how engaging your own voice may be, a fresh voice—whether that of Thomas Jefferson, Ruth Bader Ginsburg, or Alice Walker—may provide a refreshing change of tone.

But, of course, there are dangers:

- The words of authorities may be taken out of context or otherwise distorted.
- The authorities may not be authorities on the present topic.

Quite rightly we are concerned with what Jefferson said, but it is not clear that his words can be fairly applied, on one side or the other, to such an issue as abortion or drilling for oil in Alaska. Quite rightly we are concerned with what Einstein said, but it is not clear that his eminence as a physicist constitutes him an authority on, say, world peace.

## Statistics

**Statistics**, another important form of evidence, are especially useful in arguments concerning social issues. For example, if we want to argue for raising the driving age, we will probably do some research and will offer statistics about the number of accidents caused by people in certain age groups.

But a word of caution: The significance of statistics may be difficult to assess. For instance, opponents of gun control legislation have pointed out, in support of the argument that such laws are ineffectual, that homicides in Florida *increased* after Florida adopted gun control laws. Supporters of gun control laws cried "foul," arguing that in the years after adopting these laws Miami became (for reasons having nothing to do with the laws) the cocaine capital of the United States, and the rise in homicide was chiefly a reflection of murders involved in the drug trade. That is, a significant change in the population has made a comparison of the figures meaningless. This objection seems plausible, and probably the statistics therefore should carry little weight.

# A Note on Definition in the Persuasive Essay

To argue a point or to explain an idea, writers frequently need to provide definitions. Defining the terms of an argument is one of the persuasive writer's most useful strategies: A writer making an argument for or against abortion would be likely at some point in the essay to define the term "life."

The words may be *specialized* or unfamiliar to the writer's intended audience—for example, the words "venture capitalist" or "enterprise zones." Or a writer might define a word that the audience may think it knows but that (in the writer's opinion) the audience may misunderstand. For instance, you might argue that the words "insurgent" and "terrorist" are not synonyms, and then go on to define each word, showing the differences between them.

In addition to defining a word because it is specialized ("venture capitalist"), or because we want to distinguish it from another word ("insurgent" and "terrorist"), we may define a word because the word has many meanings and we want to make sure that readers take the word in a particular way. A word like "ability," for example, may require defining in a discussion of the Scholastic Aptitude Test. To argue that the SAT does or does not measure "academic ability," the writer and reader need, in a sense, to agree on a specific meaning for "ability." This kind of definition, where the writer specifies or stipulates a meaning ("By *ability* I mean . . ."), is called a **stipulative definition**.

The word *stipulate*, by the way, comes from a Latin word meaning "to bargain." Explaining a word's *etymology*, its history or its origin, as we have just done, is often an aid in definition.

In short, when defining a word or term, writers have many options, and they need to take into account their own purposes in writing and their readers' needs.

# How Much Evidence Is Enough?

If you allow yourself ample time to write your essay, you probably will turn up plenty of evidence to illustrate your arguments, such as examples drawn from your own experience and imagination, from your reading, and from your talks with others. Evidence will not only help to clarify and to support your assertions, but it will also provide a concreteness that will be welcome in a paper that might be on the whole fairly abstract. Your sense of your audience will have to guide you as you select your evidence. Generally speaking, a single example may not fully illuminate a difficult point, and so a second example, a clincher, may be desirable. If you offer a third or fourth example you probably are succumbing to a temptation to include something that tickles your fancy. If it is as good as you think it is, the reader probably will accept the unnecessary example and may even be grateful. But before you heap up examples, try to imagine yourself in your reader's place, and ask if the example is needed. If it is not needed, ask yourself if the reader will be glad to receive the overload.

One other point: On most questions, say on the value of bilingual education or on the need for rehabilitation programs in prisons, it's not possible to make a strictly logical case, in the sense of an absolutely airtight proof. Don't assume that it is your job to make an absolute proof. What you are expected to do is to offer a reasonable argument.

# Two Kinds of Reasoning: Induction and Deduction

We have just said that you are expected to offer a reasonable argument, which means that your essay will probably demonstrate two kinds of thinking, inductive and deductive. **Induction** is the process of reasoning from particular to general, or drawing a conclusion about all members of a class from a study of some members of the class. Every elephant I have seen is grayish, so by induction (from Latin for "lead into," "lead up to") I conclude that all elephants are grayish. And here we get to what is called *logos*, reasoning, as opposed to *pathos*, emotion.

Here's another example: I have met ten graduates of Vassar College and all are females, so I conclude that all Vassar graduates are females. This conclusion, however, happens to be incorrect; Vassar originally admitted only women, but it now admits men. Induction is valid only if the sample is representative.

Because we can rarely be certain that a sample is representative, induced conclusions are usually open to doubt. Still, we live our lives largely by induction; we have dinner with a friend, we walk the dog, we write home for money—all because these actions have produced certain results in the past and we assume that actions of the same sort will produce results consistent with our earlier experience. Nelson Algren's excellent advice must have been arrived at inductively: "Never eat at a place called Mom's, and never play cards with a man called Doc." In developing our argument, we draw on experience—"Policy X has been successful in all ten instances where it was tried, so we can assume it will probably succeed here too"—but we must understand that we are not dealing with certainties.

**Deduction** (from Latin for "lead down from") is the process of reasoning from premises to a logical conclusion. Here is the classic example:

"All men are mortal" (the major premise);

"Socrates is a man" (the minor premise);

"Therefore Socrates is mortal" (the conclusion).

Such an argument, which takes two truths and joins them to produce a third truth, is called a *syllogism* (from Greek for "a reckoning together"). Deduction moves from a general statement to a specific application; it is, therefore, the opposite of induction, which moves from specific instances to a general conclusion.

Notice that if a premise of a syllogism is not true, one can reason logically and still come to a false conclusion. Example: All teachers are members of a union; Jones is a teacher; therefore Jones is a member of a union. Although the formal process of reasoning is correct here, the major premise is false—not all teachers are members of a union—and so the conclusion is worthless. (Jones may or may not be a member of a union.) In other words, "Garbage in, garbage out."

# Avoiding Fallacies

> "If it were so, it would be; but as it isn't,
> it ain't. That's logic."
>
> —*Tweedledee, Through the Looking-Glass*

*Fallacies* (from a Latin verb meaning "to deceive") are logical errors in reasoning.

To persuade readers to accept your opinions, you must persuade them that you are reliable; if your argument includes fallacies, thoughtful readers will not take you seriously. Here are nine fallacies to avoid:

1. **False authority.** Be cautious about presenting as evidence the opinions or ideas of sources who are not authorities on the topic in question—for example, a heart surgeon speaking on politics. Some former authorities are no longer authorities because the problems have changed or because their views are outmoded. Adam Smith, Jefferson, Eleanor Roosevelt, and Einstein remain persons of genius, but an attempt to use their opinions when you are examining modern issues—even in their fields—may be questioned.

2. **False quotation.** Represent your source's point accurately. For example, you may find someone who grants that "there are strong arguments in favor of abolishing the death penalty," but if she goes on to argue that, on balance, the arguments in favor of retaining it seem stronger to her, it would be dishonest to quote only the words that imply that she favors abolishing it.

3. **Suppression of evidence.** Be sure to consider evidence that runs counter to your own argument. Failure to confront the opposing evidence will be noticed; your readers will keep wondering why you do not consider this point or that, and may consequently dismiss your argument. *Concede to the opposition what is due it and then outscore the opposition:* If you confront the opposition, you will almost surely strengthen your own argument. As Edmund Burke said 200 years ago, "He that wrestles with us strengthens our nerves, and sharpens our skill. Our antagonist is our helper."

4. **Generalization from insufficient evidence.** When rereading the draft of your argument, identify each generalization and ask yourself if a reasonable reader is likely to agree that the generalization is adequately supported by persuasive evidence.

A visitor to a college may sit in on three classes, each taught by a different instructor, and may find all three stimulating. Can she generalize and say that the teaching at this college is excellent? Are three classes a sufficient sample? If all three are offered by the Biology Department, and if the Biology Department includes only five instructors, perhaps she can tentatively say that the teaching of biology at this institution is good. If the Biology Department contains twenty instructors, perhaps she can still say, though more tentatively, that this sample indicates that the teaching of biology is good. But what does the sample say about the teaching of other subjects at the college? Well—nothing, really.

5. **The genetic fallacy.** Don't assume that something can necessarily be explained in terms of its birth or origin. "He wrote the novel to make money, so it can't be any good" is not a valid inference. The value of a novel does not depend on the author's motivations in writing it. Neither do the highest motivations guarantee the quality of the product.

6. **Begging the question and circular reasoning.** Both terms refer to assuming the truth of the point that you should prove. The term "begging the question" is a bit odd, and it's often misused, as in the following sentence: "His habit of robbing banks begs the question of whether he thought he'd never be caught." The phrase actually means, in effect, "You, like a beggar, are asking me to grant you something at the outset."

Consider these examples: "The barbaric death penalty should be abolished"; "This senseless language requirement should be dropped." Both of these statements beg the question, or *assume what they should prove*—that the death penalty is barbaric, and that the language requirement is senseless. You can of course make assertions such as these, but you must go on to prove them.

Circular reasoning is usually an extended form of begging the question. What ought to be proved is covertly assumed. Example: "X is the best-qualified candidate for the office, because the most informed people say so." Who are the most informed people? Those who recognize X's superiority. Another example: "I feel sympathy for her because I identify with her." Despite the "because," no reason is really offered. What follows "because" is merely a restatement, in slightly different words, of what precedes it.

7. **Post hoc ergo propter hoc** (Latin for "after this, therefore because of this"). Don't assume that because X precedes Y, X must cause Y. For example: "He went to college and came back a boozer; college corrupted him." He might have taken up liquor even if he had not gone to college.

8. **Argumentum ad hominem** (Latin for "argument toward the man"). Here the argument is directed toward the person rather than toward the issue. Don't shift from your topic to your opponent. A speaker

argues against stem cell research, and her opponent, instead of facing the merits of the argument, attacks the character or the associations of the opponent: "You're a Catholic, aren't you?"

9. **False assumption.** Consider the Scot who argued that Shakespeare must have been a Scot. Asked for his evidence, he replied, "The ability of the man warrants the assumption." Or take a statement such as "She goes to Yale, so she must be rich." Possibly the statement is based on faulty induction (the writer knows four Yale students, and all four are rich), but more likely the writer is just passing on a cliché. The Yale student in question may be on a scholarship, or struggling to earn the money, or backed by parents of modest means who for eighteen years have saved money for her college education.

The errors we have discussed are common. In revising, try to spot them and eliminate or correct them. You have a point to make, and you should make it fairly. If it can be made only unfairly, you do an injustice not only to your reader but also to yourself. You don't want to be like the politician whose speech had a marginal note: "Argument weak; shout here."

MANKOFF

*"Look, maybe you're right, but for the sake of argument let's assume you're wrong and drop it."*

© The New Yorker Collection 1983. Robert Mankoff from Cartoonbank.com. All Right Reserved.

# Wit

In addition to using sound argument and other evidence, writers often use wit, especially irony, to persuade. In irony, the words convey a meaning somewhat different from what they explicitly say. Wry understatement is typical. Here, for instance, is Thoreau explaining why in *Walden*, his book about his two years in relative isolation at Walden Pond, he will talk chiefly about himself:

> In most books, the *I*, or first person, is omitted; in this it will be retained; that, in respect to egotism, is the main difference. We commonly do not remember that it is, after all, always the first person that is speaking. I should not talk so much about myself if there were anybody else whom I knew as well. Unfortunately, I am confined to this theme by the narrowness of my experience.

Notice the wry apology in Thoreau's justification for talking about himself: He does not know anyone else as well as he knows himself. Similarly, in "unfortunately" ("Unfortunately, I am confined to this theme by the narrowness of my experience") we again hear a wry voice. After all, Thoreau knows, as we know, that *no one* has experience so deep or broad that he or she knows others better than himself or herself. Thoreau's presentation of himself as someone who happens not to have had the luck of knowing others better than himself is engagingly clever.

## Avoiding Sarcasm

Because writers must, among other things, persuade readers that they are humane, sarcasm has little place in persuasive writing. Although desk dictionaries usually define sarcasm as "bitter, caustic irony" or "a kind of satiric wit," if you think of a sarcastic comment that you have heard, you will probably agree that "a crude, sneering remark" is a better definition. Lacking the wit of good satire and the carefully controlled mockery of irony, sarcasm usually relies on gross overstatement and intends simply to humiliate. *Sarcasm* is derived from a Greek word meaning "to tear flesh" or "to bite the lips in rage," altogether an unattractive business. Sarcasm is unfair, for it dismisses an opponent's arguments with ridicule rather than with reason; it is also unwise, for it turns the reader against the speaker or writer. Readers hesitate to ally themselves with a writer who apparently enjoys humiliating the opposition. A sarcastic remark can turn the hearers against the speaker and arouse sympathy for the victim. In short, sarcasm usually doesn't work.

# Tone and Ethical Appeal

Although this chapter is chiefly about persuasion in the sense of rational discourse—the presentation of reasons in support of a thesis or conclusion—there are other forms of persuasion. We've already mentioned one of them: the *appeal to emotion*. The *appeal to force* is another: As Al Capone put it, "You can get a lot more done with a kind word and a gun, than with a kind word alone." But, in a sense, kind words themselves can do quite a lot. The writer's **tone**, or voice, matters. A moment ago we cautioned against the use of sarcasm on the grounds that the satirist is perceived as an unattractive character, and this caution can now be put into a larger context, something that Aristotle called the **ethical appeal**, from *ethos*, the Greek word for "character." The ethical appeal is based on the idea that effective speakers and writers convey by their tone the suggestion that they are good people, specifically that they are

- informed,
- intelligent,
- benevolent, and
- honest.

Because they are perceived as trustworthy, their words inspire confidence in their listeners and their readers. When we read an argument, we hear or sense a *voice* or *persona* behind the words, and our assent to the argument depends partly on the extent to which we trust this speaker, this voice, this character.

How can you inspire this trust? To begin with, you should indeed be informed, intelligent, benevolent, and honest. Still, possession of these qualities does not guarantee that you will convey them in your writing. You will have to revise your drafts so that these qualities become apparent to your audience—so that nothing in your essay causes your reader to doubt your knowledge, intelligence, good intentions, and integrity. A blunder in logic, a misleading quotation, a sarcastic remark—all such slips can cause readers to withdraw their trust from the writer.

It's generally not persuasive to present as villains or fools all persons who hold views different from your own, especially if some of them are your readers. Recognize opposing views, assume they are held in good faith, state them fairly, and be temperate in arguing your own position: "If I understand their view correctly . . ."; "It seems reasonable to conclude that . . ."; "Perhaps, then, we can agree that . . ."

**A RULE FOR WRITERS**

When you argue, be courteous and be respectful of your topic, of your audience, and of the people who hold views you are arguing against.

# Critical Thinking: Assumptions and Implications

To **think critically** is to adopt a skeptical or questioning view, not only of claims and evidence—the elements of the argument that are stated explicitly—but also of **assumptions** and **implications**, elements of an argument that are often left unstated. Assumptions are the ideas upon which an argument is based. It may be helpful to think of an assumption as what comes *before* an argument. Implications are consequences. One could think of implications as what comes *after*: what will happen if a proposal is enacted, or a new course of action is accepted, or a different way of thinking is adopted.

For example, many people once assumed that lawmakers should not get paid, or paid well. The idea was that a man (it was also assumed that women should not be making laws) should seek public office not to make money but rather to serve the community. The idea is high-minded, but one of its consequences, or implications, was that only the rich could afford to run for, and to hold, office. Experience proved that many officeholders, however high-minded, had chiefly their own interests at heart. They may indeed have thought that their actions were always for the good of the nation, but inevitably they tended to see things from a particular point of view, the point of view of the rich, in America more specifically the point of view of rich, white Protestant males.

It is easy to be skeptical when we hear the opinions of others— "What is your evidence for that?" "Says who?" "Why should I grant your assumptions, even for the sake of argument?" "That's fine, but have you considered the implications of your proposal?"—but it is difficult for us to question our own assumptions because they seem so obviously true.

**Thinking critically** involves questioning even your own cherished assumptions, things that seem self-evident, obvious, or clearly true. It involves imagining yourself as someone who does not share these assumptions, and then questioning the arguments you have presented and considering their implications. For example, are the statistics you current? Even if they are, can they be interpreted differently? To ᵗch questions of others may open you to the charge of negative- ᵘt the charge is unfair if you adopt the same questioning manner you consider your own arguments. In short, to think critically is to be skeptical not only of the assumptions, arguments, and conclusions of others but also of your own—thus to remain open to assuming a modified or new position.

## Organizing an Argument

As we have said earlier, writers find out what they think partly by means of the act of putting words on paper. But in presenting arguments for their readers, writers rarely duplicate their own acts of discovery. To put it another way, the process of setting forth ideas, and supporting them, does not follow the productive but untidy, repetitive, often haphazard process of preliminary thinking. For instance, a point that did not strike us until the middle of the third draft may, in the final version, appear in the opening paragraph. Or an example that seemed useful early in our thinking may, in the process of revision, be omitted in favor of a stronger example. Through a series of revisions, large and small, we try to work out the best strategy for persuading our readers to accept our reasoning as sound, our conclusion as valid. Unfortunately, we find that an argument cannot be presented either as it occurs to us or all at once.

No simple formula governs the organization of all effective argumentative essays. An essay may begin by announcing its thesis and then set forth the supporting reasons. Or it may begin more casually, calling attention to specific cases, and then generalize from these cases. Probably it will go on to reveal an underlying unity that brings the thesis into view, and from here it will offer detailed reasoning that supports the thesis.

As the writer of a persuasive essay, you almost always have to handle, in some sequence or other, the following matters:

- The context of the argument (for instance, an explanation of why the issue should be considered, or reconsidered)
- The thesis
- The evidence that supports the thesis
- The counterevidence
- The response to counterclaims and counterevidence (either a refutation or a concession that there *is* merit to the counterclaims but not as much as to the writer's thesis)

- Some sort of reaffirmation, perhaps that the topic needs attention or that the thesis advanced is the most plausible or the most workable or the most moral, or that the ball is now in the reader's court

Three methods of organizing arguments are fairly common, and one or another may suit an essay you're working on.

1. Begin with the context of the argument, then set forth the thesis statement and work from the simplest argument up to the most complex, taking account of opposing arguments as you set forth your own arguments. Such an arrangement will keep your reader with you, step by step.

2. After setting forth the context and your thesis, arrange the arguments in order of increasing strength. The danger in following this plan is that you may lose the reader from the start because you begin with a weak argument. Avoid this problem by telling your reader that indeed the first argument is relatively weak (if it is terribly weak, it isn't an argument at all, so scrap it), but that you offer it for the sake of completeness or because it is often given, and that you will soon give the reader far stronger arguments. Face the opposition to this initial argument, grant that opposition as much as it deserves, and salvage what is left of the argument. Then proceed to the increasingly strong arguments, devoting at least one paragraph to each. Introduce each argument with an appropriate transition ("another reason," "even more important," "most convincing of all"). State it briefly, summarize the opposing view, and then demolish this opposition. With this organization, your discussion of each of your own arguments ends affirmatively.

3. After sketching the background and stating your thesis in an introductory paragraph, mass all of the opposing arguments, and then respond to them one by one.

## CHECKLIST for Revising Drafts of Persuasive Essays

- ☐ Are the terms clearly defined? (See p. 171.)
- ☐ Is the thesis stated promptly and clearly? (See pp. 180–81.)
- ☐ Are the assumptions likely to be shared by your readers? If not, are they reasonably argued rather than merely stated? (See pp. 179–80.)
- ☐ Are the facts verifiable? Is the evidence reliable? (No out-of-date statistics, no generalizations from insufficient evidence?) (See pp. 165, 167–71.)
- ☐ Is the reasoning sound? (See pp. 172–76.)

- ☐ Are the authorities really authorities on this matter? (See pp. 170, 174.)
- ☐ Are all of the substantial counterarguments recognized and effectively responded to? (See p. 185.)
- ☐ Does the essay make use, where appropriate, of concrete examples? (See pp. 167–69.)
- ☐ Is the organization effective? Does the essay begin in a compelling way, keep the thesis in view, and end interestingly? (See pp. 180–81.)
- ☐ Is the tone appropriate? (Present yourself as fair-minded, and assume that those who hold a view opposed to yours are also fair-minded.) (See p. 178.)

## Persuasion at Work: Two Professors Consider Laptops in the Classroom

Following are two essays, the first arguing that students should be prohibited from using laptops in the classroom, the second arguing against the prohibition. After each essay we offer a brief analysis of the writer's persuasive strategies.

Carlo Rotella is a Professor of English at Boston College where he also directs the American Studies Program. His scholarly interests include urban studies and boxing, subjects he writes about for both academic and popular readers. "Tuition Lost on the Techno-Dependent" was published in the *Boston Globe* in 2010.

---

CARLO ROTELLA

# Tuition Lost on the Techno-Dependent

1    Having banned laptops from my college classroom, I was feeling a little like a technology crab, an aging nostalgist for longhand note-taking, long-playing records, and slow-dialing phones. I stopped feeling bad about it, though, after I dropped by the class of a colleague who allows laptops.

2    It was in a theater-style lecture hall, with rows of desks rising away from the podium. From where I stood in the back, I had a good, down-slope view of the screens of students' laptops. One guy

seemed to be taking notes on the lecture until a message popped up. He typed a response, sent it, read the response to his response, typed again. Then he took out his phone and, sheltered by his open laptop, began texting.

3      Another student craned forward for a better view of the sports highlights on the screen of a student in the row ahead, which caught the attention of a third student a couple of rows back of them, who then tried to go to the same site on his own laptop. I could see others shopping, watching videos, reading the news. Many appeared to be taking class-related notes at least some of the time, but I didn't see any who stuck to note-taking all the time. And when they were actually taking notes, they didn't seem to be actively listening to the argument of the lecture with concentrated intellect so much as transcribing the professor's words in a sort of secretarial fugue state.[1]

4      I don't deny that the laptop and its cousins have a lot to contribute in the classroom. I accept many of the arguments in favor: greatly expanded access to texts and supporting materials, ease of communication, and so on. You don't need to convince me that, in principle, it's a potentially important innovation. But it takes time to adjust to technological change, and we're not even close to adjusted yet.

5      First, our manners haven't caught up with our machinery. I'm reminded of that every time I see the tableau of two people at a table in a restaurant, one staring vacantly into space while the other talks into or stares at a cellphone. People with otherwise decent manners, people who in a face-to-face situation would never turn away from you in mid-sentence to take a gander at some porn, will do it without thinking twice if a battery-powered machine signals to demand their attention. And it's not like I'm laying this all on college students. In some ways, the middle-aged are more defenseless. If I had my email up on the computer built into the podium in the room where I teach, I'd probably sneak a look at it from time to time while I was lecturing.

Second, the myth of multitasking hasn't been exploded as thoroughly as it needs to be. Someday soon, if all goes well, to be caught multitasking in public will be as embarrassing as to be caught littering or sticking your hand down your pants to relieve an itch.

---

[1] A fugue state is a kind of trance. In psychiatry it is defined as a temporary state in which one's sense of identity is lost; experiences that occur during the state are forgotten once it is over.

But we're not there yet, even though study after study shows that what feels like getting lots of different stuff done at the same time is usually little more than giving in to distraction that leads to incompetence. I don't know that it's absolutely impossible for a human being to pay attention to an electronic screen and another human (or, say, traffic) at the same time, and perhaps in time we may learn to do it properly, but right now it's beyond us: you have to pick one or the other because you can't do both.

6    You have to pick, and it's not an abstract choice. College costs a lot. I teach at BC, where a year's tuition, fees, room, and board currently add up to $52,624. What are the students paying for? What can't they get online for free? In my end of the academy, the humanities, it comes down to one thing, in essence: the other people in the room, teachers, and fellow students. We can debate whether that's worth the price tag, and we can debate the relative value of lectures and seminars (I think the best mix in the humanities is some of the former and a lot of the latter), but you're paying for the exclusive company of fellow thinkers who made it through the screening processes of admissions and faculty hiring. That's it. You can get everything else online, and you can of course do the reading on your own.

7    Your money buys you the opportunity to pay attention to the other people on campus and to have them pay attention to you—close, sustained, active, fully engaged attention, undistracted by beeps, chimes, tweets, klaxons, ring tones, ads, explosions, continuous news feeds, or other mind-jamming noise. You qualify for admission, you pay your money, and you get four years—maybe the last four years you'll ever get—to really attend to the ideas of other human beings, thousands of years' worth of them, including the authors of the texts on the syllabus and the people in the room with you.

8    You can spend the rest of your life surfing the web, emailing, texting. You've got one shot at college. So, at least until the novelty wears off (probably not in my lifetime), that means no laptops in my classroom.

## An Analysis of Rotella's Argument

Carlo Rotella's **tone** is casual, direct, and engaging as he argues against classroom laptop use. He confesses to feeling like a "technology crab" in his opening paragraph; the phrase is **witty**, as is his image of himself as someone who misses such old-fashioned things as rotary phones. (The opening is also disarming: He admits he's old and nostalgic before his readers can accuse him of being these things.) The second and third paragraphs, in which Rotella describes disengaged students typing and texting during class, provide **evidence** from Rotella's experience that supports his position. That position is clear, of course, in his opening paragraph. He doesn't articulate his **thesis**, however, until the second half of the essay, when he says (in paragraph 6) that students must choose between their electronic devices, and the teachers and class-mates whose "attention" costs students $52,524 per year. He develops his thesis in paragraph 7, where he argues that the right choice is "to pay attention to the other people on campus and to have them pay at-tention to you—close, sustained, active, fully engaged attention, undis-tracted by beeps, chimes, tweets, klaxons, ring tones, ads . . . or other mind-jamming noise." Before he gets to his **thesis**, he acknowledges in paragraph 4 the **counterargument** that laptops have their uses in the classroom (e.g. "expanded access to texts"). He counters this point with two **claims of fact**. He says first (in paragraph 5) that "our manners haven't caught up with our machinery"—in other words, that we haven't yet figured out how to manage online and in-person relationships simul-taneously. In paragraph 6, he makes his second **claim**, that we can't do two things at once anyway. He supports this claim with a reference to "studies," which he mentions in passing but doesn't specify.

We find Rotella's argument compelling—but we also find compelling Elena Choy's argument against prohibiting laptops in the classroom. As you read her essay, consider how she and Rotella might respond to each other's main claims.

---

ELENA CHOY

# Laptops in the Classroom?
# No Problem

*Elena Choy has taught economics at several community colleges. Her essay was first published in the* Little, Brown Reader, Twelfth Edition, *in 2010.*

1     Someone—I forget who—said, "A teacher is someone who never says anything once." I myself have quoted this comment many

times—in the classroom, during conferences, at faculty meetings, and now in print. We teachers are a varied bunch; some of us are much more interesting than others, but probably all of us repeat ourselves more than we should or are sometimes boring in other ways, at least to certain students. If, then, during one of our lectures a student wants to surf the web or to play poker online, well, who am I to say that she or he hasn't the right to do so? We all claim that we value individual thinking, that we want students to think for themselves. Why, then, do we object when they decide they want to tune us out?

2      Let me try to give a reasoned statement of my position, a statement that will take account of the contrary position. In fact, I'll begin with what I take to be the arguments in *favor* of banning laptops. I believe the chief arguments are these: (1) the upraised lids of laptops distract the instructor, and they often prevent the instructor from making eye-contact with the students; (2) laptops distract other students, who cannot help but see what is on the screens—for instance video games; (3) students who use laptops to take notes take overly extensive notes, so they are doing stenography rather than thinking—rather, one might almost say, than paying real attention to the significant content of the course; (4) because they are so busy taking notes, laptop users tend not to participate in whatever discussion there may be in the course because they are too busy taking notes.

3      Let's look at each of these arguments, beginning with the first. I grant that I am not keen about seeing lots of upraised tops, but (a) the large majority of my students, even in a big lecture course, are not using laptops, and I therefore can make plenty of eye-contact; (b) I am delighted to see that students are taking notes, or at least I think they are taking notes; (c) if they are playing poker or shopping online, well, that's their business. They have paid their tuition, and it's up to them to decide how to spend their money and their time. I am not Big Brother; I don't think it is appropriate for me to assume that those with laptops are not taking notes. In any case, if they are not, it surely is not for me to tell them how to use their time in class, provided they are not disturbing others.

4      Which gets to the second argument offered in favor of banning laptops, that they distract other students. Do the users of laptops in class significantly damage other students? If so, of course laptops should be banned, just as we ban smoking in the classroom. I have heard students say that the poker games they see on the screens of other students prevent them from paying attention to the lecturer,

but I find it hard to take this objection seriously. Such students should stop peeking, should discipline themselves, should look at the lecturer, and should occupy themselves by taking own notes.

5    The third objection, that students who use laptops are engaged in stenography rather than in thoughtful thinking, seems to me to be equally without force. Different students have different methods of learning: Some students find it useful to take abundant notes, others take very few notes, perhaps preferring to think about what is being said while it is being said. Indeed, some students have different methods for different courses: I can easily imagine hearing a lecture that I would like to preserve fairly extensively, a lecture perhaps filled with facts and figures, *but I can also easily imagine hearing an equally stimulating lecture that is not of the sort that I would find myself taking extensive notes on*—an occasional memorable phrase might be all that I might jot down. A wise student might well adopt different methods for different lecturers. It doesn't follow, then that every student who uses a laptop will take too many notes.

6    The fourth reason offered on behalf of banning laptops is that the note-takers tend not to participate in whatever discussion there may be in class. My response is twofold: First, in lecture classes the discussion inevitably is an extremely minor part of the class, perhaps a few minutes of discussion at the end, or possibly one or two questions that are handled during the course of the lecture. At most only three or four students can participate, so we cannot in good faith argue that the laptop user, by remaining relatively silent, is hurting himself or herself, or is depriving other students of the benefit of his or her contribution. And, for that matter, even in smaller classes, let's say or ten or fifteen, we should respect the wishes of a student who prefers not to speak much in class. In twenty years of teaching I have had three students who approached me after the first meeting of a smallish class, and explained that for one reason or another they preferred not to be called on. Ordinarily in such classes I say that part of the grade will depend upon class participation, but in their cases, because they raised the matter at the outset, I respected their wishes—I do not think it is my job to demand that shy people overcome their shyness—and I based the grade entirely on their three papers, their midterm and their final examinations—just as I base the grades in my large lecture courses. Obviously some courses—let's say Spoken Spanish—require oral participation, but in most classes I think we can comply with a student who requests that he or she not be called on to speak.

7    Finally, and with some hesitation, at his late stage in my essay I want to introduce a new point. It has been my experience that the call to ban laptops chiefly comes not from students but from their professors, my colleagues. Sometimes my colleagues say that they are disturbed by the lack of eye-contact, and I sympathize with them; I know what it is to see a raised lid rather than a student's face. Sometimes they say that the students are engaged in stenography, not in thinking, and I can understand this objection, too, though; as I have indicated, I think different methods of note-taking work well for different students. When I was a student, in pre-laptop days, I confess, I took abundant notes in certain courses. My colleagues may say that they are concerned with helping students to *learn,* or *think,* not to be stenographers, but this sort of stenography served me well I think in some of the courses I took. It is not up to professors to prohibit students from taking the kinds of notes that the students think will be useful. We can give advice about taking notes, about preparing for the examination, and so forth, but we go too far when we prohibit students from taking notes in the way they find most useful.

8    In any case, and here I come to a dangerous point, I think that the chief reason instructors suggest that laptops be banned is one that they do not state, and maybe they are not even aware of. I think they fear that most students who use laptops are not taking notes, but are engaged in activities unrelated to the course—instant messaging, e-mailing, shopping, playing poker, and so on. But if students are in fact doing these things, what is the cure? Banning laptops? I don't think so. If the instructor is so boring that the students use laptops to shop and to write letters, well, when the laptops are banned the students will probably bring in crossword puzzles or exercises from other courses (for instance, Spanish vocabulary lists to be memorized) or whatever, and continue to ignore the lecturer.

9    I am saying, with much embarrassment, that a professor should ask himself a hard question: If students in my courses are using laptops for purposes unrelated to the course, what am I doing wrong? Perhaps we should videotape a lecture or two so that we can see and hear what we look like and sound like, or perhaps ask a colleague to visit our class and evaluate it. It may be that if we saw ourselves, we should understand why the student has chosen to act independently. It might be that we too would prefer online poker.

## An Analysis of Choy's Argument

Like Rotella, Choy begins with a witty, disarming opening, a joke at her own expense about boring professors. She states her position in this paragraph too: She does not object to laptop use in her classroom. Before fully presenting her **thesis**, however, she lists, in paragraph 2, four counterarguments, and discusses them in order in the four subsequent paragraphs. In paragraph 3, she disagrees with the **claim of fact** that laptop use distracts professors, and offers three reasons: She is not distracted; she's happy to see students taking notes; and it's not her business to tell students what to do. In paragraph 4, she considers the **claim of fact** that other students are distracted by laptop use; she rejects this claim, making a **claim of policy**: Students must simply control themselves around their electronic devices. In paragraph 5, she alludes to the claim that critics like Rotella make—that students take notes mindlessly, in a "secretarial fugue state"—and rejects it too, noting that "different students have different methods of learning," and some lectures are worth the detailed notes. In paragraph 6, she disputes a **claim of fact**, that laptop users don't contribute to class discussions, with another claim of fact: Lectures don't call for much discussion anyway.

Choy gets to her **thesis** gradually in the last three paragraphs of the essay, perhaps because she knows her colleagues won't like it. In paragraph 7, she notes that most objections to laptops come from professors, not students. In paragraph 8, she comes to the "dangerous point" that instructors wish to ban laptops because they fear that their students aren't paying attention to them. She develops this point, stating her **thesis** in the final paragraph, where she suggests that if students aren't paying attention, the professors (who as she noted in paragraph 1 can be pretty boring) have only themselves to blame.

As we have seen in the two preceding essays, offering airtight proof on a controversial mater may be an impossible proposition. Virginia Woolf put it this way: "When a subject is highly controversial . . . one cannot hope to tell the truth. One can only show how one came to hold whatever opinion one does hold."

# Writing the Research Essay

> Research is formalized curiosity. It is poking and prying with a purpose.
>
> —Zora Neale Hurston

## Writing Research Essays

Research essays are also sometimes called "researched essays" or "documented essays"; they are based on *sources*, and you'll write them in many of your college courses. Even an essay that is primarily persuasive or analytical may be in part based on research. For example, if you have been asked to write an essay in which you state your position on Facebook's privacy settings, or on the degree to which using Google affects your ability to concentrate, you will probably need to take into consideration the arguments of others who have written on the topic. (Note that Steven Pinker quotes from sources even in the very brief essay we reprint in Chapter 7.) If you've been asked to analyze a novel by Kate Chopin, it may be useful to read what current literary critics have said about it. If you don't consider any source, you risk taking an uninformed position. Considering what others have said and developing your own position in relation to their ideas are central to academic writing.

Not everyone likes research, of course. There are hours spent reading books and articles that prove to be contradictory or irrelevant. When the project is large, you may feel that there isn't enough time to read all the material that's available—or even to get your hands on it. Regardless of the scope of the project, some of the books may be dull.

The twentieth-century Irish poet William Butler Yeats, though an inde-fatigable worker on projects that interested him, engagingly expressed an indifference to the obligation that confronts every researcher: to look carefully at all the relevant evidence. Running over the possible reasons that Jonathan Swift did not marry (that he had syphilis, for instance, or that he feared he would transmit a hereditary madness), Yeats says: "Mr. Shane Leslie thinks that Swift's relation to Vanessa was not pla-tonic, and that whenever his letters speak of a cup of coffee they mean the sexual act; whether the letters seem to bear him out I do not know, for those letters bore me."

Though research sometimes requires one to read boring things, those who engage in it feel, at other times, an exhilaration, a sense of triumph at becoming expert on something. When you know what oth-ers have said about your topic, you are in a position to say: "Here is how other people have thought about this question; their ideas are all very interesting, but I see the matter differently. Let me tell you what *I* think."

In the example below, the second paragraph of a research essay we reprint in full in the next chapter, a student does just that. In the essay, Beatrice Cody argues against interpretations of Chopin's novel *The Awakening* as a feminist political statement—the prevailing view. Instead, she contends that the suicide of Chopin's protagonist, Edna Pontellier, "resulted from the torments of her individual psyche, her in-ability to cope with the patriarchal expectations, which most women in fact were able to tolerate."

> It is difficult to say how Chopin wished *The Awakening* to be interpreted. Heroines who ex-plore their own individuality(with varying de-grees of success and failure)abound in her work (Shinn 358); Chopin herself, though married, was a rather nontraditional wife who smoked cigarettes, and, like Edna Pontellier, took walks by her-self (Nissenbaum 333-34). One might think there-fore that Chopin was making a political statement in *The Awakening* about the position of women in society based on her own rejection of that posi-tion. But aside from slim biographical evidence and the assertions of some critics such as Larzer Ziff and Daniel S. Rankin that Chopin sympathized with Edna, we have no way of knowing whether she

> regarded this protagonist as a victim of sexist
> oppression or simply, to quote her family doctor
> in the novel itself, as "a sensitive and highly
> organized woman [. . .who] is especially peculiar"
> (66). It is therefore necessary to explore the two
> possibilities, using evidence from the novel to
> determine whether Edna Pontellier's awakening is
> political or peculiarly personal in nature.

Note the authority with which the student writes as she (respectfully) calls into question the conclusions of others who have written about the novel she's studied and researched. She has read enough to know that the biographical evidence supporting a feminist reading of *The Awakening* is "slim"; she has found enough evidence to say (persuasively, we think) that "It is . . . necessary to explore" the matter further. She knows a lot about her topic. She has become, over the course of several weeks, a kind of expert on it.

There can be great satisfaction in knowing enough about a topic to contribute to the store of knowledge and ideas about it. There can also be great satisfaction in simply learning to use the seemingly infinite resources now available to researchers—in print or electronic form—as well as in learning to document and to acknowledge your research accurately and responsibly.

## Primary and Secondary Materials

As we noted in Chapter 7, sources are usually divided into two categories, primary and secondary. A **primary source** is the real subject of study; a **secondary source** is a critical or historical account written about a primary source. For example, if you want to know whether Shakespeare's attitude toward Julius Caesar was highly traditional or highly original, or a little of each, you would read *Julius Caesar*, other Elizabethan writings about Caesar, and translations of Latin writings known to the Elizabethans. These are primary sources. In addition to these, you would read secondary sources such as modern books on Shakespeare and on Elizabethan attitudes toward Rome and toward monarchs.

Similarly, the primary material for an essay on Chopin's novel *The Awakening* is of course the novel itself; the secondary material consists of such things as biographies of Chopin and critical essays on the novel. But the line between these two kinds of sources is not always sharp. For example, if you are concerned with the degree to which *The Awakening* is autobiographical, primary materials include not only the novel and also Chopin's comments on her writing but perhaps also the comments of people who knew her. Thus, the essays—based on interviews with Chopin—that two of her friends published in newspapers probably can be regarded as primary material because they were contemporary with the novel and because they give direct access to Chopin's views, while the writings of later commentators constitute secondary material.

## What to Do with Sources

When you use sources, you are not simply emptying on the table the contents of a shopping cart filled at the scholar's supermarket, the library. You are cooking a meal. You must have a point, an opinion, a thesis. A thesis, as we noted in Chapter 1, is an idea about which intelligent readers might *disagree*. When you use sources in a research essay, you are working to establish and develop such an idea in the context of what others have thought about your topic. Your readers should feel they are moving toward the thesis with you, rather than reading a report, an anthology of commentary on a topic. Writers of reports—the kind of paper many of us wrote in high school—tend to use sources in one way: to *support* their main point. (And often, the main point turns out to have been made in one or more of the sources.) When you write a research essay, on the other hand, you use sources in a range of ways, among them:

- To establish the context of an argument, the position *against* which you'll be arguing.
- To provide the history of a problem or idea or event, or helpful background information—on an author's life, for example.
- To provide evidence to support a claim you're making.
- To provide evidence to support—or to dispute—a claim made by another critic or scholar or researcher.

Research makes you an expert on your topic; you now know what others have to say about it. But as you have thought about what the secondary sources have said about your primary material, it's likely that you've noticed contradictions and gaps, that you agree with some opinions and arguments and disagree with others, and that you've begun to develop your own ideas about your topic.

# Developing a Research Topic

Your instructor may assign a topic, in which case you'll be saved some work. (On the other hand, you may find yourself spending a lot of time with material you don't find exciting. On yet another hand, you may become interested in something you'd otherwise never have known about.) More likely, you'll need to develop your own topic, a topic related to the subject of the course for which the research essay has been assigned. Some possibilities:

- Perhaps you've read Maxine Hong Kingston's *The Woman Warrior* (1976) for a Women's Studies course and you have become interested in Confucian or Buddhist ideas that inform the narrative.
- Perhaps your government course has touched on the internment of Japanese Americans during World War II and you'd like to know more about what happened.
- Perhaps you've read Chopin's *The Awakening* for a literature course and you're wondering what readers thought about the novel when it was first published.

Any of these interests could well become a topic for a research essay. But how do you find the relevant material?

## Finding Sources

We can't give you a roadmap or a recipe for finding the sources you need. The number of possible topics is infinite, as is the number of sources. Research approaches vary widely. And the Internet—the vast interconnection of computer networks that has made an extraordinary amount of information available to researchers and everyone else—complicates things further. By its very nature, the Internet is constantly changing; guides to research on the Internet are generally outdated even before they're even published.

Nevertheless, we do have some general suggestions. One good rule of thumb is to begin with what you already know, with what you already have at hand. For instance, the textbook for your government course may cite official documents on the relocation and internment of Japanese Americans. Or your edition of Chopin's *The Awakening* may contain an introduction that references some critical essays on the novel; it's also likely to contain a selected bibliography, a list of books and articles about Chopin and her work. If you have already identified a few titles, you can go directly to your library's online catalog and begin your search there. (We'll have a bit more to say about online searches in a moment.)

If, however, you know very little about the topic, and haven't yet identified any possible sources (let's say you know nothing or almost nothing about Confucianism, but Maxine Hong Kingston's *The Woman Warrior* has made you want to learn about it), it's not a bad idea to begin with an encyclopedia—the *Encyclopaedia Britannica*, perhaps—which you'll find online through your library's e-resources Web page, and in hardcopy form in the library's reference area. In addition to providing basic information about your topic, encyclopedia articles usually include cross-references to other articles within the encyclopedia, as well as suggestions for further reading. These suggestions can help you begin to compose a list of secondary sources for your essay. And of course you need not limit yourself to one encyclopedia. There are hundreds of invaluable specialized encyclopedias, such as *Encyclopedia of Anthropology, Encyclopedia of Crime and Justice, Encyclopedia of Psychology, Encyclopedia of Religion* (a good place to go for an introduction to Confucianism), and *Kodansha Encyclopedia of Japan*. Several of them are certain to be available in your library's reference area or through your library's central information system.

## The Library's Central Information System

All libraries used to work in more or less the same way. Each one had a card catalog, a set of hundreds of little drawers containing thousands (even millions) of alphabetically arranged three-by-five cards. When you wanted a book, you went to the card catalog and looked it up by title, author, or subject. Because books would differ from library to library, the cards would also differ, but the system in every library was pretty much the same.

Of course, online catalogs have now replaced card catalogs in college, university, and public libraries. And the online catalog constitutes only a tiny fraction of the information available to you through your institution's library. With the help of enormous databases such as JSTOR, LexisNexis, and Project Muse, you can search thousands of academic journals, newspapers, and magazines. From a computer terminal in your library (or from home via an Internet connection), you can access bibliographies and indexes, full-text versions of encyclopedias, dictionaries, and academic journals, the catalogs of *other* libraries—and much more.

Unlike card catalogs, each library's central information system is a bit different. Resources differ from one library to the next. And like the Internet itself, your library's central information system is changing every day. For these reasons, perhaps the best advice we can give you about learning to find books and articles in your library is to go to your college or university's research librarian and ask for help.

## Evaluating Web Sources, and a Note on Wikipedia

As we've noted, the Internet can be a tremendous resource for researchers. But because anyone, anywhere, can post pretty much anything, the information available on the Internet can be difficult to evaluate. When you're working with secondary sources that have been published in print, for the most part you're working with material that experts in that field have judged to be worth reading. Before it's published, an article in a journal such as *Society* or *College English*, for example, will have been read by a number of reviewers (most or all of them college professors in the field), as well as by members of an advisory board and several editors. If *Society* or *College English* is in your institution's library—and we bet it is—it's there in part because librarians have decided it is worth including in the serials collection. An article in one of these journals may have weaknesses, but several experts have thought it was pretty good.

Much of the information available on the Internet has not been similarly vetted. Advertisements coexist with course syllabi. By entering the relevant keyword into a search engine such as Google or Yahoo! you could (if you wanted to) access a chat group on Lady Gaga as easily as you could find photographs of people's pets. Or an interview with Jamaica Kincaid. Or the full text of *Romeo and Juliet*. Or an essay on your research topic, written by your professor—or by the person who sits next to you in your biology class.

How do you judge what may be worth considering? In part by using the analytic skills we discuss elsewhere in this book. This advice may be particularly useful when it comes to evaluating Wikipedia entries. Wikipedia, the enormous online encyclopedia that's one of the Web's most-visited sites, has both defenders and critics. Anyone with Web access can write *or change* pretty much any Wikipedia entry at any time. It's therefore not safe to assume that a given article has been written by

*"On the Internet, nobody knows you're a dog."*
© The New Yorker Collection 1993. Peter Steiner from cartoonbank.com. All Rights Reserved.

a reputable scholar in the field. (It may well have been written or edited by that person sitting next to you in biology—on her laptop, during today's lecture.) For this reason, many professors tell their students not to use Wikipedia as a source. They argue that reliable sources are written by experts and evaluated, before publication, by other experts, and that Wikipedia is too often simply wrong. On the other hand, Wikipedia can be helpful as a source of sources. Professors who take this position say that (like such traditional encyclopedias as *Britannica Online*) Wikipedia can provide a foundation for research, especially through the links and bibliographies that appear at the end of many entries. But many of its defenders also agree that—like traditional encyclopedias—it can at best provide a foundation; it cannot provide a substitute for the information and ideas discovered through research itself. We believe that there is some truth to both sides of the debate. All information provided by Wikipedia (like everything else on the Web—or in print, for that matter) must be read critically. In the words of Horatio Crane from television's *CSI: Miami* (we checked this on Wikipedia): Trust, but verify.

The following checklist will help you focus your analysis.

### CHECKLIST for Evaluating Web Sites

- ☐ Who produced the site (a teacher, a commercial entity, a student)?
- ☐ Who sponsored the site?
- ☐ For whom is the author writing? Who is the intended audience?
- ☐ Can you tell if the author of the document is an authority in the field? (Perhaps the document is linked to the author's home page.)
- ☐ Does he or she reference other critics or writers? Good ones?
- ☐ Is the text well written?
- ☐ Do arguments seem well supported, or is the document full of vague generalizations?
- ☐ When was the site created or last updated?

For more on this matter, we recommend (appropriately enough) that you consult documents available on the Web, such as "Evaluating Information Found on the Internet" (http://www.library.jhu.edu/researchhelp/general/evaluating/index.html). It *should* still be available— but that's the other problem with Internet sources: What's here today may be gone tomorrow.

## Reading and Taking Notes on Secondary Sources

Almost all researchers—professionals as well as beginners—find that they end up with some notes that are irrelevant, and, on the other hand, find, when drafting the paper, that they vaguely remember certain material they now wish they had taken notes on. Especially in the early stages of a project, when the topic and thesis may still be relatively unfocused, it's hard to know what is noteworthy and what is not. You simply have to flounder a bit.

It may be helpful to skim an article or book all the way through the first time around without taking notes. By the time you reach the end, you may find it isn't noteworthy. Or you may find a useful summary near the end that will contain most of what you can get from the piece. Or you may find that, having a sense of the whole, you can now quickly reread the piece and take notes on the chief points that concern you.

Even if you follow this procedure, a certain amount of inefficiency is inevitable; therefore, plenty of time should be allowed. And it's worth keeping in mind that different people really do work differently. We list here three strategies for taking notes; we suspect that, over time, you'll develop your own.

- Take notes using four-by-six-inch cards, writing on one side only, because material on the back of a card is usually neglected when you come to write the paper. (Taking notes by hand offers several advantages—not least of which is that you don't need a computer to do it.)
- Take notes on your computer, keeping a separate file for each book or article. Material can be easily moved from one file to another as the organization of the essay begins to take shape.
- Don't take notes—or take very few notes. Photocopy secondary material you think you might use, *if it is brief*, and annotate that material as you read and think about it. Material from electronic sources can be downloaded and annotated as well. In fact, it's advisable to download any information you access online. Online sources can disappear; but if you download the source, you'll be able to check it if necessary, and you will be able to produce it if there are any questions about your use of it. The disadvantage here is obvious: it can be all too easy to collect a mountain of information. But there are two big advantages. Passages from the sources are transcribed or moved only once, into the draft itself, so there's less risk of mistakes and distortions. And the research—the collecting of information—can go very quickly.

## A RULE FOR WRITERS

It's crucial that you think carefully about the material you're collecting and that you annotate it thoroughly. If you don't—that is, if you merely download and print—you'll find yourself with a pile of paper, and no idea of what to do with it.

## A Guide to Note-Taking

1. **Scan the work before you start taking notes.** Before assiduously taking notes from the first paragraph onward, or highlighting

long passages, try to get a sense of the author's thesis. You may find an early paragraph that states the thesis outright; you may also find a concluding paragraph that offers a summary of the evidence that supports the thesis. Having gained a general idea of the work, you can now take notes sparingly while you read the material carefully and critically.

2. **Read critically.** Read thoughtfully, continually asking yourself if the author supports assertions with adequate evidence. Be especially sure to ask what can be said *against* assertions that coincide with your own beliefs. The heart of critical thinking is a willingness to face objections to one's own ideas.

3. **Be sure to record enough bibliographic information about the source to make it easy for you to locate it later on.** Doing so will make drafting the Works Cited list easier. *Note:* Such software tools as EndNote and RefWorks can help with compiling the list of citations, and some research librarians recommend them, especially for large research projects. Generally, students may access them through their library's home page.

4. **Write summaries, not paraphrases** (that is, write abridgments rather than restatements, which in fact may be as long as or longer than the original). As we note in our chapter on using sources, there is rarely any point to paraphrasing. Generally speaking, either quote exactly (and put the passage in quotation marks, with a notation of the source, including the page number or numbers) or summarize, reducing a page or even an entire article or chapter of a book to a few sentences that can be written on a notecard, typed into your computer, or squeezed into the margin of a photocopied page. Even when you summarize, record your source (including the page numbers) so that you can give appropriate credit in your essay.

5. **Quote sparingly.** You are not simply transcribing what you read; rather you are assimilating knowledge and you are thinking, and so for the most part your source should be chewed and digested rather than swallowed whole. Thinking now, while taking notes, will also help you later to avoid plagiarism. If, on the other hand, when you take notes you simply copy material at length, later when you are writing the essay you may be tempted to copy it yet again, perhaps without giving credit. Likewise, if you simply photocopy pages from articles or books, or download material from the Internet, and then merely underline some passages without annotating your reading, you probably will not

be thinking; you will just be underlining. But if you make a terse summary you will be forced to think and to find your own words for the idea.

6. **Quote accurately.** After copying a quotation, check your transcription against the original, and correct any misquotation. Verify the page number also. If a quotation runs from the bottom of, say, page 306 to the top of 307, make a distinguishing mark (for instance two backslashes after the last word of the first page), so that if you later use only part of the quotation, you will know the page on which it appeared.

7. **Use ellipses to indicate the omission of any words within a sentence.** If the omitted words are at the end of the quoted sentence, put a period immediately at the point where you end the sentence, and then add three spaced periods.

```
    If the. . .words are at the end of the quoted
    sentence, put a period immediately at the point
    where you end. . . .
```

8. **Use square brackets to indicate your additions to the quotations.** Here is an example:

```
Here is an [uninteresting] example.
```

9. **Do not change even an occasional word when copying a passage, even if you think you will be later putting it into your own words.** Notes of this sort may find their way into your essay, your reader will sense a style other than your own, and suspicions (and perhaps even charges) of plagiarism will follow. (For a detailed discussion of plagiarism, see pp. 122–29.)

10. **Comment on your notes.** Consider it your obligation to *think* about the material as you take notes, evaluating it and using it as a stimulus to further thought. For example, you may want to say "Tyler seems to be generalizing from insufficient evidence," or "Corsa made the same point five years earlier"; but make certain that later you will be able to distinguish between these comments and the notes summarizing or quoting your source. A suggestion: Surround all comments recording your responses with double parentheses, thus: ((Is there evidence for this assertion?)).

# Writing the Essay

Beyond referring you to the rest of this book, we can offer only eight pieces of advice:

1. **With a tentative thesis in mind, begin by rereading your notes and sorting them by topic.** Put together what belongs together. Don't hesitate to reject interesting material that now seems irrelevant or redundant. After sorting, re-sorting, and rejecting, you will have a kind of first draft without writing a draft.

2. **From your notes, make a first outline.** Although you can't yet make a paragraph outline, you may find it useful to make a fairly full rough outline, listing not only the sequence of points but also the quotations that you will use. In sketching the outline, of course, you will be guided by your *thesis*. As you worked, you probably modified your tentative ideas in the light of what your further research produced, but by now you ought to have a relatively firm idea of what you want to say. Without a thesis you will have only the basis for a *report*, not a potential essay. See the following rough outline of the essay on Kate Chopin's *The Awakening* that we present on pages 207–21.

Rough outline for Awakening paper:

1. Set up thesis: most critics and readers see The Awakening as a novel that criticizes men's oppression of women, but maybe Edna is just crazy.

2. Evidence that other side ("feminist" argument) is reasonable
   —Chopin's biography
   —Chopin's other work

3. Why other side is wrong
   —family doctor says Edna is "peculiar"
   —Chopin never took a clear position on what made Edna kill herself

4. Analysis of text: passages that support "feminist" reading
   —Edna's husband's behavior, plus what critics claim about the novel

5. Analysis of text: passages that support my reading
   —show evidence of Edna's mental illness (she's always falling asleep)

6. What Chopin herself said about the book (her "Retraction")
   —explain why it's hard to interpret
   —propose conclusion: Edna's tragedy is partly "political" and partly "personal"

3. **Transcribe or download quotations, even in the first draft, exactly as you want them to appear in the final version.** Of course, this takes some time, and the time will be wasted if, as may well turn out, you later see that the quotation is not really useful. (On the other hand, the time has not really been wasted, since it helped you ultimately to delete the unnecessary material.)

If at this early stage you just write a note reminding yourself to include the quotation—something like "here quote Jackson on undecided voters"—when you reread the draft you won't really know how the page sounds. You won't, for instance, know how much help your reader needs by way of a lead-in to the quotation, or how much discussion should follow. Only if you actually see the quotation are you in the position of your audience, and it's a good idea to try to imagine your audience, even at this early stage.

4. **Include, right in the body of the draft, all of the relevant citations.** This way when you come to revise, you don't have to start hunting through your notes to find who said what, and where. (Such tools as RefWorks and EndNote, which we discuss briefly on page 200, may be helpful at this stage as well.)

5. **Resist the urge to include every note in your essay.** As we suggest in Chapter 1, writing is a way of discovering ideas. Consequently, as you write your first draft, your thesis will inevitably shift, and notes that initially seemed important will now seem irrelevant. Don't stuff them into the draft, even if you're concerned about meeting a page requirement: Readers know padding when they see it.

6. **Resist the urge to do more research.** As you draft, you may also see places where another piece of evidence, another reference to a source, or another example would be useful. And you may feel compelled to head back to the library. We think that for now you should resist that urge too: It may simply be procrastination in disguise. Continue writing this first draft if possible, and plan to incorporate new material in a later draft.

7. **As you revise your draft, make sure that you do not merely tell the reader "A says . . . B says . . . C says . . . ."** Rather, by using a lead-in or signal phrase such as "A claims," "B provides evidence that,"

"according to C," "D concedes that," you help the reader to see the role of the quotation in your paper. Further, after quoting or summarizing a source, you should normally comment on it, thereby making clear the relation between your own ideas and those of the source. For more on incorporating quotations into your essay, see pages 118–22.

8. **When you have completed your draft, try making a paragraph outline of what you've written so far:** doing so can help you to see if there are gaps in your reasoning or your evidence. See the following paragraph outline of Beatrice Cody's final draft. Note that Roman numerals indicate the major topics of the essay; capital letters indicate major claims; and numbers indicate specific evidence that supports and develops those claims.

> Outline of Completed Draft of Politics and
> Psychology in *The Awakening*
> Thesis: Edna Pontellier's suicide resulted
> from the torments of her individual psyche, her
> inability to cope with the patriarchal expecta-
> tions that most women tolerated.
>
> I. Introduction: Edna's story seems to pose no
> problem for feminist reader, but the story is
> more complicated than it seems.
>    A. Reasons to support "feminist" reading of
>    Edna as oppressed
>       1. Seems a victim of "Feminine Mystique"
>       2. Many Chopin heroines were strong, inde-
>       pendent women
>       3. Chopin herself was a nontraditional wife
>       4. Biographers and critics claim that
>       Chopin sympathized with Edna
>    B. Reasons to question this reading
>       1. No direct evidence that Chopin did in
>       fact sympathize with Edna
>       2. Family doctor in novel describes Edna as
>       "peculiar"
>
> II. Textual evidence that supports the "feminist"
> reading
>    A. Edna's husband is sexist and domineering
>       1. Expects her to take care of children
>       2. Expects her to be a decoration in his home

B. Critics agree
   1. Ziff: Husband and children not seen as essential in women's lives
   2. Fluck: Edna's behavior (sleeping, dozing) is "radical retreat"
III. Textual evidence that suggests Edna's tragedy is unique, or "personal"
  A. Individual personality developed in context of dysfunctional family
    1. Alcoholic father
    2. "Middle-child" syndrome
    3. Marries workaholic man
  B. *Awakening* looks more like mental illness than emotional independence
    1. Hears voices
    2. Described as having two selves
IV. Conclusion: Chopin fused "personal" and "political"
  A. Chopin's post-publication "Retraction" points in both directions
  B. Chopin hinted that leisure plus mental instability doomed Edna
  C. Few options open to women; men dominate women in social structure

## CHECKLIST for Revising Drafts of Research Essays

☐ Is the tentative title informative and focused?

☐ Does the paper make a point, or does it just accumulate other people's ideas? (See pp. 190–92.)

☐ Does it reveal the thesis early? (See pp. 200, 202–04.)

☐ Are claims supported by evidence? (See pp. 192–204.)

☐ Are all the *words* and *ideas* of the sources accurately attributed? (See pp. 199–201.)

☐ Are quotations introduced adequately with signal phrases (such as "according to Ziff," or "Smith contends," or "Johnson points out") to indicate who is speaking? (See p. 203.)

☐ Are all of the long quotations necessary, or can some of them be effectively summarized? (See p. 200.)

☐ Are quotations discussed adequately? (See p. 203; see also Chapter 8, "Analyzing Texts.")

□ Write an outline of the completed draft to check its organization. Does the paper advance in orderly stages? Can your imagined reader easily follow your thinking? (See pp. 202–05.)

□ Is the documentation in the correct form? (See Chapter 13, "Documenting Sources.")

# A Sample Research Essay (MLA Format)

At the beginning of this chapter, we noted that Beatrice Cody used her research to help her develop her *own* position on the novel. As you read her essay, be alert to the range of sources Cody has chosen and to the range of ways in which she uses them: to establish the critical position she'll be arguing against, to give helpful background on Chopin's life, to provide information on the responses of Chopin's contemporaries to the novel, and so on.

*Note:* Cody uses the Modern Language Association (MLA) form of in-text citations, which are clarified by a list headed "Works Cited." We explain the MLA system in detail in Chapter 13, "Documenting Sources." In that chapter we also explain and illustrate the American Psychological Association (APA) form of in-text citations, and we offer information on several other systems of documentation.

1/2"

Beatrice Cody

Ms. Bellanca

Writing 125

12 April 2011

Politics and Psychology in

*The Awakening*

*Title announces focus and scope of essay.*

1    At first glance, Kate Chopin's novel *The Awakening* (1899) poses no problem to the feminist reader. It is the story of Edna Pontellier, a woman living at the turn of the century who, partly through a half-realized summer romance, discovers that sensual love, art, and individuality mean more to her than marriage or motherhood. When she concludes that there can be no compromise between her awakened inner self and the stifling shell of her outer life as a wife and mother, she drowns herself. In such a summary, Edna appears to be yet another victim of the "Feminine Mystique" described by Betty Friedan in the 1960s, a mind-numbing malaise afflicting the typical American housewife whose husband and society expected her to care for family at the expense of personal freedom and fulfillment. However, it is possible that the events leading to Edna's tragic death were not caused solely by the expectations of a sexist society pre-dating Friedan's model, in which a wife was not only dutiful to but also the "property" of her husband (Culley 119),

*Plot summary helps orient readers unfamiliar with novel.*

← 1" →                                    ← 1" →

↑ 1" ↓

COLLEGE WRITING

*Citation includes title because there are two works by Chopin on Works Cited list.*

and a mother not only stayed home but also sacrificed even the "essential" for her children (Chopin *Awakening* 48). Perhaps Edna's suicide resulted from the torments of her individual psyche, her inability to cope with the patriarchal expectations that most women in fact were able to tolerate.

*Clear statement of thesis.*

*Citation 2 includes name because author isn't cited in the sentence itself.*

It is difficult to say how Chopin wished *The Awakening* to be interpreted. Heroines who explore their own individuality (with varying degrees of success and failure) abound in her work (Shinn 358); Chopin herself, though married, was a rather nontraditional wife who smoked cigarettes, and, like Edna Pontellier, took walks by herself (Nissenbaum 333—34). One might think therefore that Chopin was making a political statement in *The Awakening* about the position of women in society based on her own rejection of that position. But aside from slim biographical evidence and the assertions of some critics such as Larzer Ziff and Daniel S. Rankin that Chopin sympathized with Edna, we have no way of knowing whether she regarded this protagonist as a victim of sexist oppression or simply, to quote her family doctor in the novel itself, as "a sensitive and highly organized woman . . . [who] is especially peculiar" (66). It is therefore necessary to explore the two possibilities, using

*Sources are paraphrased here. Although the words of the sources aren't used, ideas must be acknowledged.*

*Brackets around "who" indicate that word has been added.*

*Citation includes page number because title and author are clear from context.*

evidence from the novel to determine whether Edna Pontellier's awakening is political or peculiarly personal in nature.

3      It does not take a deeply feminist awareness to detect the dominant, controlling stance Edna's husband, Leonce, assumes in their marriage. Throughout the novel Chopin documents the resulting injustices, both great and small, which Edna endures. In one instance Leonce comes home late at night after Edna has fallen asleep, and, upon visiting their sleeping children, concludes that both of them are feverish. He wakes Edna so that she may check on them, despite her assertion that the children are perfectly well. He chides her for her "inattention" and "habitual neglect of the children" (7)—rather than respecting her ability as their mother to judge the state of their health or attending to them himself—and reduces her to tears. She defers to his judgment, looking at the boys as he had asked, and, finding them entirely healthy, goes out to the porch where "an indescribable oppression . . . filled her whole being with a vague anguish" (8). Though in some ways inconsequential, actions such as these epitomize Leonce Pontellier's attitude toward women and particularly toward his wife. It is his belief that she has a certain role and specific duties

*. . . (three spaced periods) indicate that words have been omitted from sentence.*

(those of a woman) which must be done
well—according to his (a man's) standards.
Although he would probably claim to love
Edna, he does not seem to regard her as an
autonomous individual; she is the mother of
his children, the hostess of such "callers"
as he deems appropriate (i.e., the ones who
will bring him influence and esteem) (51)
and essentially another decoration in his
impeccably furnished house (50). When Edna's
awakening leads her to abandon household
chores in favor of painting, Chopin exposes
Leonce's sexism:

> Mr. Pontellier had been a rather
> courteous husband so long as he
> met a certain tacit submissiveness
> in his wife. But her new and
> unexpected line of conduct
> completely bewildered him . . .
> her absolute disregard for her
> duties as a wife angered him. (57)

4        It would seem from such evidence
that Chopin intended *The Awakening* to
depict the wrongs that women suffered at
the hands of men in her society. Taking
this cue from Chopin, many twentieth-century
critics choose to view it in a political
light. Larzer Ziff, for example, claims
that the novel "rejected the family as
the automatic equivalent of feminine self

*Prose quotations longer than four typed lines are indented one inch from the left margin and double-spaced.*

*Block quotations are not enclosed within quotation marks. Note that the period precedes the parenthetic citation in a block quotation.*

fulfillment, and on the very eve of the
twentieth century it raised the question of
what woman was to do with the freedom she
struggled toward" (175). Winfried Fluck,
noting Edna's "preference for semi-conscious
states of being . . . sleeping, dreaming,
dozing, or the moment of awakening" (435),
argues that she is enacting "a radical retreat
from the imprisonment of all social roles"
(435). Marie Fletcher states that "[Edna's]
suicide is the last in a series of rebellions
which structure her life, give it pathos, and
make of the novel . . . an interpretation of
the 'new woman'" (172)—"the emerging
suffragist/woman professional of the late
nineteenth century" (Culley 118). Even in 1899
an anonymous reviewer in the *New Orleans
Times-Democrat* noticed the political implications of the novel, declaring in his own
conservative way that

> a woman of twenty-eight, a wife
> and twice a mother who is pondering
> upon her relations to the world
> about her, fails to perceive that
> the relation of a mother to her
> children is far more important than
> the gratification of a passion
> which experience has taught her
> is . . . evanescent, can hardly be
> said to be fully awake. (150)

*Cody quotes opposing views. Note smooth integration of quoted passages. The verbs "claims," "noting," and "states" clearly signal quotations.*

COLLEGE WRITING

5          These critics lead us to focus on the
socio-political implications of the novel, and
on the questions it raises about a woman's
role and responsibility: when if ever does a
woman's personal life become more important
than her children? or, how does Edna embody
the emancipated woman? But I believe that more
than just the social pressure and politics of
the late nineteenth century were acting on
Edna. It was the inherent instability of her
own psyche, exacerbated by the oppression she
suffered as a woman, that drove her to swim
out to her death at the end of *The Awakening*.

6          Despite the feminist undertones

*Clear transition ("despite").*

discernible in Chopin's work, a strong sense
prevails that Edna's tragedy is unique, a
result of her own psychology, not only of
societal oppression. Throughout the novel
Chopin describes Edna's agitated state
of mind and drops hints about her upbringing
and family life before marriage. Upon piecing
all the clues to her personality together
one gets a troubling, stereotypical picture.
Edna's widowed father is a stern colonel
from Kentucky who "was perhaps unaware
that he had coerced his own wife into her
grave" (71). From the scenes in which he
appears one deduces that he is harsh and
authoritative with his family; the narrator's
comment about his wife implies that perhaps

*In this paragraph and the next, Cody develops her argument by analyzing the text of the novel.*

he was abusive (no doubt psychologically, possibly physically) as well. He gambles compulsively on horseracing (69), which denotes an addictive personality. He also makes his own very strong cocktails—"toddies"—which he drinks almost all day long (71). He retains the appearance of sobriety, however, which indicates a high tolerance built up over much time. From this evidence one may assume that he suffers from alcoholism.

7     The rest of Edna's family—two sisters—fit the mold of the dysfunctional family that a violent, alcoholic parent tends to create. Her oldest sister seems to be the hyperresponsible, over-functioning "perfect" daughter. She served as a surrogate mother to Edna and her younger sister, and is described by Edna's husband as the only daughter who "has all the Presbyterianism undiluted" (66). Edna's younger sister is, predictably, exactly the opposite: Leonce Pontellier describes her as a "vixen" (66). She has rebelled against all of the rules and expectations that the eldest daughter obeys and fulfills. Edna, the middle child, is hence a curious case. Chopin tells us that "even as a child she had lived her own small life all within herself" (15). In such family situations the

middle child is usually rather introverted.
Whereas the two other siblings strive
compulsively either to correct or create
problems, the sibling in the middle passively

*Evidence
from experts
offered in
support of
thesis.*

escapes from her painful family situation
by withdrawing into herself (Seixas and
Youcha 48—49).

8       So far this simplistic but relatively
reliable delineation of personalities works
for Edna's character. Later in life she
perpetuates the patterns of her dysfunctional
family by marrying a man who almost mirrors
her father in personality; he is simply a
workaholic rather than an alcoholic. Edna
gives birth to two children, "a responsibility
which she had blindly assumed" (20) in her
typically passive way. The first time she
truly examines her role in this marriage and
indeed in the world at large occurs on Grand
Isle, a resort island where she and her family
are vacationing for the summer. There she
begins to spend a great deal of time with a
young man named Robert Lebrun, and a mutual
desire gradually arises between them. This
desire, and the general sensuality and open-
ness of the Creole community to which she is
exposed, bring about Edna's sexual, artistic,
and individual awakening. Although the reader
is excited and inspired by this awakening
in Edna—a woman learning to shed the fetters

COLLEGE WRITING

of both her oppressive marriage and society in general—the way it takes control of her life is disturbingly reminiscent of mental illness. She becomes infatuated with Robert, devotes an inordinate amount of time to painting, and seeks out classical music, which wracks her soul in a torturous ecstasy.

Throughout her awakening, she experiences myriad moods and feelings that she had never felt before in her docile, passive state. Many of these moods manifest themselves in the form of mysterious, troubling voices: "the voices were not soothing that came to her from the darkness and the sky above and the stars" (53); "she felt like one who has entered and lingered within the portals of some forbidden temple in which a thousand muffled voices bade her begone" (84). Behind the veil of metaphor here one can detect hints of an almost schizoid character. Chopin even describes Edna as two selves, which naturally befits a woman undergoing an emotional transformation, but which also denotes a distinctly schizophrenic state of mind: "she was becoming herself and daily casting aside that ficttious self which we assume like a garment with which to appear before the world" (57); "she could only realize that she herself—her present self—was in some way different from the other self" (41). Chopin phrases her descriptions of Edna in such a way that they could in fact describe either a woman gaining her emotional autonomy or a woman losing her mind.

10    As compelling as I find the suggestion of Edna's insanity, I must admit that her struggle between selfhood and motherhood is one too common to all women to be passed off as the ravings of a madwoman. As to which interpretation she preferred, Chopin offered few clues. For example, in February 1898 Chopin responded to a question, posed by the society page of the *St. Louis Post-Dispatch*, about the possible motives for a recent rash of suicides among young high-society women. Rather than the pressure of society as a likely motive, she suggests a "highly nervous" disposition (qtd. in Toth 120). Indeed, she asserts that "leadership in society is a business . . . there is nothing about it that I can see that would tend to produce an unhealthy condition of mind. On the contrary, it prevents women from becoming morbid, as they might, had they nothing to occupy their attention when at leisure" (qtd. in Toth 120). Perhaps, then, we are to suppose that a combination of psychic instability and extensive leisure, rather than the oppression of her society, caused Edna

*Parenthetic reference to an indirect source. (The quotation from Chopin appears on page 120 of Toth's book.)*

to take her own life. And yet this same response in the *Post-Dispatch* includes a counter-question to the editor: "Business men commit suicide every day, yet we do not say that suicide is epidemic in the business world. Why should we say the feeling is rife among society women, because half a dozen unfortunates, widely separated, take their own lives?" (qtd. in Toth 120). Her implicit criticism of the double standard suggests that Chopin was aware of the politics of gender relations in her own society in addition to the existence of an "hysterical tendency" in some women (qtd. in Toth 120). One cannot therefore discount the possibility that Chopin meant Edna's suicide to be in part a reaction to her society's rigid and limiting expectations of women.

11     Chopin received such harsh criticism of Edna Pontellier's sexual freedom and attitude toward family that, when *The Awakening* was published, if not before, she must have had some idea of how controversial the issue of her protagonist's personal freedom really was: her hometown library banned the book, and Chopin herself was banned from a St. Louis arts club (Reuben). Her critics tend to believe that she sympathized unreservedly with her headstrong heroine; but even the

*Citation of online source. (Source is unpaginated, so citation gives only the author's name.)*

retraction she published soon after her novel does not reveal whether she viewed Edna as oppressed or mentally ill. Apparently written for the benefit of her scandalized reviewers, the retraction ironically relieves Chopin of all responsibility for Edna's "making such a mess of things and working out her own damnation" (159). Again, as in her ambiguous response to the *Post-Dispatch*, Chopin leaves curious readers unsatisfied, and the motive of Edna's suicide unclear.

12      It is left to the reader therefore to decide whether Edna is a martyr to a feminist cause—the liberation of the American housewife—or the victim of a psychological disturbance that drives her to suicide. I believe that it is best not to dismiss either possibility. To begin with, one cannot deny that in the nineteenth century few options other than marriage and child-rearing were open to women. These narrow options were the result of a societal structure in which men socially, economically, and sexually dominated women. In the twenty-first century we can look back at Chopin's time and feel confident in condemning this state of affairs, but from contemporary criticism of *The Awakening* alone, it is clear that this political view was not so widely accepted at the turn of the century. Perhaps Chopin had an unusually clear

and untimely insight into what we now consider the sexism of her society, but she chose to condemn it only implicitly by portraying it as a fact of life against which her unbalanced heroine must struggle and perish. As Larzer Ziff puts it, "Edna Pontellier is trapped between her illusions and the condition which society arbitrarily establishes to maintain itself, and she is made to pay" (175). Chopin fused the political and the personal in Edna Pontellier, who, like most women in the world, suffers not only from the pressures of a society run by and for men, but also from her own individual afflictions.

*Sources are listed in alphabetical order by author.*

*"Works Cited" is centered.*

*Three hyphens indicate another work by the author named immediately above.*

*Second and subsequent lines of entry are indented 5 spaces.*

*Online source (paginated).*

*Signed entry in a reference work with alphabetically arranged entries.*

*Begin Works Cited list on new page. Continue pagination.*

*Short form of citation. Articles by Culley and Fletcher are reprinted in the Norton edition of* The Awakening. *The full citation for the volume appears under Chopin.*

Cody 14

Works Cited


Chopin, Kate. *The Awakening*. 1899. Ed. Margaret Culley. New York: Norton, 1976. Print.

---."Retraction." 1899. Rpt. in *The Awakening*. By Kate Chopin. 159. Print.

Culley, Margaret. "The Context of *The Awakening*." In *The Awakening*. By Kate Chopin. 119–22. Print.

Fletcher, Marie. "The Southern Woman in the Fiction of Kate Chopin." Rpt. in *The Awakening*. By Kate Chopin. 170–73. Print.

Fluck, Winfried. "'The American Romance' and the Changing Functions of the Imaginary." *New Literary History* 27.3 (1996): 415–57. *Project Muse*. Web. 1 Apr. 2011.

"New Publications." *New Orleans Times-Democrat*. Rpt. in *The Awakening*. By Kate Chopin. 150. Print.

Nissenbaum, Stephen. "Chopin, Kate O'Flaherty." *Notable American Women, 1607–1950: A Biographical Dictionary*. Cambridge, MA: Harvard University Press, 1971. Print.

Rankin, Daniel S. "Influences upon the Novel." Rpt. in *The Awakening*. By Kate Chopin. 163–65. Print.

*Online source (unpaginated).*

Reuben, Paul P. "Chapter 6: 1890—1910: Kate Chopin (1851—1904)." *PAL: Perspectives in American Literature—A Research and Reference Guide.* Web. 2 Apr. 2011.

Seixas, Judith S., and Geraldine Youcha. *Children of Alcoholism: A Survivor's Manual.* New York: Harper, 1985. Print.

Shinn, Thelma J. "Kate O'Flaherty Chopin." *American Women Writers: A Critical Reference Guide from Colonial Times to the Present.* New York: Unger, 1979 ed. Print.

*Journal article.*

Toth, Emily. "Kate Chopin on Divine Love and Suicide: Two Rediscovered Articles." *American Literature* 63 (1991): 115—21. Print.

Ziff, Larzer. Excerpt from *The American 1890s: Life and Times of a Lost Generation,* 279-305. Rpt. in *The Awakening.* By Kate Chopin. 173—75. Print.

## An Analysis of Cody's Use of Sources

In our introductory comments, we noted that Cody uses sources in a range of ways in this essay. Here, we will point to some of the specific ways in which she uses the ideas of others to develop her argument about the novel and to enrich her analysis of it:

- In paragraph 1, Cody alludes to Betty Friedan's concept of the "Feminine Mystique" to help explain the prevailing interpretation of the novel. Note that the reference to Freidan is general; the idea of the "Feminine Mystique" is treated as **common knowledge.**

- In paragraph 2, Cody draws on Chopin's biography to help develop the interpretation she'll be arguing against. She's **granting the opposition what's due to it**; she's establishing the merit of the point of view against which she's arguing. (One wouldn't, after all, want to waste time arguing against a foolish position.) She also **quotes the authorities**, the critics Ziff and Rankin, she'll go on to dispute.
- At the end of paragraph 2, Cody **quotes a passage from the novel**, **evidence** that helps **support** her thesis (stated at the end of paragraph 1) that Edna's suicide in part "resulted from the torments of her individual psyche."
- In paragraphs 3 and 4, Cody **analyzes evidence** from the novel, from contemporary reviews, and from current criticism, that **does not support** her argument, but rather supports the "socio-political" interpretation of *The Awakening*. (Again, she's establishing the merit of the **counterargument**.)
- In paragraph 6, Cody **analyzes** the text of the novel, focusing now on **evidence** that **supports** her position—for example, Chopin's representation of Edna's family members.
- In paragraph 7, Cody refers to what might be called **expert testimony**: a discussion in a psychology textbook that supports her interpretation of Edna's dysfunctional family as a cause of Edna's own disturbed psyche.
- In paragraph 10, Cody quotes from Chopin herself to give a somewhat different perspective on Edna's character; she thereby enriches her analysis of Chopin's protagonist.
- In paragraph 12, Cody uses a quotation from Larzer Ziff, a critic she's been disagreeing with until now, in part to support her larger point. We note that at the end of the essay she develops a position that strikes a balance between the argument she's been putting forth, and the prevailing view of the novel. Our last impression of Cody, therefore, is that she is a thoughtful and reasonable critic.

# A Sample Research Essay (APA Format)

In the following research essay, student Jacob Alexander uses the APA form of in-text citations, which are clarified by a list headed "References." Our annotations in the margins of the essay point to noteworthy features of Alexander's use of sources and of the system of citation; a brief analysis of the essay follows it. For instructions on using the APA citation format, see Chapter 13, "Documenting Sources," pages 294–330.

*Quadruple space*

Nitrite: Preserventative or Carcinogen?

Jacob Alexander

Writing 1B: Environmental Issues

Professor Louis

May 2, 2011

*Triple space*

Abstract

*Quadruple space*

*Abstract appears on separate page after title page. Do not indent first line of paragraph.*

←—1"—→

Sodium nitrite, added to cured meats and smoked fish as a color fixative, can combine in meat and in the stomach to form a powerful carcinogen. Some argue that restrictions placed in recent years by the FDA on nitrite use have significantly reduced the health threat nitrite poses; however, recent research suggests that it may still be a significant cancer cause. The public must remain cautious about nitrite consumption.

←—1"—→

223

COLLEGE WRITING

224

Nitrite: Preservative or Carcinogen?

1       According to Julie Miller Jones, a
professor of food and nutrition and the author
of *Food Safety*, "average Americans eat their
weight in food additives every year" (cited in
Murphy, 1996, p. 140). There are approximately
fifteen thousand additives currently in use
(National Cancer Institute Fact Sheet [NCI],
1996); many of them are known to be dangerous.
Of these, nitrites may be among the most
hazardous of all. In this country, ham, bacon,
corned beef, salami, bologna, lox, and other
cold cuts and smoked fish almost invariably
contain sodium nitrite. In fact, one-third of
the federally inspected meat and fish we
consume—more than seven billion pounds of it
every year—contains this chemical (Jacobson,
1987, p. 169).

2       Just how dangerous are nitrites, and why—
if they really *are* dangerous—does the food
industry still use them? Both questions are
difficult to answer. Some experts say that
nitrites protect consumers from botulism, a
deadly disease that can be caused by spoiled
food, and that "the benefits of nitrite additives
outweigh the risks" (Edlefsen & Brewer, no date).
Others argue that the dangers nitrites once
posed have been significantly reduced—even
eliminated—by restrictions placed on their use by
the Food and Drug Administration. Nevertheless,
the evidence has long suggested that nitrites are
linked to stomach cancer; recent research has

*Page number and short form of title appear on every page*

*An indirect reference. Alexander consulted Murphy, who quotes Jones.*

*Citation gives author because Jacobson is not named in the text. Note format: author, date of publication, and page number preceded by a "p."*

*This online source did not provide a date of publication.*

*A reference
to two
sources. The
writer is
summarizing
whole
works, so no
page
numbers are
given.*
linked nitrites to leukemia and brain tumors as

well (Warrick, 1994; Legator & Daniel, 1995).

Perhaps the only certain conclusions one can

reach are that the effects of nitrite on the

*Clear
statement of
thesis.*

human body are still to some degree uncertain—

and that to protect themselves, consumers must be

cautious and informed.

3        That nitrite is a poison has been clear

for almost three decades. In 1974, Jacqueline

Verrett, who worked for the FDA for fifteen

years, and Jean Carper reported on several

instances of people poisoned by accidental

overdoses of nitrites in cured meats:

*Quotations
of more
than forty
words must
be indented
one inch
from the left
margin.
Block
quotations
do not
require
quotation
marks at
beginning
and end.*
> In Buffalo, New York, six persons were
> hospitalized with "cardiovascular
> collapse" after they ate blood sausage
> which contained excessive amounts of
> nitrites. . . . In New Jersey, two persons
> died and many others were critically
> poisoned after eating fish illegally
> loaded with nitrites. In New Orleans, ten
> youngsters between the ages of one and a
> half and five became seriously ill . . .
> after eating wieners or bologna
> overnitrited by a local meat-processing
> firm; one wiener that was obtained later
> from the plant was found to contain a
> whopping 6,570 parts per million. In
> Florida, a three-year-old boy died after
> eating hot dogs with three times greater
> nitrite concentration than the government
> allows. (pp. 138—39)

*Note that a
period
precedes the
parenthetical
citation in a
block quote.*

4       The chemical has the unusual and difficult-to-replace quality of keeping meat a fresh-looking pink throughout the cooking, curing, and storage process (Assembly of Life Science, 1982, p. 3). The nitrous acid from the nitrite combines with the hemoglobin in the blood of the meat, fixing its red color so that the meat does not turn the tired brown or gray natural to cured meats.

5       Unfortunately, it does much the same thing in humans. Although most of the nitrite passes through the body unchanged, a small amount is released into the bloodstream. This combines with the hemoglobin in the blood to form a pigment called methemoglobin, which cannot carry oxygen. If enough oxygen is incapacitated, a person dies. The allowable amount of nitrite in a quarter pound of meat has the potential to incapacitate between 1.4 and 5.7 percent of the hemoglobin in an average-sized adult (Verrett & Carper, 1974, pp. 138–39). One of the problems with nitrite poisoning is that infants under a year, because of the quantity and makeup of their blood, are especially susceptible to it.

6       If the consumer of nitrite isn't acutely poisoned (and granted, such poisonings are rare), his or her blood soon returns to normal and this particular danger passes: the chemical, however, has long-term effects, as research conducted in the 1970s clearly established. Nitrite can cause headaches in people who are especially sensitive to it, an upsetting symptom

considering that in rats who ate it regularly
for a period of time, it has produced lasting
"epileptic like" changes in the brain—
abnormalities which showed up when the rats
were fed only a little more than an American
fond of cured meats might eat (Wellford, 1973,
p. 173). Experiments with chickens, cattle,
sheep, and rats have shown that nitrite, when
administered for several days, inhibits the
ability of the liver to store vitamin A and
carotene (Hunter, 1972, p. 90). And finally,
Nobel laureate Joshua Lederberg points out that,
in microorganisms, nitrite enters the DNA.
"If it does the same thing in humans," he says,
"it will cause mutant genes." Geneticist Bruce
Ames adds, "If out of one million people, one
person's genes are mutant, that's a serious
problem. . . . If we're filling ourselves now
with mutant genes, they're going to be around for
generations" (cited in Zwerdling, 1971,
pp. 34–35).

7       By far the most alarming characteristic of
nitrite, however, is that in test tubes, in
meats themselves, in animal stomachs, and in
human stomachs—wherever a mildly acidic
solution is present—it can combine with amines
to form nitrosamines. And nitrosamines are
carcinogens. Even the food industry and the
agencies responsible for allowing the use of
nitrite in foods admit that nitrosamines cause
cancer. Edlefsen and Brewer, writing recently
for the National Food Safety Database, note that

*An online
source. (The
authors and
title are
named in
the sentence;
the source
has no date
or page
numbers.)*

"over 90 percent of the more than 300 known nitrosamines in foods have been shown to cause cancer in laboratory animals." They continue: "No case of human cancer has been shown to result from exposure to nitrosamines," but they acknowledge that "indirect evidence indicates that humans would be susceptible" (no date).

8      It is important to note that nitrite alone, when fed to rats on an otherwise controlled diet, does not induce cancer. It must first combine with amines to form nitrosamines. Considering, however, that the human stomach has the kind of acidic solution in which amines and nitrites readily combine, and considering as well that amines are present in beer, wine, cereals, tea, fish, cigarette smoke, and a long list of drugs including antihistamines, tranquilizers, and even oral contraceptives, it is hardly surprising to find that nitrosamaines have been found in human stomachs.

9      When animals are fed amines in combination with nitrite, they develop cancer with a statistical consistency that is frightening, even to scientists. Verrett and Carper report that after feeding animals 250 parts per million (ppm) of nitrites and amines, William Lijinsky, a scientist at Oak Ridge National Laboratory,

> found malignant tumors in 100 percent of
> the test animals within six months. . . .
> "Unheard of," he says. . . . "You'd
> usually expect to find 50 percent at
> the most. And the cancers are all over

the place—in the brain, lung, pancreas, stomach, liver, adrenals, intestines. We open up the animals and they are a bloody mess." [He] believes that nitrosamines, because of their incredible versatility in inciting cancer, may be the key to an explanation for the mass production of cancer in seemingly dissimilar populations. In other words, nitrosamines may be a common factor in cancer that has been haunting us all these years. (1974, p. 136)

Verrett and Carper (1974, pp. 43–46) list still more damning evidence. Nitrosamines have caused cancer in rats, hamsters, mice, guinea pigs, dogs, and monkeys. It has been proven that nitrosamines of over a hundred kinds cause cancer. Nitrosamines have been shown to pass through the placenta from the mother to cause cancer in the offspring. Even the lowest levels of nitrosamines ever tested have produced cancer in animals. When animals are fed nitrite and amines separately over a period of time, they develop cancers of the same kind and at the same frequency as animals fed the corresponding nitrosamines already formed.

10     To address these problems (and in response to intense public concern), in 1978, the FDA ruled that a reducing agent, such as ascorbic *This online* acid, must be added to products containing *source did* *not provide a* nitrite; the reducing agent inhibits the *date of* *publication.* formation of nitrosamines (Edlefsen & Brewer, no

date). And in the last two decades, at least, the furor over nitrite seems as a consequence to have abated. In fact, a 1997 article published by the International Food Information Council Foundation (a group primarily sponsored by the food industry, according to information provided by its Web site) celebrates nitrite as a "naturally derived" substance that, according to the American Academy of Sciences, has never been found to cause cancer. On the contrary, the anonymous author states, nitrite does many good things for consumers; it may even help to fight cancer: "it safeguards cured meats against the most deadly foodborne bacterium known to man" and helps with "promoting blood clotting, healing wounds and burns and boosting immune function to kill tumor cells."

*No citation is given here because all information is included in the sentence itself.*

11      Other experts are less certain that reducing agents have entirely solved the nitrosamine problem. The *Consumer's Dictionary of Food Additives* notes that one common agent, sodium ascorbate, which is added to the brine in which bacon is cured, "offers only a partial barrier because ascorbate is soluble in fatty tissues" (Winter, 1994, p. 282). But in the wake of several studies it is unclear that "inhibiting" the formation of nitrosamines actually makes nitrites safe to consume.

12      *The Los Angeles Times* reports that one of these studies, conducted by John Peters, an epidemiologist at USC, found that "children who eat more than 12 hot dogs per month have nine

times the normal risk of developing childhood
leukemia" (Warrick, 1994). Interestingly, the
study was focused not on nitrites, but rather on
electromagnetic fields. "Dietary exposure to
processed or cured meats was part of a little
side questionnaire to our study on electromagnetic fields," Peters said. "We were as
surprised as anyone by the hot dogs findings.

*An indirect*
*reference.*
*The writer*
*quotes*
*Warrick*
*quoting* 13
*Peters.*

. . . It was the biggest risk for anything we saw
in the study—about four times the risk for
EMF's" (cited in Warrick, 1994).

In another of these recent studies, hot
dogs were linked to brain tumors: researchers
found that "children born to mothers who ate at
least one hot dog per week while pregnant have
twice the risk of developing brain tumors, as do
children whose fathers ate too many hot dogs

*Authors are*
*named in the*
*sentence and*
*the online*
*source isn't*
*paginated.*
*Only*
*publication*
*date is cited.*

before conception" (Warrick, 1994). Dr. M. Legator
and Amanda Daniel comment that "these studies
confirm thirty years' worth of scientific research
on the cancer causing properties of preserved
meats and fish" (1995).

14         The question, then, is why nitrite
continues to be used in so much of the meat
Americans consume. Although nitrite adds a small
amount to flavor, it is used primarily for
cosmetic purposes. Food producers are of course
also quick to point out that nitrite keeps
people safe from botulism in cured meats, an
argument to which the public may be particularly
susceptible because of a number of recent and
serious food scares. Nevertheless, some evidence

WRITING THE RESEARCH ESSAY

231

suggests that the protection nitrite offers is
both unnecessary and ineffective.

15        Michael Jacobson explains the preservative
action of nitrite:

> Nitrite makes botulinum spores sensitive
> to heat. When foods are treated with
> nitrite and then heated, any botulinum
> spores that may be present are killed. In
> the absence of nitrite, spores can be
> inactivated only at temperatures that ruin
> the meat products. . . . Nitrite's
> preservative action is particularly
> important in foods that are not cooked
> after they leave the factory, such as ham,
> because these offer an oxygen-free
> environment, the kind in which botulinum
> can grow. The toxin does not pose a danger
> in foods that are always well cooked, such
> as bacon, because the toxin would be
> destroyed in cooking.
>
> Laboratory studies demonstrate
> clearly that nitrite can kill botulinum,
> but whether it actually does in
> commercially processed meat has been
> called into question. Frequently, the
> levels used may be too low to do
> anything but contribute to the color.
> (1987, p. 165)

Bratwurst and breakfast sausage are manufactured now without nitrite because they don't
need to be colored pink; bacon is always cooked
thoroughly enough to kill off any botulinum

spores present. Certainly there are other ways
of dealing with botulism. High or low temperature prevents botulism. What nitrite undoubt-
edly does lower, however, is the level of care
and sanitation necessary in handling meat.

16          Clearly, the use of nitrite adds immeasur-
ably to the profit-making potential of the meat
industry, but why does the federal government
allow this health hazard in our food? In the
first place, nitrite and nitrate have been used
for so long that it is hard for lawmakers to get
past their instinctive reaction, "But that's the
way we've always done it." Indeed, the Romans
used saltpeter, a nitrate, to keep meat and, as
early as 1899, scientists discovered that the
nitrate breaks down into nitrite and that it is
the nitrite which actually preserves the red

*Note that a*
*reference to a*
*single page is*
*preceded by*
*"p." and that*
*a reference to*
*two or more*
*pages is*
*preceded by*
*"pp."*

color in meats (Jacobson, 1987, pp. 164–65).
Thus, by the time the U.S. Department of Agri-
culture and the Food and Drug Administration got
into the business of regulating food, they
tended to accept nitrite and nitrate as givens.

A second reason for the inadequacy of
regulation is that government mechanisms for
protecting the consumer are full of curious
loopholes. In 1958 Congress passed the Food
Additive Amendment, including the Delaney
Clause, which clearly states that additives
should be banned if they induce cancer in laboratory animals. Unfortunately, however, the
amendment does not apply to additives that were
in use before it was passed, so, since nitrite

and nitrate had already been in use for a long
time, they were automatically included on the
list of chemicals "Generally Recognized as
Safe." To complicate matters further, nitrite
in meat is regulated by the USDA, while
nitrite in fish is under the jurisdiction of
the FDA. And these agencies generally leave it
to industry—the profit-maker—to establish
whether or not an additive is safe. The final
irony in this list of governmental errors is
that the FDA depends heavily, for "independent" research and advice, on the food commit-
tees of the National Academy of Sciences,
which Daniel Zwerdling claims are "like a
Who's Who of the food and chemical industry"
(1971, p. 34). (This, of course, is the organization cited in the anonymous Web posting
quoted above, the organization that holds that
"nitrite levels in cured meat have not been
linked to the development of human cancers.")

17      Clearly, consumers need to be informed;
clearly, it is unwise to count on government
agencies for protection against the dangers food
additives may pose. Some experts continue to
argue that nitrite is safe enough; Edelfson and
Brewer, for example, cite a 1992 study by J. M.
Jones that suggests that drinking beer exposes a
consumer to more nitrite than does eating
bacon—and that new car interiors are a significant source of nitrite as well.[1] Others recom-

*Because the author is named in the sentence, the citation gives only the date and page number.*

*An explanatory footnote.*

[1] Presumably the exposure here results from
contact, not ingestion.

mend caution. One expert advises: "If you must
eat nitrite-laced meats, include a food or
drink high in vitamin C at the same time—for
example, orange juice, grapefruit juice,
cranberry juice, or lettuce" (Winter, 1994, p.
282). And, in fact, a study by a committee
organized by the National Academy of Sciences
strongly implies (Assembly, 1982, p. 12) that
the government should develop a safe
alternative to nitrites.

18          In the meantime, the chemical additive
industry doesn't seem very worried that alternatives, such as biopreservatives, will pose a
threat to its profits. An industry publication,
"Chemical Marketing Reporter," recently
reassured its readers by announcing that
"around 82.5 million pounds of preservatives,
valued at $133 million, were consumed in the
US in 1991." The report also stated that
"though the trend toward phasing out controversial preservatives like sulfites, nitrates
and nitrites continues, natural substitutes
remain expensive and often less than
effective, making biopreservatives a distant
threat" (Tollefson, 1995).

  References

            Assembly of Life Science. (1982). *Alternatives to*
*Second and*
*subsequent*            *the current use of nitrite in food.*
*lines of entries*
*are indented*          Washington, DC: National Academy Press.
*five spaces.*
            Edlefsen, M., & Brewer, M. S. (n.d.). *The*                     *Use "n.d."*
                                                                            *when date is*
                        *national food safety database.*                   *unavailable.*

                        Nitrates/Nitrites. Retrieved from

                        http://www.foodsafety.org

*Capitalize*    Hunter, B. T. (1972). *Fact/book on food additives*
*only the first*
*word in*               *and your health.* New Canaan, CT: Keats.
*book and*
*article titles.*International Food Information Council

                        Foundation. (1997). Nitrite: keeping

                        food safe. *Food Insight.* Retrieved

                        from http://ific.org/foodinsight

            Jacobson, M. F. (1987). *Eater's digest.*

                        Washington, DC: Center for Science in the
*An online*
*version*               Public Interest.
*of a*
*newspaper* Legator, M., & Daniel, A. (1995). Reproductive
*article.*
*Capitalize all*        systems can be harmed by toxic exposure.
*important*
*words in*              *Galveston County Daily News.* Retrieved
*newspaper and*
*periodical titles.*    from http://www.galvnews.com

            Murphy, K. (1996, May 6). Do food                          *An online*
                                                                        *version of a*
                        additives subtract from health?                 *magazine*
                                                                        *article. Note*
                        *Business Week*, p. 140.                        *that the year*
                                                                        *precedes the*
            National Cancer Institute (1996, June).                     *month and date*
                                                                        *in the*
                        *NCI fact sheet.* Food additives.               *parentheses*
                                                                        *following the*
                        Retrieved from http://nisc8a.upenn.edu/         *author.*

                        pdghtml/6/eng/600037.html

Tollefson, C. (1995, May 29). Stability

preserved; preservatives; food

additives '95. *Chemical Marketing

Reporter 247*(22) SR28.

*A book by two authors. Note use of ampersand between authors' names.*

Verrett, J., & Carper, J. (1974). *Eating may

be hazardous to your health.* New York:

Simon and Schuster.

Warrick, P. (1994, June 8). A frank

discussion. *Los Angeles Times*, E1.

Welford, H. (1973). *Sowing the wind; a

report from Ralph Nader's Center for

Study of Responsible Law on food

safety and the chemical harvest.* New

York: Bantam.

Winter, R. (1994). *A consumer's dictionary

of food additives* (Updated 4th ed.).

New York. Crown.

Zwerdling, D. (1971, June). Food pollution.

*Ramparts, 9*(11), 31–37, 53–54.

*Use "p." or "pp." when citing books or newspapers, but not periodicals. Ramparts is a periodical.*

# An Analysis of Alexander's Use of Sources

Jacob Alexander's **research essay** argues persuasively against eating foods preserved with sodium nitrite even as Alexander acknowledges that the dangers of nitrites haven't been established with absolute certainty. His **balanced, reasonable tone** and his range of **sources** help to establish his credibility. He cites industry and government publications, experts in the field, reference works, news articles, and a variety of other sources. Readers are inclined to trust someone who considers lots of evidence, even evidence that runs counter to his position. We know that at least one reader found his argument convincing: Alexander's writing instructor reports that she hasn't eaten a hot dog since she read his essay.

Here, we will point to some of the specific ways Alexander develops his argument.

- Paragraphs 1–3 capture the reader's attention by **establishing that there is a problem**, one that affects almost everyone. Paragraph 1 **introduces the problem** of food additives by quoting an **authority** (a "professor of food and nutrition") and offering a striking piece of information, that people eat their weight in additives each year. Paragraph 2 **develops the problem** by presenting the writer's research questions (how dangerous are additives, and—if they are dangerous—why are they still used?) and offering **evidence** from authorities on both sides. Paragraph 3 **develops the problem** further by presenting frightening **evidence** of deaths due to nitrites.

- Paragraphs 4–10 present the writer's **research** on what nitrites do: how they preserve meat (paragraph 4); how they affect the blood (paragraph 5) and the genes (paragraph 6); and how they may cause cancer in humans (paragraphs 7–10). The writer offers a particularly damning piece of **evidence** in paragraph 7 when he cites the food industry's report that nitrosamines, which form when nitrites and amines combine in the body, cause cancer. The food industry of course profits from preservatives and can be expected to defend nitrites whenever possible, so the admission powerfully supports Alexander's position.

- Paragraphs 11–12 look at the Food and Drug Administration's response, in the 1970s, to public concerns about nitrites and at various experts' current thinking about them. Alexander notes that a bulletin published by a food industry group in the late 1990s celebrates nitrite as a "naturally derived" substance that may in fact fight cancer—an interesting **counterargument**, but one that seems weak after all the evidence to the contrary. Paragraphs 13–14 present frightening information from current studies that again link nitrites and cancer; the link establishes a **transition** (in paragraph 15) to a discussion of the second part of Alexander's **research question**: why are nitrites still used?

■ Paragraphs 16–18 explore and develop this question: Botulism-killing nitrites make lower standards of sanitation possible for meat producers and increase industry profits—but given the dangers, why does the *government* permit their use? The answers: long practice, and regulatory loopholes. Paragraph 19 presents Alexander's **conclusion** that consumers must be wary. (We like the touch of **wit** in the explanatory footnote to this paragraph.) And paragraph 20—the final paragraph—ends with a chilling **quotation** from a chemical industry publication reassuring its readers that nitrites are here to stay. No summary or further commentary is needed from Alexander; the quotation strikes just the right conclusive note.

# PART THREE
# A Writer's Handbook

# 11

# Punctuating Sentences

SPEAKERS CAN RAISE OR LOWER THE VOLUME OR PITCH OF THEIR voices; they can speak a phrase slowly and distinctly and then (making a parenthetical remark, perhaps) quicken the pace. They can wave their arms, pound a table, or pause, meaningfully. But writers, physically isolated from their audience, can do none of these things. Nevertheless, they can embody some of the tones and gestures of speech—in the patterns of their written sentences, and in the dots, hooks, and lines of punctuation that clarify those patterns.

Punctuation clarifies, first of all, by removing or reducing ambiguity. Consider this headline from a story in a newspaper:

SQUAD HELPS DOG BITE VICTIM

Of course, there is no real ambiguity here—only a laugh—because the stated meaning is so clearly absurd, and on second reading we supply the necessary hyphen in *dog-bite*. But other ill-punctuated sentences may be troublesome rather than entertaining. Take the following sentence:

He arrived late for the rehearsal didn't end until midnight.

Almost surely you stumbled in the middle of the sentence, thinking that it was about someone arriving tardily at a rehearsal, and then, since what followed made no sense, you probably went back and mentally added the comma (by pausing) at the necessary place:

He arrived late, for the rehearsal didn't end until midnight.

Punctuation helps to keep your reader on the right path. And the path is your train of thought. If your punctuation is faulty, you unintentionally point the reader off your path and toward dead-end streets and quagmires.

Even when punctuation is not the key to meaning, it usually helps you get your meaning across neatly. Consider the following sentence:

> There are two kinds of feminism—one is the growing struggle of women to understand and change the shape of their lives and the other is a narrow ideology whose adherents are anxious to clear away whatever does not conform to their view.

The sentence is clear enough, but by changing the punctuation it can be sharpened. Because a dash usually indicates an abrupt interruption—it usually precedes a sort of afterthought—a colon would be better. The colon, usually the signal of an amplification of what precedes it, here would suggest that the two classifications are not impromptu thoughts but carefully considered ones. Second, and more important, in the original version the two classifications are run together without any intervening punctuation, but since the point is that the two are utterly different, it is advisable to separate them by inserting a comma or semicolon, indicating a pause. A comma before "and the other" would do, but probably a semicolon (without the "and") is preferable because it is a heavier pause, thereby making the separation clearer. Here is the sentence, revised:

> There are two kinds of feminism: one is the growing struggle of women to understand and change the shape of their lives; the other is a narrow ideology whose adherents are anxious to clear away whatever does not conform to their view.

The right punctuation enables the reader to move easily through the sentence.

Although punctuation helps a reader to move through a sentence, it must be admitted that some of the rules of punctuation do not contribute to meaning or greatly facilitate reading. For example, in American usage a period never comes immediately after quotation marks; it precedes quotation marks, thus:

> "If you put the period inside the closing quotation mark," the writing instructor said, "I will give you an A."

If you put the period after the closing quotation mark, the meaning remains the same, but you are also informing your reader that you don't know the conventions of American usage—conventions all writers in the United States are expected to adhere to. A pattern of such errors will diminish your authority as a writer: Your reader, noticing that you don't know where to put the period in relation to the quotation mark, may well begin to wonder what else you don't know. Conversely, demonstrating that you know the rules will help to gain your reader's confidence and establish your authority as a writer.

### A Word on Computer Grammar and Punctuation Checks

Word-processing programs include a tool that can check grammar and punctuation. At your request, the program will flag sentences that look faulty and offer suggestions for correcting mistakes. These programs can be very helpful: They can draw your attention to sentence fragments, to problems with plurals and possessives, even to passive verbs. But they don't catch everything, and they don't always know how to fix the problems they identify.

Our advice: Use the tool if you have it, but don't let it do your editing for you. Check the program's suggestions against your own knowledge and the advice offered in this book.

# Three Common Errors: Fragments, Comma Splices, and Run-On Sentences

### Fragments and How to Correct Them

A **fragment** is a part of a sentence set off as if it were a complete sentence:

> Because I didn't care.
> Being an accident.
> Later in the week.

Fragments are common in speech, but they are used sparingly in writing, usually for emphasis. A fragment used carelessly in writing often looks like an afterthought—usually because it *was* an afterthought—that is, an explanation or other addition that belongs to the previous sentence.

With appropriate punctuation (and sometimes with no punctuation at all), a fragment can usually be connected to the previous sentence:

**Incorrect**

Many nineteenth-century horror stories have been made into films. Such as *Dracula* and *Frankenstein*.

**Correct**

Many nineteenth-century horror stories have been made into films, such as *Dracula* and *Frankenstein*.

**Incorrect**

A fragment often looks like an afterthought. Perhaps because it *was* an afterthought.

**Correct**

A fragment often looks like an afterthought—perhaps because it *was* an afterthought.

**Incorrect**

He hoped to get credit for two summer courses. Poetry and Accounting.

**Correct**

He hoped to get credit for two summer courses: Poetry and Accounting.

**Incorrect**

Many schools are putting renewed emphasis on writing. Because SAT scores have declined for ten years.

**Correct**

Many schools are putting renewed emphasis on writing because SAT scores have declined for ten years.

Notice in these examples that, depending upon the relationship between the two parts, the fragment and the preceding statement can be joined by a comma, dash, or colon, or by no punctuation at all.

Notice also that unintentional fragments often follow subordinating conjunctions, such as *because* and *although*. Subordinating conjunctions introduce a subordinate (dependent) clause; such a clause cannot stand as a sentence. Here is a list of the most common subordinating conjunctions:

| | | |
|---|---|---|
| after | provided | when |
| although | since | where |
| because | though | whereas |
| before | unless | while |
| if | until | |

## How to Correct Comma Splices and Run-on Sentences

An error known as a **comma splice** or **comma fault** results when a comma is mistakenly placed between two independent clauses that are not joined by a coordinating conjunction: *and, or, nor, but, for, yet, so.* If the comma is omitted, the error is called a **run-on sentence.**

Here are some examples of the two errors:

### Comma Splice (or Comma Fault)

In the second picture the man leans on the woman's body, he is obviously in pain.

### Run-on Sentence

In the second picture the man leans on the woman's body he is obviously in pain.

Run-on sentences and comma splices may be corrected in five principal ways:

**1. Use a period to create two sentences:**

In the second picture the man leans on the woman's body. He is obviously in pain.

**2. Use a semicolon:**

In the second picture the man leans on the woman's body; he is obviously in pain.

**3. Use a comma and a coordinating conjunction (*and, or, nor, but, for, yet, so*):**

In the second picture the man leans on the woman's body, and he is obviously in pain.

**4. Make one of the clauses dependent (subordinate). Use a subordinating conjunction such as *after, although, because,***

*before, if, provided, since, though, unless, until, when, where, whereas, while:*

In the second picture the man leans on the woman's body because he is in pain.

5. **Reduce one of the independent clauses to a phrase, or even to a single word:**

In the second picture the man, obviously in pain, leans on the woman's body.

Run-on sentences and comma splices are especially common in sentences containing transitional words or phrases such as the following:

| | | |
|---|---|---|
| also | furthermore | in fact |
| besides | hence | nevertheless |
| consequently | however | therefore |
| for example | indeed | whereas |

When these words join independent clauses, the clauses cannot be linked by a comma.

### Incorrect

She argued from faulty premises, however the conclusions happened to be correct.

Here are five correct revisions, following the five rules we have just given. (In the first two revisions we place "however" after rather than before "the conclusions" because we prefer the increase in emphasis, but the grammatical point is the same.)

### Correct

1. She argued from faulty premises. The conclusions, however, happened to be correct. [Two sentences]

2. She argued from faulty premises; the conclusions, however, happened to be correct. [Semicolon]

3. She argued from faulty premises, but the conclusions happened to be correct. [Coordinating conjunction: *but*]

4. Although she argued from faulty premises, the conclusions happened to be correct. [Subordinating conjunction: *although*]

5. She argued from faulty premises to correct conclusions. [Reduction of an independent clause to a phrase]

The following sentence contains a comma splice:

> The husband is not pleased, in fact, he is embarrassed.

How might it be repaired?

# The Period

Periods are used to mark the ends of sentences (or intentional sentence fragments) other than questions and exclamations:

> A sentence normally ends with a period.
> She said, "I'll pass."
> Yes.
> Once more, with feeling.

But a sentence within a sentence is punctuated according to the needs of the longer sentence. Notice, in the following example, that a period is *not* used after "pass."

> She said, "I'll pass," but she said it without conviction.

Periods are used with abbreviations of titles and terms of reference:

> Dr.  Mr.  Mrs.  Ms.  i.e.  e.g.  etc.
> p.  pp.  (for "page" and "pages")

But when the capitalized initial letters of the words naming an organization are used in place of the full name, the periods are commonly omitted:

> CBS  CORE  IBM  NBA  UCLA  UNICEF  USAF

Periods are also used to separate chapter from verse in the Bible:

> Genesis 3.2   Mark 6.10

For further details on references to the Bible, see page 259.

# The Question Mark

Use a question mark after a direct question:

> Do you have a Twitter account?

Do not use a question mark after an indirect question, or after a polite request:

> He asked if I have a Twitter account.
> Would you please explain why you don't have a Twitter account.

# The Colon

The colon has four uses:

- to introduce a list or series of examples
- to introduce an amplification or explanation of what precedes the colon
- to introduce a quotation (though a quotation can be introduced by other means)
- to indicate time

Now let's look at each of those four uses.

1. **The colon may introduce a list or series:**

Students are required to take one of the following sciences: biology, chemistry, geology, physics.

2. **The colon may introduce an explanation.** It is almost equivalent to *namely* or *that is*. What is on one side of the colon more or less equals what is on the other side. The material on either side of the colon can stand as a separate sentence:

She explained her fondness for wrestling: she did it to shock her parents.

The forces which in China created a central government were absent in Japan: farming had to be on a small scale, there was no need for extensive canal works, and a standing army was not required to protect the country from foreign invaders.

Many of the best of the Civil War photographs must be read as the fossils of earlier events: The caissons with their mud-encrusted wheels, the dead on the field, the empty landscapes, all speak of deeds already past.

*—John Szarkowski*

Notice in the last example that the writer uses a capital letter after the colon; the usage is acceptable when a complete sentence follows the colon, as long as that style is followed consistently throughout a paper.

3. **The colon, like the comma, may be used to introduce a quotation;** it is more formal than the comma, setting off the quotation to a greater degree.

The black sculptor Ed Wilson tells his students: "Malcolm X is my brother, Martin Luther King is my brother, Eldridge Cleaver is my brother! But Michelangelo is my grandfather!"

*—Albert E. Elsen*

**4. A colon is used to separate the hour from the minutes when the time is given in figures:**

9:15   12:00

**5. Colons (like semicolons) go outside of closing quotation marks if they are not part of the quotation:**

"There is no such thing as a free lunch": The truth of these words is confirmed every day.

## The Semicolon

There are four main uses of the semicolon. Sheridan Baker (in *The Practical Stylist*) summed them up in this admirable formula: "Use a semicolon where you could also use a period, unless desperate." Correctly used, the semicolon can add precision to your writing; it can also help you out of some tight corners.

**1. You may use a semicolon instead of a period between closely related independent clauses not joined by a coordinating conjunction:**

All happy families resemble one another; every unhappy family is unhappy in its own fashion.

*—Leo Tolstoy*

The demands that men and women make on marriage will never be fully met; they cannot be.

*—Jessie Bernard*

When a cat washes its face it does not move its paw; it moves its face.

In each of the examples the independent clauses might have been written as sentences separated by periods; the semicolon pulls the statements together, emphasizing their relationship. Alternatively, the statements might have been linked by coordinating conjunctions (*and, or, nor, but, for, yet, so*). For example:

The demands made upon marriage will never be fully met for they cannot be.

When a cat washes its face it does not move its paw, but it moves its face.

The sentences as originally written, using semicolons, have more bite.

2. **You *must* use a semicolon (rather than a comma) if you use a *conjunctive adverb* to connect independent clauses.** (A conjunctive adverb is a transitional word such as *also, consequently, furthermore, however, moreover, nevertheless, therefore.*)

His hair was black and wavy; however, it was false.

We don't like to see our depressed relative cry; nevertheless, tears can provide a healthy emotional outlet.

She said "I do"; moreover, she repeated the words.

Take note of the following three points:

- A comma goes after the conjunctive adverb.
- Semicolons (like colons) go outside of closing quotation marks if they are not part of the quotation.
- A conjunctive adverb requires a semicolon to join independent clauses. A comma produces a comma splice:

**Incorrect**

His hair was black and wavy, however, it was false.

3. **You may use a semicolon to separate a series of phrases with internal punctuation:**

He had a car, which he hadn't paid for; a wife, whom he didn't love; and a father, who was unemployed.

4. **Use a semicolon between independent clauses linked by coordinating conjunctions if the sentence would otherwise be difficult to read, because it is long and complex, or because it contains internal punctuation:**

In the greatest age of painting, the nude inspired the greatest works; and even when it ceased to be a compulsive subject, it held its position as an academic exercise and a demonstration of mastery.

(Often it is preferable to break up such sentences, or to recast them.)

# The Comma

The comma (from the Greek word meaning "to cut") indicates a relatively slight pause within a sentence. If after checking the rules you are still uncertain whether or not to use a comma in a given sentence, read the sentence aloud and see if it sounds better with or without a pause;

you can then add or omit the comma. A women's shoe store in New York has a sign on the door:

NO MEN PLEASE.

If the proprietors would read the sign aloud, they might want to change it to

NO MEN, PLEASE

When you are typing, always follow a comma with a space.

For your reference, here is a guide to the following pages, which summarize the correct uses of the comma:

**1. Independent clauses (unless short) joined by a coordinating conjunction (*and, or, nor, but, for, yet, so*) take a comma before the conjunction:**

Most students see at least a few football games, and many go to every game of the season.

Most students seem to have an intuitive sense of when to use a comma, but in fact the "intuition" is the result of long training.

If the introductory independent clause is short, the comma is usually omitted:

She ran but she couldn't catch up.

**2. An introductory subordinate clause or long phrase is usually followed by a comma:**

Having revised his manuscript for the third time, he went to bed.

In order to demonstrate her point, the instructor stood on her head.

If the introductory subordinate clause or phrase is short, say four words or fewer, the comma may be omitted, provided no ambiguity results from the omission:

Having left he soon forgot.

But compare this last example with the following:

Having left, the instructor soon forgot.

If the comma is omitted, the sentence is misread. Where are commas needed in the following sentences?

When Shakespeare wrote comedies were already popular.

While he ate his poodle would sit by the table.

As we age small things become killers.

3. **A subordinate clause or long modifying phrase tacked on as an afterthought is usually preceded by a comma:**

Buster Keaton fell down a flight of stairs without busting, thereby gaining his nickname from Harry Houdini.

By the time he retired, Hank Aaron had 755 home runs, breaking Babe Ruth's record by 41.

With afterthoughts, the comma may be omitted if there is a clear sequence of cause and effect, signaled by such words as *because, for,* and *so.* Compare the following examples:

In 1601 Shakespeare wrote *Hamlet,* probably his best-known play.

In 1601 Shakespeare wrote *Hamlet* because revenge tragedy was in demand.

4. **A pair of commas can serve as a pair of unobtrusive parentheses.** Be sure not to omit the second comma:

The earliest known paintings of Christ, dating from the third century, are found in the catacombs outside of Rome.

Medicare and Medicaid, the chief sources of federal support for patients in nursing homes, are frequently confused.

Under this heading we can include a conjunctive adverb (a transitional adverb such as *also, besides, consequently, however, likewise, nevertheless, therefore*) inserted within a sentence. These transitional words are set off between a pair of commas:

Her hair, however, was stringy.

If one of these words begins a sentence, the comma after it is optional. Notice, however, that the presence of such a word as "however" is not always a safeguard against a run-on sentence or comma splice; if the word occurs between two independent clauses and it goes with the second clause, you need a semicolon before it and a comma after it:

His hair was black and wavy; however, it was false.

(See the discussion of comma splices on pp. 246–48.)

5. **Use a comma to set off a nonrestrictive modifier.** A nonrestrictive modifier, as the following examples will make clear, is a sort of parenthetical addition; it gives supplementary information about the subject, but it can be omitted without changing the subject. A restrictive modifier, however, is not supplementary but essential; if a restrictive modifier is omitted, the subject becomes more general. In Dorothy Parker's celebrated poem,

Men seldom make passes
At girls who wear glasses.

"who wear glasses" is a restrictive modifier, narrowing or restricting the subject down from "girls" to a particular group of girls, those who wear glasses. That is, the subject is *not* "girls," but the narrower or more limited group, "girls who wear glasses."

Here is a *non*restrictive modifier:

For the majority of immigrants, who have no knowledge of English, language is the chief problem.

Now here is a restrictive modifier:

For the majority of immigrants who have no knowledge of English, language is the chief problem.

These sentences say different things. The first version says—in addition to its obvious message that language is the chief problem—that the majority of immigrants have no knowledge of English. The second version makes no such assertion; it talks not about the majority of immigrants but only about a more restricted group—the majority of those immigrants who have no knowledge of English.

Now look at another example:

Shakespeare's shortest tragedy, *Macbeth,* is one of his greatest plays.

In this sentence, "*Macbeth*" is nonrestrictive because the subject is already as restricted as possible; Shakespeare can have written only one "shortest tragedy." That is, "*Macbeth*" is merely an explanatory equivalent of "Shakespeare's shortest tragedy" and it is therefore enclosed in commas. (A noun or noun phrase serving as an explanatory equivalent to another, and in the same syntactical relation to other elements in the sentence, is said to be in apposition.) But compare

Shakespeare's tragedy *Macbeth* is one of his greatest plays.

with the misleadingly punctuated sentence,

Shakespeare's tragedy, *Macbeth,* is one of his greatest plays.

The first of these is restrictive, narrowing or restricting the subject "tragedy" down to one particular tragedy, and so it rightly does not separate the modifier from the subject by a comma. The second, punctuated so that it is nonrestrictive, falsely implies that *Macbeth* is Shakespeare's only tragedy.

Here is an example of a nonrestrictive modifier correctly punctuated:

Women, who constitute 50.7 percent of the population and 53 percent of the electorate, constitute only 16.6 percent of the House of Representatives and 17 percent of the Senate.

In the next two examples, the first illustrates the correct use of commas after a nonrestrictive appositive, and the second illustrates the correct omission of commas after a restrictive appositive:

Hong Yee Chiu, a Chinese-American physicist, abbreviated the compound adjective *quasi-stellar* to *quasar.*

The Chinese-American physicist Hong Yee Chiu abbreviated the compound adjective *quasi-stellar* to *quasar.*

6. **Words, phrases, and clauses in series take a comma after each item except the last.** The comma between the last two items may be omitted if there is no ambiguity:

Photography is a matter of eyes, intuition, and intellect.
She wrote plays, poems, and stories.
He wrote plays, sang songs, and danced jigs.
She wrote a wise, witty, humane book.

But adjectives in a series may cause difficulty. The next two examples correctly omit the commas:

a funny silent film
a famous French professor

In each of these last two examples, the adjective immediately before the noun forms with the noun a compound that is modified by the earlier adjective. That is, the adjectives are not a coordinate series (what is funny is not simply a film but a silent film; what is famous is not simply a professor but a French professor) and so commas are not used. Compare:

a famous French professor
a famous, arrogant French professor

In the second example, only "famous" and "arrogant" form a coordinate series. If in doubt, see if you can replace the commas with "and"; if you can, the commas are correct. In the example given, you could insert "and" between "famous" and "arrogant" but not between "arrogant" and "French."

Commas are not needed if all the members of the series are connected by conjunctions:

He ate steak for breakfast and lunch and supper.

7. **Use a comma to set off direct discourse:**

"It's a total failure," she said.
She said, "It's a total failure."

But do not use a comma for indirect discourse:

She said that it is a total failure.
She said it is a total failure.

8. **Use a comma to set off "yes" and "no":**

No, I will turn in my essay tomorrow.

9. **Use a comma to set off words of address:**

Look, Bill, you should turn in your essay today.

10. **Use a comma to separate a geographical location within another geographical location:**

She was born in Brooklyn, New York, in 1895.

Another way of putting it is to say that a comma is used after each unit of an address, except that a comma is *not* used between the name of the state and the zip code.

11. **Use a comma to set off the year from the month or day:**

He was born on June 10, 1996, at Morristown Memorial Hospital.

No comma is needed if you use the form "10 June 1996."

12. **Note the position of the comma when used with other punctuation:** If a comma is required with parenthetic material, it follows the second parenthesis:

Because Japan was secure from invasion (even the Mongols were beaten back), its history is unusually self-contained.

The only time a comma may precede a parenthesis is when parentheses surround a digit or letter used to enumerate a series:

Questions usually fall into one of three categories: (1) true-false, (2) multiple choice, (3) essay.

A comma always goes inside closing quotation marks unless the quotation is followed by a parenthesis:

"Sayonara," he said.
"Sayonara" (Japanese for "goodbye"), he said.

# The Dash

The dash—more specifically, the em dash—indicates an abrupt break or pause. Your computer will probably insert the dash automatically if you type two hyphens without hitting the space bar before, between, or after. (If your computer does not automatically insert the em dash, you will need to locate it on your program's list of special characters.)

1. **The words within dashes function as parenthetic material (material that is not essential).** By setting material within dashes—an emphatic form of punctuation—the writer gives the material more emphasis than it would get within parentheses:

The bathroom—that private place—has rarely been the subject of scholarly study.

The Great Wall of China forms a continuous line over 1400 miles long—the distance from New York to Kansas City—running from Peking to the edge of the mountains of Central Asia.

**Note:** If the material between two dashes is deleted, the remaining words still form a grammatical sentence.

2. **A dash can serve, somewhat like a colon, as a pause before a series.** It is more casual than a colon:

The earliest Shinto holy places were natural objects—trees, boulders, mountains, islands.

Each of the brothers had his distinct comic style—Groucho's double-talk, Chico's artfully stupid malapropisms, Harpo's horseplay.

—*Gerald Mast*

A dash is never used next to a comma, and it is used before a period only to indicate that the sentence is interrupted.

Why, they couldn't hit an elephant at this dist—.

—*General John Sedgewick, (last words)*

Overuse of the dash—even only a little overuse—gives writing an unpleasantly agitated—even explosive—quality.

# Parentheses

Let's begin with a caution: Avoid using parentheses to explain pronouns:

In his speech he (Hamlet) says . . .

If "he" needs to be explained by "Hamlet," omit the "he" and just say "Hamlet."

1. **Use parentheses for subordinate material.** What is enclosed in parentheses functions as a casual aside, less essential than similar material set off in commas, less vigorously spoken than similar material set off in dashes:

While guest curator for the Whitney (he has since returned to the Denver Art Museum), Feder assembled a magnificent collection of masks, totems, paintings, clothing, and beadwork.

Another caution: Avoid an abundance of these interruptions, and avoid a long parenthesis within a sentence (you are now reading a simple example of this annoying but common habit of writers who have trouble sticking to the point) because the reader will lose track of the main sentence.

2. **Use parentheses to enclose digits or letters in a list that is given in running text:**

The exhibition included (1) decorative screens, (2) ceramics, (3) ink paintings, (4) kimonos.

3. **Do not confuse parentheses with square brackets.** The latter are used around material you add to a quotation (see p. 201).

4. **For the use of parentheses in documentation, see Chapter 13, "Documenting Sources."**

5. **Note the position of other punctuation with a parenthesis.** The example under rule 2 is the rare exception to the rule that within a sentence, punctuation other than quotation marks never immediately precedes an opening parenthesis. Note also that in the example under rule 1, the comma *follows* the closing parenthesis:

While guest curator for the Whitney (he has since returned to the Denver Art Museum), Feder assembled a magnificent collection of masks, totems, paintings, clothing, and beadwork.

If an entire sentence is in parentheses, put the final punctuation (period, question mark, or exclamation mark) inside the closing parenthesis.

# Italics

It used to be the case that in typewritten material underlining was equivalent to italics: The underlining told the typesetter to set the underlined words in italic type. Typewriters and typesetters are rare things these days, and so the rule has changed. According to current guidelines of the Modern Language Association, underlining is no longer acceptable.

1. **Italicize the name of a book, magazine, newspaper, painting, play, pamphlet, plane, spacecraft, ship, train, movie, radio or television program, compact disk, audiocassette, record album, statue, Web site, or online database**. Do not italicize names of sacred works such as the Bible, the Koran, and Acts of the Apostles, or political documents such as the Magna Carta and the Declaration of Independence. Notice that when you write about a newspaper or periodical whose title begins with the article "the," the convention is to give the article in lowercase Roman letters (e.g., "the *New Yorker*").

**Note:** Titles of shorter works, or works contained within longer works, are usually enclosed in quotation marks. The list of such titles includes poems, essays, chapter titles, songs, short story titles, and encyclopedia entries. Although one might assume otherwise, the titles of manuscripts and dissertations—unpublished material, in other words—are also enclosed in quotation marks.

2. **Use italics only sparingly for emphasis.** Sometimes this method of indicating your tone of voice is exactly right:

> In 1911 Jacques Henri Lartigue was not merely as unprejudiced as a child; he *was* a child.
>
> —*John Szarkowski*

3. **Use italics for foreign words that have not become a part of the English language:**

> Acupuncture aims to affect the *ch'i,* a sort of vital spirit that circulates through the bodily organs.

But:

> He ate a pizza.
> She behaved like a prima donna.
> Avoid clichés.

4. **You may use italics in place of quotation marks to indicate that you are providing a clarification or definition:**

> Honolulu means *safe harbor.*

5. **You may also use italics to identify a word or term to which you wish to call special attention:**

> Claude Lévi-Strauss tells us that one of the great purposes of art is that of *miniaturization.* He points out that most works of art are miniatures, being smaller (and therefore more easily understood) than the objects they represent.

## Capital Letters

Certain obvious conventions—the use of a capital for the first word in a sentence, for names (of days of the week, holidays, months, people, countries), and for words derived from names (such as pro-French)—need not be discussed here.

1. **Titles of works in English are usually given according to the following formula.** Use a capital for the first letter of the first word, for the first letter of the last word, and for the first letter of all other words that are not articles, conjunctions, or prepositions:

*The Rise and Fall of the Third Reich*
*A Midsummer Night's Dream*
*Up and Out*
"The Short Happy Life of Francis Macomber"
*A Short Guide to College Writing*

2. **Use a capital for a quoted sentence within a sentence, but not for a quoted phrase (unless it is at the beginning of your sentence) and not for indirect discourse:**

He said, "You can even fool some of the people all of the time."
He said you can fool some people "all of the time."
He said that you can even fool some of the people all of the time.

3. **Use a capital for a rank or title preceding a proper name or for a title substituting for a proper name:**

She said she was Dr. Perez.
He told President Obama that the Vice President was away.

But:

Why would anyone wish to be president?
Washington was the first president.

4. **Use a capital when the noun designating a family relationship is used as a substitute for a proper noun:**

If Mother is busy, ask Tim.

But:

Because my mother was busy, I asked Tim.

5. **Formal geographical locations (but not mere points on the compass) are capitalized:**

North America
Southeast Asia
In the Southwest, rain sometimes evaporates before touching
the ground.
Is Texas part of the South?
The North has its share of racism.

But:

> The wind came from the south.
> Texas is bordered on the north by Arkansas, Oklahoma, and New Mexico.

Do *not* capitalize the names of the seasons:

> spring   summer   winter   fall

## The Hyphen

The hyphen has three uses, all drawing on the etymology of the word *hyphen*, which comes from the Greek for "in one," "together."

1. **Use a hyphen to attach certain prefixes to root words.** *All-, pro-, ex-,* and *self-* are the most common of these (*all-powerful, ex-wife, pro-labor, self-made*), but note that even these prefixes are not always followed by a hyphen. If in doubt, check a dictionary. Prefixes before proper names are always followed by a hyphen:

> anti-Semite   pro-NATO   un-American

Prefixes ending in *i* are hyphenated before a word beginning with *i*:

> anti-intellectual   semi-intelligible

A hyphen is normally used to break up a triple consonant resulting from the addition of a prefix:

> ill-lit

2. **Use a hyphen to tie compound adjectives into a single visual unit:**

> out-of-date theory
> twenty-three books
> a no-smoking area
> eighteenth- and nineteenth-century novels

But if a compound modifier follows the modified term, it is usually not hyphenated:

> The theory was out of date.

3. **Use a hyphen to join some compound nouns:**

> Scholar-teacher   philosopher-poet

*Note:* **Use an en dash, which is shorter than an em dash (see pp. 257–58) but longer than a hyphen, to indicate a span of dates or page numbers.** (The en dash is located on your program's list of special characters.)

1957–59
pp. 162–68

# The Apostrophe

Use an apostrophe to indicate the possessive, to indicate a contraction, and to form certain unusual plurals.

1. **The most common way to indicate the possessive of a singular noun is to add an apostrophe and then an s:**

a dog's life    a week's work    Marx's doctrines

But some authorities suggest that for a proper noun of more than one syllable that ends in *s* or another sibilant (*cks, x, z*), it is better to add only an apostrophe:

Sophocles' plays    Chavez' ideas

When in doubt, say the name aloud and notice if you are adding an *s*. If you are adding an *s* when you say it, add an apostrophe and an *s* when you write it. Our own strong preference, however, is to add an apostrophe and an *s* to all singular proper nouns:

Jones's book    Kansas's highways

Possessive pronouns, such as *his, hers, its, theirs, ours,* do not take an apostrophe:

The cat shed its fur.
The book is hers, not his or theirs.

(*Exception:* Indefinite pronouns take an apostrophe, as in "one's hopes" and "others' opinions.")

For plurals ending in *s*, add only an apostrophe to indicate the possessive:

the boys' father    the Smiths' house    the Joneses' car

If the plural does not end in *s*, add an apostrophe and an *s:*

women's clothing    mice's eyes

© Original Artist. Reproduction rights obtainable from www.CartoonStock.com

Don't try to form the possessive of the title of a work (for example, of a play, a book, or a film): Write "the imagery in *The Merchant of Venice*" rather than "*The Merchant of Venice*'s imagery." Using an apostrophe gets you into the problem of whether to italicize the *s*. Similarly, if you use an apostrophe for a work normally enclosed in quotation marks (for instance, a short story), you can't put the apostrophe and the *s* after the quotation marks, but you can't put it inside either.

2. **Use an apostrophe to indicate the omitted letters or numbers in contractions:**

She won't.
It's time to go.
the class of '05

3. **Until recently an apostrophe was used to make plurals of words that do not usually have a plural and (this is optional) to make the plurals of digits and letters:**

Her speech was full of if's and and's and but's.
I got two A's and two B's.
the 1920's

This use of the apostrophe is no longer standard, but it remains acceptable.

# Abbreviations

In general, avoid abbreviations except in footnotes and except for certain common ones listed below. And don't use an ampersand (&) unless it appears in material you are quoting or in a title. Abundant use of abbreviations makes an essay sound like a series of newspaper headlines. Usually, for example, *United States* is better than *U.S.*, except when an adjective: the U.S. army.

1. **Abbreviations, with the first letter capitalized, are used before a name:**

Dr. Bellini          Ms. Smith          St. Thomas

But:

The doctor took her temperature and eighty dollars.

2. **Degrees that follow a name are abbreviated:**

B.A.          D.D.S          M.D.          Ph.D.

3. **Other acceptable abbreviations include:**

AD          BC          BCE CE          A.M.          P.M          e.g.          i.e.

(By the way, *e.g.* means *for example*; *i.e.* means *that is*; the two ought not to be confused. See pp. 277 and 280.)

4. **The name of an agency or institution.** For instance, the Congress of Racial Equality, International Business Machines, and Southern Methodist University may be abbreviated by using the initial letters, capitalized and usually without periods (CORE, IBM, SMU). It is advisable to give the name in full when first mentioning it (not everyone knows that AARP means American Association of Retired Persons, for instance) and to use the abbreviation in subsequent references.

# Numbers

1. **Write numbers out if you can do so in fewer than three words; if you cannot, use figures:**

> sixteen    seventy-two    ten thousand    one-sixth
> 10,200    10,200,000
> There are 336 dimples on a golf ball.

But write out round millions and billions to avoid a string of zeros:

> a hundred and ten million

For large round numbers you can also use a combination of figures and words:

> The cockroach is about 250 million years old.

However, if a number begins a sentence, note that it should always be written out:

> Two hundred and fifty million years ago the cockroach first appeared on earth.

2. **Use figures in dates, addresses, decimals, percentages, page numbers, and hours followed by a.m. or p.m.:**

> February 29, 1900    .06 percent    6 percent    8:16 A.M.

But hours unmodified by minutes are usually written out, followed by *o'clock*:

> Executions in England regularly took place at eight o'clock.

3. **Use an apostrophe to indicate omitted figures:**

> class of '98
> the '90s (but the *nineties*)

4. **Use an en dash to indicate a span:**

> 1975–79
> 10–20

In giving inclusive numbers, give the second number in full for the numbers up through ninety-nine (2–5, 8–11, 28–34). For larger numbers, give only the last two digits of the second number (101–06, 112–14) unless the full number is necessary (198–202).

5. **Dates can be given with the month first, followed by numerals, a comma, and the year:**

February 10, 1999

or they can be given with the day first, then the month, and then the year (without a comma after the day or month):

10 February 1999

6. **BC follows the year, but AD precedes it:**

10 BC
AD 200

The abbreviations BC and AD are falling out of favor and are being replaced with BCE ("before the common era") and CE ("common era"). Both abbreviations follow the year.

7. **Roman numerals are less used than formerly.** Capital Roman numerals were used to indicate a volume number, but volume numbers are now commonly given in Arabic numerals. Capital Roman numerals are still used, however, for the names of individuals in a series (Elizabeth II) and for the primary divisions of an outline; lowercase Roman numerals are used for the pages in the front matter (table of contents, foreword, preface, etc.) of a book. The old custom of citing acts and scenes of a play in Roman numerals and lines in Arabic numerals (II.iv.17–25) is still preferred by many instructors, but the use of Arabic numerals throughout (2.4.17–25) is gaining acceptance.

# Using the Right Word

The difference between the right word and the almost right word is the difference between lightning and a lightning bug.

—Mark Twain

SOME THINGS ARE SAID OR WRITTEN AND SOME ARE NOT. More precisely, anything can be said or written, but only some things are acceptable to the ears and minds of readers. "She don't know nothing about it" has been said and will be said again, but readers who encounter such a sentence will probably judge the speaker as an uneducated person with little of interest to say—and immediately tune out.

Although such a double negative is not acceptable today, it used to be: Chaucer's courteous Knight "never spoke no baseness," and Shakespeare's courtly Mercutio, in Romeo and Juliet, "will not budge for no man." But things have changed; what was acceptable in the Middle Ages and the Renaissance (for example, emptying chamber pots into the gutter) would not be acceptable now. And some of what was once unacceptable has become acceptable. At the beginning of the twentieth century, grammarians suggested that one cannot use drive in speaking of a car; one drives (forces into motion) an ox, or even a person ("He drove her to distraction"), but not a machine. A century of usage, however, has erased all objections.

This chapter presents a list of expressions that, although commonly used, set many teeth on edge. Several decades from now, some of these expressions may be as acceptable as "drive a car," but we are writing for today, and we might as well try to hold the attention of today's readers by following today's taste in language.

# A Note on Idioms

An *idiom* (from a Greek word meaning "peculiar") is a fixed group of words, peculiar to a given language. Thus, in English we say, "I took a walk," but Germans "make a walk," Spaniards "give a walk," and Japanese "do a walk." (If we think the German, Spanish, and Japanese expressions are odd, we might well ask ourselves where it is that we take a walk to.) If a visitor from Argentina says, in English, that she "gave a walk," she is using unidiomatic English, just as anyone who says he knows a poem "at heart" instead of "by heart" is using unidiomatic English.

Probably most unidiomatic expressions use the wrong preposition, as in the following examples:

| Unidiomatic | Idiomatic |
| --- | --- |
| comply to | comply with |
| superior with | superior to |

Sometimes while we write, or even while we speak, we are unsure of the idiom and we pause to try an alternative—"parallel with?" "parallel to?"—and we don't know which sounds more natural, more idiomatic. At such moments, more often than not, either is acceptable, but if you are in doubt, check a dictionary. (The *American Heritage Dictionary* has notes on usage following the definitions of hundreds of its words.)

In any case, if you are a native speaker of English, when you read your draft you will probably detect unidiomatic expressions such as superior with; that is, you will hear something that sounds odd, and so you will change it to something that sounds familiar, idiomatic—here, superior to. If any unidiomatic expressions remain in your essay, the trouble may be that an effort to write impressively has led you to use unfamiliar language. A reader who sees such unidiomatic language may sense that you are straining for an effect. Try rewriting the passage in your own voice.

If English is not your first language and you are not yet fluent in it, plan to spend extra time revising and editing your work. Check prepositional phrases with special care. In addition to using a college edition of an English-language dictionary, consult reference works designed with the international or bilingual student in mind. One compact book our students find particularly useful is Michael Swan's *Practical English Usage*, published by Oxford University Press. But don't neglect another invaluable resource: students who are native speakers. They will usually be able to tell you whether a phrase sounds right, though they may not know why.

DILBERT © Scott Adams/Dist. By United Feature Syndicate, Inc.

# A Writer's Glossary

**a, an**   Use *a* before words beginning with a consonant ("a book") or with a vowel sounded as a consonant ("a one-way ticket," "a university"). Use *an* before words beginning with a vowel ("an egg") including those beginning with a *silent h* ("an egg," "an hour"). If an initial *h* is pronounced, *a* is normal ("a history course") but if the accent is not on the first syllable, *an* is acceptable, as in "an historian."

**above**   Try to avoid writing *for the above reasons, in view of the above,* or *as above.* These expressions sound unpleasantly legalistic. Substitute *for these reasons,* or *therefore,* or some such expression or word.

**academics**   Only two meanings of this noun are widely accepted: (1) "members of an institution of higher learning," and (2) "persons who are academic in background or outlook." Avoid using it to mean "academic subjects," as in "Students should pay attention not only to academics but also to recreation." *Revised:* "Students should pay attention not only to their courses but also to recreation."

**accept, except**   *Accept* means "to receive with consent." *Except* means "to exclude" or "excluding."

**affect, effect**   *Affect* is usually a verb, meaning (1) "to influence, to produce an effect, to impress," or (2) "to pretend, to put on," as in "He affected an English accent." Psychologists use it as a noun for "feeling" ("The patient experienced no affect"). *Effect,* as a verb, means "to bring about" ("The workers effected the rescue in less than an hour"). As a noun, *effect* means "result" ("The effect was negligible").

**African American, African-American**   Both forms are acceptable to denote an American of African ancestry. In recent years these words have generally been preferred to *black,* although even on this point the consensus continues to shift.

**aggravate**   To worsen, to increase for the worse, as in "Smoking aggravated the irritation." Although it is widely used to mean "annoy" ("He aggravated me"), many readers are annoyed by such a use.

**all ready, already**   *All ready* means "everything is ready." *Already* means "by this time."

**all right, alright**   The first of these is the preferable spelling; for some readers it is the only acceptable spelling.

**all together, altogether**   *All together* means that members of a group act or are gathered together ("They voted all together"); *altogether* is an adverb meaning "entirely," "wholly" ("This is altogether unnecessary").

**allusion, reference, illusion**   An *allusion* is an implied or indirect reference. "As Lincoln says" is a *reference* to Lincoln, but "As a great man has said," along with a phrase quoted from the Gettysburg Address, constitutes an *allusion* to Lincoln. *Allusion* has nothing to do with *illusion* (a deception). Note the spelling (especially the second i) in "disillusioned" ("left without illusions, disenchanted").

**almost**   See *most.*

**a lot**   Two words (not *alot*).

**ambiguous, ambivalent**   *Ambiguous* refers to things that are unclear; a*mbivalent* refers to people who are uncertain. One could say that the reasons for Hamlet's inaction are ambiguous; his famous soliloquy, which begins with the question, "to be, or not to be," suggests his ambivalence.

**among, between**   See *between.*

**amount, number**   *Amount* refers to bulk or quantity: "A small amount of gas was still in the tank." Use *number,* not *amount,* to refer to separate (countable) units: "He did not know the number of gallons that the tank held."

**and etc.**   Because *etc.* is an abbreviation for et cetera ("and others"), the *and* in *and etc.* is redundant. (See also the entry on *et cetera.*)

**and/or**   Acceptable, but a legalism and unpleasant sounding. Often *or* by itself will do, as in "students who know Latin or Italian." When *or* is not enough ("Scripts for the second season of *The Sopranos* were written by Todd Kessler and/or David Chase") it is better to recast

("Scripts for the second season of *The Sopranos* were written by Todd Kessler or David Chase, or both").

**ante, anti** *Ante* means "before" (*antebellum*, "before the Civil War"); *anti* means "against" (*antivivisectionist*). Hyphenate *anti* before capitals (*anti-Semitism*) and before i (*anti-intellectual*).

**anxious** Best reserved for uses that suggest anxiety ("He was anxious before the examination"), though some authorities now accept it in the sense of "eager" ("He was anxious to serve the community").

**anybody** One word ("Do you know anybody here?"). If two words (*any body*), you mean any corpse ("Several people died in the fire, but the police cannot identify any body").

**any more, anymore** *Any more* is used as an adjective: "I don't want any more meat" (here *any more* says something about meat). *Anymore* (one word) is used as an adverb: "I don't eat meat anymore" (here *anymore* says something about eating).

**anyone** One word ("Why would anyone think that?"), unless you mean "any one thing," as in "Here are three books; you may take any one." *Anyone* is an indefinite singular pronoun meaning *any person*: "If anyone has a clue, he or she should call the police." In an astounding advertisement, the writer moved from *anyone* (singular) to *their* (third person plural) to *your* (second person): "Anyone who thinks a Yonex racquet has improved their game, please raise your hand."

**area of** Like *field of* and *topic of* ("the field of literature," "the topic of politics"), *area of* can usually be deleted. "The area of marketing" equals "marketing."

**around** Avoid using *around* in place of *about:* "He wrote it in about three hours." See also *centers on.*

**as, like** *As* is a conjunction; use it in forming comparisons, to introduce clauses. (A clause has a subject and a verb.)

*You can learn to write, as you can learn to swim.*
*Huck speaks the truth as he sees it.*

*Like* is a preposition; use it to introduce prepositional phrases:

*He looks like me.*
*Like Hamlet, Laertes has lost a father.*
*She thinks like a lawyer.*

A short rule: use *like* when it introduces a noun *not* followed by a verb: "Nothing grabs people like *People*."

Writers who are fearful of incorrectly using *like* resort to cumbersome evasions: "He eats in the same manner that a pig eats." But there's nothing wrong with "He eats like a pig."

**Asian, Oriental**   *Asian* as a noun and as an adjective is the preferred word. *Oriental* (from *oriens*, "rising sun," "east") is in disfavor because it implies a Eurocentric view—that is, that things "oriental" are east of the European colonial powers who invented the term. Similarly, Near East, Middle East, and Far East are terms that are based on a Eurocentric view. No brief substitute has been agreed on for *Near East* and *Middle East*, but *East Asia* is now regarded as preferable to *Far East*.

**as of now**   Best deleted, or replaced by *now*. Not "As of now I don't smoke," but "Now I don't smoke" or "I don't smoke now" or "I don't smoke."

**aspect**   Literally, "a view from a particular point," but it has come to mean *topic*, as in "Several aspects should be considered." Try to use a sharper word; for example, "Several problems should be considered," or "Several consequences should be considered."

**as such**   Often meaningless, as in "Tragedy as such evokes pity."

**as to**   Usually *about* is preferable. Not "I know nothing as to the charges," but "I know nothing about the charges."

**bad, badly**   *Bad* used to be only an adjective ("a bad movie"), and *badly* was an adverb ("she sings badly"). In "I felt bad," *bad* describes the subject, not the verb. (Compare "I felt happy," or "I felt good about getting a raise." After verbs of appearing, such as "feel," "look," "seem," "taste," an adjective, not an adverb, is used. If you are in doubt, substitute a word for *bad*, for instance *sad*, and see what you say. Since you would say "I feel sad about his failure," you can say "I feel bad . . ."). But "badly" is acceptable and even preferred by many. Note, however, this distinction: "This meat smells bad" (an adjective describing the meat), and "Because I have a stuffed nose I smell badly" (an adverb describing my ability to smell something).

**being**   Do not use *being* as a main verb, as in "The trouble being that his reflexes were too slow." The result is a sentence fragment. See pages 244–46).

**being that, being as** A sentence such as "Being that she was a stranger . . ." sounds like an awkward translation from the Latin. Use *because.*

**beside, besides** Beside means "at the side of." Because besides can mean either "in addition to" or "other than," it is ambiguous, as in "Something besides TB caused his death." It is best, then, to use *in addition to* or *other than,* depending on what you mean.

**between** A general rule is to use the preposition *between* when two items are being discussed ("I'm trying to choose between a Blackberry and an iPhone.") and to use *among* when there are more than two ("She was among the top three candidates"). We note that some grammarians say that this rule is imprecise, and that *between* should be used when relating individual entities ("East Hanover is between Whippany, Madison, and Florham Park") and *among* should be used in relation to a collective (non-individualized) group ("There is no honor among thieves").

**biannually, bimonthly, biweekly** Every two years, every two months, every two weeks (not twice a year, etc.). Twice a year is *semiannually,* that is, "half yearly." Because *biannually, bimonthly,* and *biweekly* are commonly misunderstood, it is best to avoid them and to say "every two . . ."

**Black, black** Although one sometimes sees the word capitalized when it refers to race, most publishers use a lowercase letter, making it consistent with *white,* which is never capitalized. See also *African American.*

**can, may** When schoolchildren asked "Can I leave the room?" their teachers used to correct them thus: "You *can* leave the room if you have legs, but you *may not* leave the room until you receive permission." In short, *can* indicates physical possibility, *may* indicates permission. But because "you may not" and "why mayn't I?" sound not merely polite but stiff, *can* is usually preferred except in formal contexts.

**capital, capitol** A *capital* is a city that is a center of government. *Capital* can also mean wealth ("It takes capital to start a business"). A *capitol* is a building in which legislators meet. Notice the distinction in the following sentence: "Washington, DC, is the nation's capital; the capitol ought to have a gold dome."

**centers on, centers around** Use *centers on,* because *center* refers to a point, not to a movement around.

**Chicana, Chicano** A Mexican American (female or male, respectively; the male plural, *Chicanos,* is used for a group consisting of males and females). Although the term sometimes was felt to be derogatory, today it usually implies ethnic pride.

**collective nouns**  A collective noun, singular in form, names a collection of individuals. Examples: *audience, band, committee, crowd, jury, majority, minority, team.* When you are thinking chiefly of the whole as a unit, use a singular verb (and a singular pronoun, if any): "The majority rules"; "The jury is announcing its verdict." But when you are thinking of the individuals, use a plural verb (and pronoun, if any): "The majority are lawyers"; "The jury are divided and they probably cannot agree." If the plural sounds odd, you can usually rewrite: "The jurors are divided and they probably cannot agree."

**compare, contrast**  To *compare* is to note likenesses or differences: "Compare a motorcycle with a bicycle." To *contrast* is to emphasize differences.

**complement, compliment**  *Complement* as a noun means "that which completes"; as a verb, "to fill out, to complete." *Compliment* as a noun is an expression of praise; as a verb it means "to offer praise."

**comprise**  To include, contain, consist of: "The university comprises two colleges and a medical school" (not "is comprised of"). Conservative authorities hold that "to be comprised of" is always incorrect, and they reject the form one often hears: "Two colleges and a medical school comprise the university." Here the word should be *compose*, not *comprise*.

**concept**  Should often be deleted. For "The concept of the sales tax is regressive" write "The sales tax is regressive."

**contact**  Because it is vague, avoid using *contact* as a verb. Not "I contacted him," but "I spoke with him" or "I wrote to him," etc.

**continual, continuous**  Conservative authorities hold that *continuous* means "uninterrupted," as in "It rained continuously for six hours"; *continually* means "repeated often, recurring at short intervals," as in "For a year he continually wrote letters to her."

**contrast, compare**  See *compare.*

**could have, could of**  See *of.*

**criteria**  Plural of *criterion*; hence it is always incorrect to speak of "a criteria," or to say "The criteria is . . . ." Correct: "The criterion is simple"; "the criteria are unfair."

**data**  Plural of *datum.* Although some social scientists speak of "this data," "these data" is preferable: "These data are puzzling."

Because the singular, *datum*, is rare and sounds odd, it is best to substitute *fact* or *figure* for *datum*.

**different from**  Prefer it to *different than*, unless you are convinced that in a specific sentence *different from* sounds terribly wrong, as in "These two books are more different than I had expected." (In this example, "more," not "different," governs "than." But this sentence, though correct, is awkward and therefore it should be revised: "These two books differ more than I had expected.")

**dilemma**  A situation requiring a choice between equally undesirable alternatives; not every difficulty or plight or predicament is a *dilemma*. Not "Her dilemma was that she had nowhere to go," but "Her dilemma was whether to go out or to stay home: one was frightening, the other was embarrassing." And note the spelling (two *m*'s, no *n*).

**disinterested**  Though the word is often used to mean "indifferent," "unconcerned," "uninterested," reserve it to mean "impartial": "A judge should be disinterested."

**due to**  Some people, holding that *due to* cannot modify a verb (as in "He failed due to illness"), tolerate it only when it modifies a noun or pronoun ("His failure was due to illness"). They also insist that it cannot begin a sentence ("Due to illness, he failed"). In fact, however, daily usage accepts both. But because it almost always sounds stiff, try to substitute *because* of or *through*.

**due to the fact that**  Wordy phrase for *because*.

**each**  Although many authorities hold that *each*, as a subject, is singular, even when followed by "them" ("Each of them is satisfactory"), some authorities accept and even favor the plural ("Each of them are satisfactory"). But it is usually better to avoid the awkwardness by substituting *all* for *each*: "All of them are satisfactory." When *each* refers to a plural subject, the verb must be plural: "They each have a book"; "We each are trying." *Each* cannot be made into a possessive; you cannot say "Each's opinion is acceptable."

**effect**  See *affect*.

**e.g.**  Abbreviation for *exempli gratia*, Latin for "for example." It is thus different from *i.e.* (an abbreviation for *id est*, Latin for "that is"). "E.g." (not italicized) introduces an example: "common pets (e.g., cats, dogs, and birds) have few diseases that can be transmitted to humans." "I.e." (also not italicized) introduces a definition: "Pets (i.e., animals kept for companionship) cost Americans billions of dollars annually."

**either . . . or, neither . . . nor**  If the subjects are singular, use a singular verb: "Either the boy or the girl is lying." If one of the subjects joined by *or* or *nor* is plural, most grammarians say that the verb agrees with the nearer subject, thus: "A tree or two shrubs are enough," or "Two shrubs or a tree is enough." But because the singular verb in the second of these sentences may sound odd, follow the first construction; that is, put the plural subject nearer to the verb and use a plural verb. Another point about *either . . . or:* In this construction, "either" serves as advance notice that two equal possibilities are in the offing. Beware of putting "either" too soon, as in "Either he is a genius or a lunatic." Better: "He is either a genius or a lunatic."

**enthuse**  Objectionable to many readers. For "He enthused," say "He was enthusiastic." Use *enthuse* only in the sense of "to be excessively enthusiastic," "to gush."

**et cetera, etc.**  Latin for "and other things"; if you mean "and other people," you need *et al.,* short for *et alii.* Because etc. is vague, its use is usually inadvisable. Not "He studied mathematics, etc.," but "He studied mathematics, history, economics, and French." Or, if the list is long, cut it by saying something a little more informative than etc.—for example, "He studied mathematics, history, and other liberal arts subjects."

**everybody, everyone**  These take a singular verb ("Everybody is here"), and a pronoun referring to them is usually singular ("Everybody thinks his problems are suitable topics of conversation"), but use a plural pronoun if the singular would seem unnatural ("Everybody was there, weren't they?"). To avoid the sexism of "Everybody thinks his problems . . . ," revise to "All people think their problems . . ."

**examples, instances**  See *instances.*

**except**  See *accept.*

**exists**  Often unnecessary and a sign of wordiness. Not "The problem that *exists* here is," but "The problem here is."

**expound**  Usually a pretentious substitute for *explain* or *say.* To *expound* is to give a methodical explanation of theological matters.

**the fact that**  Wordy phrase. "Because of the fact that boys played female roles in Elizabethan drama" can be reduced to "Because boys played female roles in Elizabethan drama."

**factor**  Strictly speaking, a *factor* helps to produce a result. Although factor is often used in the sense of "point" ("Another factor to be studied is . . ."), such use is often wordy. "The possibility of plagiarism is a factor that must be considered" simply adds up to "The possibility of plagiarism must be considered." *Factor* is almost never the precise word: "the factors behind Gatsby's actions" are, more precisely, "Gatsby's motives."

**famous, notorious**   See *notorious.*

**Far East**   See *Asian.*

**farther, further**   Some purists claim that *farther* always refers to distance and *further* to time ("The gymnasium is farther than the library"; "Let us think further about this").

**fatalistic, pessimistic**   *Fatalistic* means "characterized by the belief that all events are predetermined and therefore inevitable"; *pessimistic* means "characterized by the belief that the world is evil," or, less gloomily, "expecting the worst."

**fewer, less**   See *less.*

**field of**   See *area of.*

**firstly, secondly**   Acceptable, but it is better to use *first, second.*

**former, latter**   These words are acceptable, but they are often annoying because they force the reader to reread earlier material in order to locate what *the former* and *the latter* refer to. The expressions are legitimately used to avoid repeating lengthy terms, but if you are talking about an easily repeated subject—say, Lincoln and Grant—don't hesitate to replace *the former* and *the latter* with their names. The repetition will clarify rather than bore.

**good, well**   *Good* is an adjective ("a good book"). *Well* is usually an adverb ("She writes well"). Standard English does not accept "She writes good." But standard English requires *good* after verbs of appearing, such as *seems, looks, sounds, tastes:* "it looks good," "it sounds good." *Well* can also be an adjective meaning *healthy:* "I am well."

**graduate, graduate from**   Use *from* if you name the institution or if you use a substitute word as in "She graduated from high school"; if the institution (or substitute) is not named, *from* is omitted: "She graduated in 2006." The use of the passive ("She was graduated from high school") is acceptable but sounds fussy to many.

**he or she, his or her**   These expressions are awkward, but the implicit male chauvinism in the generic use of the male pronoun ("A citizen should exercise his right to vote") may be more offensive than the awkwardness of *he or she* and *his or her.* Moreover, sometimes the male pronoun, when used for males and females, is ludicrous, as in "The more violence a youngster sees on television, regardless of his age or sex, the more aggressive he is likely to be." Do what you can to avoid the dilemma. Sometimes you can use the plural *their:* "Students are expected to hand in their papers on Monday" (instead of "The student is expected to hand in his or her paper on Monday"). Or eliminate the possessive: "The student must hand in a paper on Monday." See *man;* see also "Avoiding Sexist Language," pages 74–75.

**Hispanic, Latina, Latino**   A person who traces his or her origin to a Spanish-speaking country is a *Hispanic.* (*Hispania* was the Latin name for Spain.) But some people object to the term when applied to persons in the Western Hemisphere, arguing that it overemphasizes the European influence on ethnic identity and neglects the indigenous and black heritages. Many who object to *Hispanic* prefer to call a person of Latin-American descent a *Latina* (the feminine form) or a *Latino* (the masculine form), partly because these words are themselves Latin-American words. (The male plural, *Latinos,* commonly is used for a group consisting of males and females.) But many people object that these words too obscure the unique cultural heritages of, say, Mexican Americans, Cuban Americans, and Puerto Ricans.

**hopefully**   Commonly used to mean "I hope" or "It is hoped" ("*Hopefully,* the rain will stop soon"), but it is best to avoid what some consider a dangling modifier. After all, the rain itself is not hopeful. If you mean "I hope the rain will stop soon," say exactly that. Notice, too, that *hopefully,* is often evasive. If the president of the college says, "Hopefully, tuition will not rise next year," don't think that you have heard a promise to fight against an increase; you only have heard someone evade making a promise. In short, confine *hopefully* to its adverbial use, meaning "in a hopeful manner": "Hopefully, he uttered a prayer."

**however**   Independent clauses (for instance, "He tried" and "He failed") should not be linked with *however* preceded by a comma. Incorrect: "He tried, however he failed." What is required is a period ("He tried. However, he failed") or a semicolon before *however* ("He tried; however, he failed").

**the idea that**   Usually dull and wordy. Not "The idea that we grow old is frightening," but "That we grow old is frightening," or (probably better) "Growing old is frightening."

**identify**   When used in the psychological sense, "to associate oneself closely with a person or an institution," it is preferable to include a reflexive pronoun, thus: "He identified himself with Hamlet," *not* "He identified with Hamlet."

**i.e.**   Latin for *id est,* "that is." The English words are preferable to the Latin abbreviation. On the distinction between *i.e.* and *e.g.*, see *e.g.*

**immanent, imminent**   *Immanent,* "remaining within, intrinsic"; *imminent,* "likely to occur soon, impending."

**imply, infer**   The writer or speaker *implies* ("suggests"); the perceiver *infers* ("draws a conclusion"): "Karl Marx implied that . . . but his modern disciples infer from his writings that . . . ." Although *infer* is widely used for *imply,* preserve the distinction.

**incidence, incident**   The *incidence* is the extent or frequency of an occurrence: "The incidence of violent crime in Tokyo is very low." The plural, *incidences,* is rarely used: "The incidences of crime and of fire in Tokyo . . . ." An *incident* is one occurrence: "The incident happened yesterday." The plural is *incidents:* "The two incidents happened simultaneously."

**individual**   Avoid using the word to mean only "person": "He was a generous individual." But it is precise when it implicitly makes a contrast with a group: "In a money-mad society, he was a generous individual"; "Although the faculty did not take a stand on this issue, faculty members as individuals spoke out."

**instances**   Instead of *in many instances* use *often.* Strictly speaking an *instance* is not an object or incident in itself but one offered as an example. Thus, "another instance of his failure to do his duty" (not "In three instances he failed to do his duty").

**irregardless**   Unacceptable; use *regardless.*

**it is**   Usually this expression needlessly delays the subject: "It is unlikely that many students will attend the lecture" could just as well be "Few students are likely to attend the lecture."

**its, it's**   The first is a possessive pronoun ("The flock lost its leader"); the second is a contraction of *it is* ("It's time to go."). You'll have no trouble if you remember that the possessive pronoun its, like other possessive pronouns such as *our, his,* and *their,* does *not* use an apostrophe.

**kind of**   Singular, as in "That kind of movie bothers me" not "Those kind of movies bother me." If, however, you are really talking about more than one kind, use *kinds* and be sure that the demonstrative pronoun and the verb are plural: "Those kinds of movies bother me." Notice also that the phrase is *kind of,* not *kind of a.* Not "What *kind of a* car does she drive?" but "What *kind of* car does she drive?"

**Latina, Latino**   See *Hispanic.*

**latter** See *former.*

**lay, lie** *To lay* means "to put, to set, to cause to rest." It takes an object: "May I lay the coats on the table?" The past tense and the participle are *laid:* "I laid the coats on the table"; "I have laid the coats on the table." *To lie* means "to recline," and it does not take an object: "When I am tired I lie down." The past tense is *lay,* the participle is *lain:* "Yesterday I lay down"; "I have lain down hundreds of times without wishing to get up."

**lend, loan** The usual verb is *lend:* "Lend me a pen." The past tense and the participle are both lent. *Loan* is a noun: "This isn't a gift, it's a loan." But, curiously, *loan* as a verb is acceptable in past forms: "I loaned him my bicycle." In its present form ("I often loan money") it is used chiefly by bankers.

**less, fewer** *Less* (as an adjective) refers to bulk amounts (also called mass nouns): less milk, less money, less time. *Fewer* refers to separate (countable) items: fewer glasses of milk, fewer dollars, fewer hours.

**lifestyle, life-style, life style** All three forms are acceptable, but because many readers regard the expression as imprecise, try to find a substitute such as *values.*

© Original Artist. Reproduction rights obtainable from www.cartoonStock.com

**like, as**   See *as.*

**literally**   It means "to the letter," "exactly as stated," and "strictly in accord with the primary meaning; not metaphorically." It is not a mere intensive. "He was literally dead" means that he was a corpse; if he was merely exhausted, *literally* won't do. You cannot be "literally stewed" (except by cannibals), "literally tickled pink," or "literally walking on air."

**loose, lose**   *Loose* is an adjective ("The nail is loose"); *lose* is a verb ("Don't lose the nail").

**the majority of**   Usually a wordy way of saying *most.* Of course if you mean "a bare majority," say so; otherwise *most* will usually do. Certainly "The majority of the basement is used for a cafeteria" should be changed to "Most of the basement is used for a cafeteria." *Majority* can take either a singular verb or a plural verb. When *majority* refers to a collection—for example, a group acting as a body— the verb is singular, as in "The majority has withdrawn its support from the mayor." But when *majority* refers to members of a group acting as individuals, as in "The majority of voters in this district vote Republican," a plural verb (here, "vote") is usually preferred. If either construction sounds odd, use "most," with a plural verb: "Most voters in this district vote Republican."

**man, mankind**   The use of these words in reference to males and females sometimes is ludicrous, as in "Man, being a mammal, breast-feeds his young." But even when not ludicrous, the practice is sexist, as in "man's brain" and "the greatness of mankind." Consider using such words as *human being, person, humanity, humankind, people.* Similarly, for "manmade," *artificial* or *synthetic* may do. See also "Avoiding Sexist Language," pages 74–75.

**may, can**   See *can.*

**me**   The right word in such expressions as "between you and me" and "They gave it to John and me." It is the object of verbs and of prepositions. In fact, *me* rather than *I* is the usual form after any verb, including the verb *to be;* "It is me" is nothing to be ashamed of. See *myself.*

**medium, media**   *Medium* is singular, *media* is plural: "TV is the medium to which most children are most exposed. Other media include film, radio, and publishing." It follows, then, that *mass media* takes a plural verb: "The mass media exert an enormous influence."

**Middle East**   See *Asian.*

**might of, might have; must of, must have**   *Might of* and *must of* are colloquial for *might have* and *must have*. In writing, use the *have* form: "He might have cheated; in fact, he must have cheated."

**more**   Avoid writing a false (incomplete) comparison such as "His essay includes several anecdotes, making it more enjoyable." Delete "more" unless there really is a comparison with another essay. On false comparisons, see also *other.*

**most, almost**   Although it is acceptable in speech to say "most everyone" and "most anybody," it is preferable in writing to use "almost everyone," "almost anybody." But of course: "Most students passed."

**myself**   *Myself* is often mistakenly used for *I* or *me*, as in "They praised Tony and myself," or "Professor Chen and myself examined the dead rat." In the first example, *me* is the word to use; after all, if Tony hadn't been there the sentence would say "They praised me." (No one would say "They praised myself.") Similarly, in the second example if Professor Chen were not involved, the sentence would run "I examined the dead rat," so what is needed here is simply "Professor Chen and I examined . . . ." In general, use *myself* only when (1) it refers to the subject of the sentence ("I look out for myself"; "I washed myself") or (2) when it is an intensive ("I myself saw the break-in"; "I myself have not experienced racism").

**nature**   You can usually delete *the nature of,* as in "The nature of my contribution is not political but psychological."

**Near East**   See *Asian.*

**needless to say**   The reader may well wonder why you go on to say it. Of course this expression is used to let readers know that they are probably familiar with what comes next, but usually *of course* will better serve as this sign.

**Negro**   Capitalized, whether a noun or an adjective, though white is not. In recent years *Negro* has been replaced by *black* or *African American.*

**neither . . . nor**   See *either . . . or.*

**nobody, no one, none**   *Nobody* and *no one* are singular, requiring a singular verb ("Nobody believes this," "No one knows"), but they can be referred to by a plural pronoun ("Nobody believes this, do they?" "No one knows, do they?"). *None,* though it comes from *no one,* almost always requires a plural verb when it refers to people ("Of the ten people present, none are students") and a singular verb when it refers to things ("Of the five assigned books, none is worth reading").

**not only . . . but also**  Keep in mind these two points: (1) many readers object to the omission of "also" in such a sentence as "She not only brought up two children but practiced law"—it's preferable to write "She not only brought up two children but also practiced law"—and (2) all readers dislike a faulty parallel, as in "She not only is bringing up two children but practices law." ("Is bringing up" needs to be paralleled with "is also practicing.")

**notorious**  Widely and unfavorably known; not merely famous, but famous for some discreditable trait or deed.

**not . . . un-**  Such an expression as "not unfamiliar" is useful only if it conveys something different from the affirmative. Compare the frostiness of "I am not unfamiliar with your methods" with "I am familiar with your methods." If the negative has no evident advantage, use the affirmative.

**number, amount**  See *amount.*

**a number of**  Requires a plural verb: "A number of women are presidents of corporations." But when *number* is preceded by *the* it requires a singular verb: "The number of women who are presidents is small." (The plural noun after *number* may require a plural verb, as in "women are," but the subject of the sentence is *the number,* which itself remains singular; hence its verb is singular, as in "is small.")

**of**  Be careful not to use *of* when *have* is required. Not "He might of died in the woods," but "He might have died in the woods." Note that what we often hear as "would've" or "should've" or "must've" or "could've" is "would have" or "should have" or "must have" or "could have," not "would of," etc.

**off of**  Use *off* or *from:* "Take it off the table"; "He jumped from the bridge."

**often-times**  Use *often* instead.

**old-fashioned, old-fashion**  Only the first is acceptable.

**one**  British usage accepts the shift from *one* to *he* in "One begins to die the moment he is born," but American usage prefers "One begins to die the moment one is born." A shift from *one* to *you* ("One begins to die the moment you are born") is unacceptable. As a pronoun, *one* can be useful in impersonal statements such as the sentence about dying, at the beginning of this entry, where it means "a person," but don't use it as a disguise for yourself ("One objects to Smith's argument"). Try to avoid *one*; one *one* usually leads to another, resulting in a sentence that, in James Thurber's words, "sounds like a trombone solo" ("If one takes oneself too seriously, one begins to . . . "). See also *you*.

**one of**  Takes a plural noun, and if this is followed by a clause, the preferred verb is plural: "one of those students who are," "one of those who feel." Thus, in such a sentence as "One of the coaches who have resigned is now seeking reinstatement," notice that "have" is correct; the antecedent of "who" (the subject of the verb) is "coaches," which is plural. Coaches have resigned, though "one . . . is seeking reinstatement." But in such an expression as "one out of a hundred," the following verb may be singular or plural ("One out of a hundred is," "One out of a hundred are").

**only**  Be careful where you put it. The classic textbook example points out that in the sentence "I hit him in the eye," *only* can be inserted in seven places (beginning in front of "I" and ending after "eye") with at least six different meanings. Try to put it just before the expression it qualifies. Thus, not "Presidential aides are only responsible to one person," but "Presidential aides are responsible to only one person" (or "to one person only").

**oral, verbal**  See *verbal*.

**Oriental**  See *Asian*.

**other**  Often necessary in comparisons. "No American president served as many terms as Franklin Roosevelt" absurdly implies that Roosevelt was not an American president. The sentence should be revised to "No other American president served as many terms as Franklin Roosevelt."

**per**  Usually it sounds needlessly technical ("twice per hour") or disturbingly impersonal ("as per your request"). Preferable: "twice an hour," "according to your request," or "as you requested."

**per cent, percent, percentage**  The first two of these are interchangeable; both mean "per hundred," "out of a hundred," as in "Ninety per cent (or percent) of the students were white." *Per cent* and *percent* are always accompanied by a number (written out, or in figures). It is usually better to write out *per cent* or *percent* than to use a per cent sign (12%), except in technical or statistical papers. *Percentage* means "a proportion or share in relation to the whole," as in "A very large percentage of the student body is white." Many authorities insist that *percentage* is never preceded by a number. Do not use *percentage* to mean "a few," as in "Only a percentage of students attended the lecture"; a percentage can be as large as 99.99. It is usually said that with *per cent, percent,* and *percentage* whether the verb is singular or plural depends on the number of the noun that follows the word, thus: "Ninety percent of their books are paperbacks"; "Fifty percent of their library is worthless"; "A large percentage of their books are worthless." But some readers (including the authors of this book) prefer a singular verb after *percentage* unless the resulting sentence is as grotesque as this one: "A large percentage of the students is unmarried." Still, rather than say a "percentage . . . are," we would recast the sentence: "A large percentage of the student body is unmarried," or "Many (or "Most," or whatever) of the students are unmarried."

**per se**   Latin for "by itself." Usually sounds legalistic or pedantic, as in "Meter per se has an effect."

**pessimistic**   See *fatalistic.*

**phenomenon, phenomena**   The plural is *phenomena;* thus, "these phenomena," but "this phenomenon."

**plus**   Unattractive and imprecise as a noun meaning "asset" or "advantage" ("When he applied for the job, his appearance was a plus"), and equally unattractive as a substitute for *moreover* ("The examination was easy, plus I had studied") or as a substitute for *and* ("I studied the introduction plus the first chapter").

**politics**   Preferably singular ("Ethnic politics has been a strong force for a century"), but a plural verb is acceptable.

**precede, proceed**   To *precede* is to go before or ahead ("X precedes Y"). To *proceed* is to go forward ("The spelling lesson proceeded smoothly").

**prejudice, prejudiced**   *Prejudice* is a noun: "It is impossible to live entirely without prejudice." But use the past participle *prejudiced* as an adjective: "They were prejudiced against me from the start."

**preventative, preventive**   Both are acceptable but the second form is now used by writers on medicine ("preventive medicine"); *preventative* therefore has come to seem amateurish.

**principal, principle**  *Principal* is (1) an adjective meaning "main," "chief," "most important" ("The principal arguments against IQ testing are three"), and (2) a noun meaning "the chief person" ("Ms. Murphy was the principal of Jefferson High") or "the chief thing" ("She had so much money she could live on the interest and not touch the principal"). *Principle* is always a noun meaning "rule" or "fundamental truth" ("It was against his principles to eat meat").

**prior to**  Pretentious for *before*.

**protagonist**  Literally, the "first actor," and, by extension, the "chief actor." It is odd, therefore, to speak of "the protagonists" in a single literary work or occurrence.

**quite**  Usually a word to delete, along with *definitely, pretty, rather,* and *very*. Quite used to mean "completely" ("I quite understand") but it has come also to mean "to a considerable degree," and so it is ambiguous as well as vague.

**quotation, quote**  *Quotation* is a noun; *quote* is a verb. "I will quote Churchill" is fine, but not "these quotes from Churchill." (In fact, "quote" as a noun is gaining acceptance, but you should avoid this usage because it offends many readers.) And remember, you may *quote* one of Hamlet's speeches, but Hamlet does not *quote* them; he says them.

**rather**  Avoid use with strong adjectives. "Rather intelligent" makes sense, but "rather tremendous" does not. "Rather brilliant" probably means "bright"; "rather terrifying" probably means "frightening"; "rather unique" probably means "unusual." Use the right adjective, not *rather* and the wrong adjective.

**the reason . . . is because**  Usually *because* is enough (not "The reason they fail is because they don't study," but simply "They fail because they don't study"). Similarly, *the reason why* can usually be reduced to *why*. Notice, too, that because *reason* is a noun, it cannot neatly govern a *because* clause: not "The reason for his absence is because he was sick," but "The reason for his absence was illness."

**rebut, refute**  To *rebut* is to argue against, but not necessarily successfully. If you mean "to disprove," use *disprove* or *refute*.

**in regard to, with regard to**  Often wordy for *about, concerning,* or *on,* and sometimes even these words are unnecessary. Compare: "She knew a great deal in regard to jazz"; "She knew a great deal about jazz." Compare: "Hemingway's story is often misunderstood with regard to Robert Wilson's treatment of Margot Macomber"; "In Hemingway's story, Robert Wilson's treatment of Margot Macomber is often misunderstood."

**relate to**   Usually a vague expression, best avoided, as in "I can relate to Hedda Gabler." Does it mean "respond favorably to," "identify myself with," "interact with" (and how can a reader "interact with" a character in a play?). Use *relate to* only in the sense of "have connection with," as in "How does your answer relate to my question?" (even in such a sentence a more exact expression is preferable).

**repel, repulse**   Both verbs mean "to drive back," but only *repel* can mean "to cause distaste," "to disgust," as in "His obscenities repelled the audience."

**respectfully, respectively**   *Respectfully* means "with respect, showing respect" ("Japanese students and teachers bow respectfully to each other"). *Respectively* means "each in turn" ("Professors Arnott, Bahktian, and Cisneros teach, respectively, chemistry, business, and biology").

**seem**   Properly it suggests a suspicion that appearances may be deceptive: "He seems honest (but . . . )." Don't say "The book seems to lack focus" if you believe it does lack focus.

**semiannually, semimonthly, semiweekly**   See *biannually*.

**shall, will, should, would**   The old principle held that in the first person *shall* is the future indicative of *to be* and *should* the conditional ("I shall go," "We should like to be asked") and that *will* and *would* are the forms for the second and third persons. When the forms are reversed ("I will go," "Government of the people . . . shall not perish from the earth"), determination is expressed. But today almost nobody adheres to these principles. Indeed, *shall* (except in questions) sounds stilted to many ears.

**s/he**   This relatively new gender-free pronoun ("As soon as the student receives the forms, s/he should fill them out") is sometimes used in place of *he or she* or *she or he*, which are used to avoid the sexism implied when the male pronoun "he" is used to stand for women as well as men ("As soon as the student receives the forms, he should fill them out"). Other, less noticeable and therefore better ways of avoiding sexist writing are suggested under *he or she*. See also "Avoiding Sexist Language," pages 74–75.

**simplistic** Means "falsely simplified by ignoring complications." Do not confuse it with *simplified,* whose meanings include "reduced to essentials" and "clarified."

**since, because** Traditional objections to *since,* in the sense of "because," have all but vanished. Note, however, that when *since* is ambiguous and may also refer to time ("Since he joined the navy, she found another boyfriend"), it is better to say *because* or *after,* depending on which you mean.

**situation** Overused, vague, and often unnecessary. "His situation was that he was unemployed" adds up to "He was unemployed." And "an emergency situation" is probably an emergency.

**subjunctive** For the use of the subjunctive with conditions contrary to fact (for instance, "If I were you"), see *was, were.* The subjunctive is also used in *that* clauses followed by verbs demanding, requesting, or recommending: "She asked that the students be prepared to take a test." But because this last sort of sentence sounds stiff, it is better to use an alternative construction, such as "She asked the students to prepare for a test."

**than, then** *Than* is used chiefly in making comparisons ("German is harder than French"), but also after "rather," "other," and "else" ("I'd rather take French than German"; "He thinks of nothing other than sex"). *Then* commonly indicates time ("She took German then, but now she takes French"; "Until then, I'll save you a seat"), but it may also mean "in that case" ("It's agreed, then, that we'll all go"), or "on the other hand" ("Then again, she may find German easy"). The simplest guide: Use *than* after comparisons and after "rather," "other," "else"; otherwise use *then.*

**that, which, who** Many pages have been written on these words; opinions differ, but you will offend no one if you observe the following principles. (1) Use *that* in restrictive (that is, limiting) clauses: "The rocking chair that creaks is on the porch." (2) Use *which* in nonrestrictive (in effect, parenthetic) clauses: "The rocking chair, which creaks, is on the porch." (See pp. 254–55.) The difference between these two sentences is this: In the first, one rocking chair is singled out from several—the one that creaks; in the second, the fact that the rocking chair creaks is simply tossed in and is not added for the purpose of identifying the one chair out of several. (3) Use *who* for people in restrictive and in nonrestrictive clauses: "The women who were playing poker ignored the men"; "The women, who were playing poker, ignored the men." But note that often *that, which,* and *who* can be omitted: "The creaky rocking chair is on the porch"; "The women playing poker ignored the men." "The women, playing poker, ignored the men." In general, omit these words if the sentence remains clear.

**their, there, they're**   The first is a possessive pronoun: "Chaplin and Keaton made their first films before sound tracks were developed." The second, *there,* sometimes refers to a place ("Go there"; "Do you live there?"), and sometimes is what is known in grammar as an introductory expletive ("There are no solutions to this problem"). The third, *they're,* is a contraction of "they are" ("They're going to stay for dinner").

**this**   Often refers vaguely to "what I have been saying." Does it refer to the previous sentence, the previous paragraph, the previous page? Try to clarify by being specific: "This last point"; "This clue gave the police all they needed."

**thusly**   Unacceptable; *thus* is an adverb and needs no adverbial ending.

**till, until**   Both are acceptable, but until is preferable because *till*—though common in speech—looks literary in print. The following are *not* acceptable: *til, 'til, 'till.*

**to, too, two**   *To* is toward; *too* is either "also" ("She's a lawyer, too") or "excessively" ("It's too hot"); *two* is one more than one ("It's two feet long").

**topic of**   See *area of.*

**toward, towards**   Both are standard English; *toward* is more common in the United States, *towards* in Great Britain.

**type**   Often colloquial (and unacceptable in most writing) for *type of,* as in "this type teacher." But *type of* is not especially pleasing either. Better to write "this kind of teacher." And avoid using *type* as a suffix: "essay-type examinations" are essay examinations; "natural-type ice cream" is natural ice cream. Sneaky manufacturers make "Italian-type cheese," implying that their domestic cheese is imported and at the same time protecting themselves against charges of misrepresentation.

**unique**   The only one of its kind. Someone or something therefore cannot be "rather unique" or "very unique" or "somewhat unique."

Instead of saying "rather unique," say *rare,* or *unusual,* or *extraordinary,* or whatever seems to be the best word.

**U.S., United States**   Generally, *United States* is preferable to *U.S.,* except when used as an adjective (*U.S. Air Force*).

**usage**   Don't use *usage* where *use* will do, as in "Here Vonnegut completes his usage of dark images." *Usage* properly implies a customary practice that has created a standard: "Usage has eroded the difference between *shall* and *will.*"

**use of**   The use of *use of* is usually unnecessary. "Through the use of setting he conveys a sense of foreboding" may be reduced to "The setting conveys . . . " or "His setting conveys . . . ."

**utilize, utilization**   Often inflated for *use* and *using,* as in "The infirmary has noted that it is sophomores who have most utilized the counseling service." But when one means "find an effective use for," *utilize* may be the best word, as in (here we borrow from the *American Heritage Dictionary*) "The teachers were unable to utilize the new computers," where *use* might wrongly suggest that the teachers could not operate the computers.

**verbal**   Often used where *oral* would be more exact. *Verbal* simply means "expressed in words," and thus a *verbal agreement* may be either written or spoken. If you mean spoken, call it an *oral agreement.*

**viable**   A term from physiology, meaning "capable of living" (for example, referring to a fetus at a stage of its development). Now pretentiously used and overused, especially by politicians and journalists, to mean "workable," as in "a viable presidency." Avoid it.

**was, were**   Use the subjunctive form—*were* (rather than *was*)—in expressing a wish ("I wish I were younger") and in "if-clauses" that are contrary to fact ("If I were rich"; "If I were you . . . ").

**we**   If you mean *I,* say *I.* Not "The first fairy tale we heard" but "the first fairy tale I heard." (But of course *we* is appropriate in some statements: "We have all heard fairy tales"; "If we look closely at the evidence, we can probably agree that . . . ."). The rule: Don't use *we* as a disguise for *I.* See pages 86–87.

**well**   See *good.*

**well-known, widely known**   Athletes, performers, politicians, and such folk are not really *well-known,* except perhaps by a few of their friends and their relatives; use *widely known* if you mean they are known (however slightly) to many people.

**which** Often can be deleted. "Students are required to fill out scholarship applications which are lengthy" can be written "Students are required to fill out lengthy scholarship applications." Another example: "*The Tempest,* which is Shakespeare's last play, was written in 1611"; "*The Tempest,* Shakespeare's last play, was written in 1611," or "Shakespeare wrote his last play, *The Tempest,* in 1611." For the distinction between *which* and *that,* see also the entry on *that.*

**while** Best used in a temporal sense, meaning "during the time": "While I was speaking, I suddenly realized that I didn't know what I was talking about." While it is not wrong to use *while* in a non-temporal sense, meaning "although" (as at the beginning of this sentence), it is better to use *although* to avoid any ambiguity. Note the ambiguity in: "While he was fond of movies, he chiefly saw westerns." Does it mean "Although he was fond of movies," or does it mean "During the time when he was fond of movies"? Another point: Do not use while if you mean *and* ("First-year students take English 1–2, while sophomores take English 10–11" [substitute *and* for *while*]).

**who, whom** Strictly speaking, *who* must be used for subjects, even when they look like objects: "He guessed who would be chosen." (Here *who* is the subject of the clause "who would be chosen.") *Whom* must be used for the objects of a verb, verbal (gerund, participle), or preposition: "Whom did she choose?"; "Whom do you want me to choose?"; "To whom did he show it?" We may feel stuffy in writing "Whom did she choose?" or "Whom are you talking about?" but to use *who* is certain to annoy some readers. Often you can avoid the dilemma by rewriting: "Who was chosen?"; "Who is the topic of conversation?" See also the entry on *that.*

**whoever, whomever** The second of these is the objective form. It is often incorrectly used as the subject of a clause. Incorrect: "Open the class to whomever wants to take it." The object of "to" is not "whomever" but is the entire clause—"whoever wants to take it"— and "whoever" is the subject of "wants."

**who's, whose** The first is a contraction of *who* is ("Who's on first?"). The second is a possessive pronoun: "Whose book is it?"; "I know whose it is."

**will, would** See *shall* and also *would.*

**would**   "I would think that" is a wordy version of "I think that." (On the mistaken use of *would of* for *would have,* see also *of.*)

**you**   In relatively informal writing, *you* is ordinarily preferable to the somewhat stiff *one:* "If you are addicted to cigarettes, you may find it helpful to join Smokenders." (Compare: "If one is addicted to cigarettes, one may . . . .") But because the direct address of you may sometimes descend into nagging, it is usually better to write: "Cigarette addicts may find it helpful . . . ." Certainly a writer (you?) should not assume that the reader is guilty of vices unless the essay is clearly aimed at an audience that admits to these vices. Thus, it is acceptable to say, "If you are a poor speller," but it is not acceptable to say, to the general reader, "You should improve your spelling"; the reader's spelling may not need improvement. And avoid *you* when the word cannot possibly apply to the reader: "A hundred years ago you were faced with many diseases that now have been eradicated." Something like "A hundred years ago people were faced . . . " is preferable.

**your, you're**   The first is a possessive pronoun ("your book"); the second is a contraction of *you are* ("You're mistaken").

# Documenting Sources

## Documentation

As we noted in Chapter 7, "Using Sources," much of academic reading and writing is text-based, and texts come in a variety of forms, from print to podcasts. So that readers may evaluate your ideas and the ideas that have shaped your writing, you need to provide information about each source you use in a research essay. Among other things, readers need to know

- who wrote or produced the source in question (does the source speak with authority?);
- what exactly the source is—what form it takes (is it a print publication? an article stored in an electronic database?);
- who published or disseminated it (what publisher or other institution has endorsed it?)
- when it was published (is the information current?); and
- how to locate it. (Readers need to be able to retrace your steps. They may want to confirm that you have represented the source accurately; they may also want to learn more about the subject, and perhaps to build on your work themselves.)

The way this information is presented varies from discipline to discipline: Sociologists, for example, present the date of publication more prominently than do historians; engineers usually list their sources by number at the end of a research work and in order of their appearance in the text; and literary critics list sources alphabetically by authors' names. The systems vary; they also evolve. In the following pages we discuss in detail two of the most widely used systems of documentation:

the guidelines of the Modern Language Association (MLA) and of the American Psychological Association (APA), both updated in 2009.

At the end of this chapter, we tell you where you may locate information on other systems of documentation.

# MLA Format

## Citations Within the Text

Brief parenthetic citations within the body of the essay are made clear by a list of your sources, entitled Works Cited, appended to the essay. Thus, an item in your list of works cited will clarify a sentence in your essay such as

> According to Angeline Goreau, Aphra Behn in her novels continually contradicts "the personal politics she had defended from the outset of her career as a writer" (252).

This citation means that the words inside the quotation marks appear on page 252 of a source written by Goreau, which will be listed in Works Cited. More often than not the parenthetic citation appears at the end of a sentence, as in the example just given, but it can appear elsewhere in the sentence. Its position will depend in part on your ear, and in part on the requirement that you point clearly to the place where your source's idea ends and your point begins. (In the following example, the idea that follows the parenthetic citation is not Gardiner's, but the writer's own.)

> Judith Kegan Gardiner, on the other hand, acknowledges that Behn's work "displays its conflicts with patriarchal authority" (215), conflicts that appear most notably in the third volume of *Love Letters*.

Seven points must be made about these examples:

1. **Quotation marks:** The closing quotation mark appears after the last word of the quotation, *not* after the parenthetic citation. Because the citation is not part of the quotation, the citation is not included within the quotation marks.

2. **Omission of words (ellipsis):** If the quoted words are merely a phrase, as in the previous example, you do not need to indicate (by an ellipsis—three spaced periods) that you are omitting material before or after the quotation. But if the quotation is longer than a phrase and is not a complete sentence, you must use an ellipsis to indicate that you are omitting material. If you omit material from the middle of a sentence, indicate the omission with an ellipsis. If you omit material from the end of the sentence, indicate the omission with an ellipsis followed by a period, the sentence period. If you omit a whole sentence, the sentence period comes first, followed by an ellipsis. If you omit material from the middle of one sentence to the end of another, the sentence period *follows* the ellipsis. If the ellipsis is followed by a parenthetical citation, the sentence period follows the parenthesis. (For more on ellipses, see p. 120.)

3. **Addition of words:** On occasion, you'll need to add a word or two to a quotation clarify its meaning. If you must make such an addition—and such additions should be kept to a minimum because they're distracting—enclose the word or words in square brackets, *not* parentheses. If the quotation contains a misspelling or other error, transcribe it as it appears in the source and insert the word *sic* (Latin for "thus," as in "thus the word appears in the source; it's not my error") in italics and in square brackets. Note that the APA recommends italicizing *sic*; the MLA does not.

    Although he was born in Italy, Christopher Colombus [sic] and his voyages were funded by Spain.

4. **Punctuation with parenthetic citations:** Look again at the examples of citations from Goreau and Gardiner given a moment ago. Notice that if you follow a quotation with a parenthetic citation, any necessary period, semicolon, or comma *follows* the parenthetic citation. In the first example (citing page 252 in Goreau), a period follows the citation; in the second (citing page 215 in Gardiner), a comma. In the next example, notice that the comma follows the citation.

    Johnson insists that "these poems can be interpreted as Tory propaganda" (72), but his brief analysis is not persuasive.

If, however, the quotation itself uses a question mark or an exclamation mark, this mark of punctuation appears *within* the closing quotation mark; even so, a period follows the parenthetic citation.

Jenkins-Smith is the only one to suggest doubt:
"How can we accept such a superficial reading
of these works?" (178). He therefore rejects the
entire argument.

5. **Two or more titles by one author:** If your list of works cited includes more than one work by an author, you will have to give additional information (either in your comment or within the parenthetic citation) in order to indicate *which* of the titles you are referring to. We will go further into this on page 298.

6. **Long (or "block") quotations:** We have been talking about short quotations, which are not set off but are embedded within your own sentences. Long quotations, usually defined as more than three lines of poetry or four lines of prose, are indented one inch from the left, as in the following example.

Janet Todd explains Behn's reverence for the
Stuart monarchy:

> She was a passionate supporter of both
> Charles II and James II as not simply
> rulers but as sacred majesties, god-kings
> on earth, whose private failings in no
> way detracted from their high office. . . .
> For her, royalty was not patriarchal
> anachronism as it would be for liberated
> women writers a hundred years on, but a
> mystical state. (73)

In introducing a long quotation, keep in mind that a reader will have trouble reading a sentence that consists of a lead-in, a long quotation, and then a continuation of your own sentence. It's better to have a short lead-in ("Janet Todd explains Behn's reverence for the Stuart monarchy"), and then set off a long quotation that is a complete sentence or group of sentences and therefore ends with a period. To set off a quotation, begin on a new line, double-space and indent one inch from the left margin, and do *not* enclose the quotation within quotation marks. Put a period at the end of the quotation (since the quotation is a complete sentence or group of sentences and is not embedded within a longer sentence of your own), hit the space bar twice, and then, on the same line, give the citation in parentheses. Do *not* put a period after the parenthetic citation that follows a long quotation.

7. **Citing a summary or a paraphrase:** Even if you don't quote a source directly but use its point in a paraphrase or a summary, you will give a citation:

> Goreau notes that Behn participated in public life and in politics not only as a writer: In the 1660s she went to Antwerp as a spy for Charles II (89-90).

The basic point, then, is that the system of in-text citation gives the documentation parenthetically. Notice that in all but one of the previous examples, the author's name is given in the student's text (rather than within the parenthetic citation). But there are several other ways of giving the citation, and we shall now look at them.

## Author and Page Number in Parenthetic Citation

> Heroines who explore their own individuality (with varying degrees of success and failure) abound in Chopin's work (Shinn 358).

It doesn't matter whether you summarize (as in this example) or quote directly; the parenthetic citation means that your source is page 358 of a work by Shinn, listed in Works Cited, at the end of your essay.

## Title and Page Number in Parentheses

If, as we mentioned earlier, your list includes two or more titles by an author, you cannot in the text simply give a name and a page reference; the reader would not know to which of the titles you are referring. Let's assume that Works Cited includes two items by Larzer Ziff. In a sentence in your essay you might specify one title, saying something like, "For example, Larzer Ziff, in *The American 1890's*, claims . . . ." If, however, you do not mention the title in your lead-in, you will have to give the title (in a shortened form) in the parenthetic citation:

> Larzer Ziff, for example, claims that the novel "rejected the family as the automatic equivalent of feminine self-fulfillment" (*American* 175).

Notice in this example that *American* is a short title for Ziff's book *The American 1890's: Life and Times of a Lost Generation*. The full title is given in Works Cited, as is the title of another work by Ziff, but the short title in the parenthetic citation is enough to direct the reader to page 175 of the correct source named in Works Cited.

Notice also that when a short title and a page reference are given in parentheses, a comma is *not* used after the title.

### Author, Title, and Page Number in Parentheses

We have just seen that if Works Cited includes two or more works by an author, and if in your lead-in you do not specify which work you are at the moment making use of, you will have to give the title as well as the page number in parentheses. Similarly, if for some reason you do not in your lead-in mention the name of the author, you will have to add this bit of information to the parenthetic citation thus:

```
At least one critic has claimed that the novel
"rejected the family as the automatic equivalent
of feminine self-fulfillment" (Ziff, American 175).
```

Notice, again, that a comma does *not* separate the title from the page reference; but notice, too, that a comma *does* separate the author's name from the title. (Don't ask us why; ask the Modern Language Association.)

### A Government Document or a Work of Corporate Authorship

Treat the issuing body as the author. Thus, you would write something like this:

```
In Food Resources Today, the Commission on Food
Control concludes that there is no danger (36-37).
```

### A Work by Two or Three Authors

If a work is by *two or three authors*, give their names, either in the parenthetic citation (the first example) or in a lead-in (the second example):

```
Whereas the two other siblings strive compulsively
either to correct or create problems, the sibling
in the middle passively escapes from her pain-
ful family situation by withdrawing into herself
(Seixas and Youcha 48-49).
```

or

```
Barnet, Bellanca, and Stubbs suggest that the most
efficient way to learn about your library's online
resources is to consult a reference librarian (196).
```

If there are *more than three authors*, give the last name of the first author, followed by "et al." (an abbreviation for *et alii*, Latin for "and others"):

> Gardner et al. found that . . .

or

> Sometimes even higher levels are found (Gardner et al. 83).

### Parenthetic Citation of an Indirect Source (Citation of Material That Itself Was Quoted or Summarized in Source)

Suppose you are reading a book by Jones, and she quotes Smith, and you wish to use Smith's material. Your citation will be to Jones—the source you are using—but of course you cannot attribute Smith's words to Jones. You will have to make it clear that you are quoting not Jones but Smith, and so your parenthetic citation will look like this:

> (qtd. in Jones 84-85)

### Parenthetic Citation of Two or More Works

A semicolon, followed by a space, is used to separate two sources:

> Some scholars have speculated that Poe died of rabies, not alcoholism (Walk 44; Hayward 173).

### A Work in More Than One Volume

This is a bit tricky.

1. If you have used only one volume, in Works Cited you will specify the volume, and so in your parenthetic in-text citation you will need to give only a page number—as most of our examples illustrate.

2. If you have used more than one volume, your parenthetic citation will have to specify the volume as well as the page:

> Landsdale points out that nitrite combines with hemoglobin to form a pigment that cannot carry oxygen (2: 370).

The reference is to page 370 of volume 2 of a work by Landsdale.

3. If, however, you are citing not a page but an entire volume—let's say volume 2—your parenthetic citation would be

```
(vol. 2)
```

Or, if you did not name the author in your lead-in, it would be

```
(Landsdale, vol. 2)
```

Notice also some other points:

- When citing a volume and page, the volume number, like the page number, is given in Arabic (not Roman) numerals.
- The volume number is followed by a colon, then a space, then the page number.
- Abbreviations such as "vol." and "p." and "pp." are *not* used, except when citing a volume number without a page number, as illustrated in the last two examples.

### An Anonymous Work

For an anonymous work, give the title in your lead-in or give it in a shortened form in your parenthetic citation:

```
Official Guide to Food Standards includes
a statistical table on nitrates (362).
```

or

```
A statistical table on nitrites is available
(Official Guide 362).
```

But double-check to make sure that the work is truly anonymous. Some encyclopedias, for example, give the authors' names quietly. If initials follow the article, these are the initials of the author's name. Check the alphabetic list of authors given at the front or back of the encyclopedia.

### A Literary Work

Because classic works of literature are widely available, and your readers may have at hand editions different from the one that you have read, you can help them locate the material (if they want to check it) by giving information—for instance, a chapter number—in addition to a page reference. The following forms are customary.

1. **A novel**. In parentheses, give the page number of the edition you specify in Works Cited, followed by a semicolon, a space, and the relevant additional helpful information, such as the chapter number, or the book number (some novels are divided into "books," which themselves are then divided into chapters).

> Chopin in *The Awakening* describes the Pontelliers' house as "charming" (69; ch. 17).

or

> George Eliot characterizes Glegg effectively when in *The Mill on the Floss* she says that his "ordinary tone" was one of "sharp questioning" (235; bk. 3, ch. 4).

2. **A play**. Most instructors want the act, scene, and (if the lines are numbered) line numbers, rather than a page reference, thus:

> The Ghost, in his first encounter with Hamlet, speaks of "Murder most foul" (1.5.28).

This reference is to line 28 in the fifth scene of the first act.

If you are quoting a few words within a sentence of your own, immediately after closing the brief quotation give the citation (enclosed within parentheses), and, if your sentence ends with the quotation, put the period after the closing parenthesis.

> That Macbeth fully understands that killing Duncan is not a manly act but a villainous one is clear from his words to Lady Macbeth: "I dare do all that may become a man" (1.7.46). Moreover, even though he goes on to kill Duncan, he does not go on to deceive himself into thinking that his act was noble.

If, however, your sentence continues beyond the citation, after the parenthetic citation put whatever punctuation may be necessary (for instance, a comma may be needed), complete your sentence, and end it with a period.

This is clear from his words, "I dare do all that does become a man" (1.7.46), and he never loses his awareness of true manliness.

3. **A poem**. Preferences vary, and you can't go wrong in citing the page, but for a poem longer than, say, a sonnet (fourteen lines), most instructors find it useful if students cite the line numbers, in parentheses, after the quotations. In your first use, preface the numerals with "line" or "lines" (not in quotation marks, of course); in subsequent citations simply give the numerals. For very long poems that are divided into books, such as Homer's *Odyssey*, give the page, a semicolon, a space, the book number, and the line number(s). The following example refers to page 327 of a title listed in Works Cited; it goes on to indicate that the passage occurs in the ninth book of the poem, lines 130 to 135.

(327; 9.130–35)

Long quotations (more than three lines of poetry) are indented one inch. As we explained on page 297, if you give a long quotation, try to give one that can correctly be concluded with a period. After the period, hit the space bar three times, and then, on the same line, give the citation in parentheses.

As good an example as any of the absurdity and yet the pathos of T. S. Eliot's *Prufrock* are these lines from near the end of the poem:

Shall I part my hair behind? Do I dare to eat a peach?

I shall wear white flannel trousers, and walk upon the beach.

I have heard the mermaids singing, each to each.

I do not think that they will sing to me. (122–25)

Notice that the period here is given at the end of the quotation, *not* after the parenthetic citation of lines 122–25.

## A Personal Interview

Probably you won't need a parenthetic citation because you'll say something like

```
Cyril Jackson, in an interview, said...
```

or

```
According to Cyril Jackson...
```

and when your readers turn to Works Cited, they will see that Jackson is listed, along with the date of the interview. But if you do not mention the source's name in the lead-in, you will have to provide it within parentheses:

```
It has been estimated that chemical additives earn
the drug companies well over five hundred million
dollars annually (Jackson).
```

## Lectures

If you use in your research essay a distinctive phrase, idea, or piece of information from a class lecture or discussion, you'll want to give the speaker credit for it. If you give a signal phrase such as "In a lecture at NYU, Jones said," the parenthetic citation should include only the date of the lecture; if you don't give a signal phrase, then include the speaker's name, followed by a comma, followed by the date:

```
The museum world today, is "now parts of show biz"
(Orlofsky, Sept. 20, 2004).
```

The entry for the lecture on the Works Cited list will contain the title of the lecture—if there is one—and the place it was given.

## Electronic Sources

Follow the format for print sources. In some cases, page numbers will be available; in others, paragraphs will be numbered; in still others, no number at all will be given. E-book readers such as the Nook and the Kindle give page numbers *and* location numbers, and the page numbers aren't always stable. (In some cases, they can change depending on the orientation of the device.) *Use what you have*, indicating the author's name or the title of the source where necessary, as determined by context. When giving paragraph numbers, use the abbreviation "par" or "pars." (Use a comma to separate the abbreviation from the author's name or title.)

> One lawyer argued that Monica Lewinsky was nowhere near the White House that day (Hedges, pars. 2-3).

## A Note on Footnotes in an Essay Using Parenthetic Citations

There are two reasons for using footnotes in an essay that chiefly uses parenthetic citations.

1. In a research paper you will, of course, draw on many sources, but in other kinds of papers you may be using only one source, and yet within the paper you may often want to specify a reference to a page or (for poetry) a line number, or (for a play) to an act, scene, and line number. In such a case, to append a page headed *Work Cited*, with a single title, is silly; it is better to use a single footnote when you first allude to the source. Such a note can run something like this:

> [1]All references are to Mary Shelley, *Frankenstein*, afterword by Harold Bloom (New York: Signet, 1965).

2. Footnotes can also be used in another way in an essay that documents sources by giving parenthetic citations. If you want to include some material that might seem intrusive in the body of the essay, you may relegate it to a footnote. For example, in a footnote you might translate a quotation given in a foreign language, or in a footnote you might write a paragraph—a sort of mini-essay—in which you offer an amplification of some point. By putting the amplification in a footnote, you are signaling to the reader that it is dispensable; it is, so to speak, thrown in as something extra, something relevant but not essential to your argument.

A raised Arabic numeral indicates in the body of your text that you are adding a footnote at this point. (The "insert reference" or "insert footnote" command of your word-processing program will insert both the raised numeral and the text of your footnote in the appropriate places in your essay; simply click *insert* at the point in the text where you want the footnote to appear and follow the program's instructions.)

> Joachim Jeremias's *The Parables of Jesus* is probably the best example of this sort of book.[1]

Usually the number is put at the end of a sentence, immediately after the period, but put it earlier if clarity requires you to do so.

```
Helen Cam¹ as well as many lesser historians held
this view.
```

## The List of Works Cited

Your parenthetic documentation consists of references that become meaningful when the reader consults a list entitled *Works Cited* given at the end of your essay. We present sample entries below, but see also the list of works cited at the end of the documented essay presented in Chapter 1, "Writing the Research Essay" (pp. 220–21, 236–37).

The list of works cited continues the pagination of the essay; if the last page of text is 10, then the list begins on page 11. Your last name and the page number will appear in the upper-right corner, half an inch from the top of the sheet. Next, type "Works Cited," centered, one inch from the top, then double-space and type the first entry. Following are the governing conventions.

### Alphabetic Order

1. Arrange the list alphabetically by author, with the author's last name first.
2. List an anonymous work alphabetically under the first word of the title, or under the second word if the first word is *A, An,* or *The*, or a foreign equivalent.
3. If your list includes two or more works by one author, the work whose title comes earlier in the alphabet precedes the work whose title comes later in the alphabet.

### Form on the Page

1. Begin each entry flush with the left margin. If an entry runs to more than one line, indent five spaces for each succeeding line of the entry.
2. Double-space each entry, and double-space between entries.

### The Elements of the Citation

The information included in a citation will vary according to the medium of the source. The MLA designates three major categories of sources: print sources, Web sources, and "other common sources." For **printed books**, the basic elements include:

- Author
- Title
- Publisher
- Date and place of publication
- Medium of publication (For a book, the medium of publication is "print.")

*Note:* This last element is new, and it is included in all citations. Citations for print journals give such additional information as the name of the periodical, the series and volume numbers, the issue number, and the page range. Citations for **Web sources** give both the date of publication and the date of access: the date on which *you* located the material. (The MLA no longer requires the URL, or Web site address, unless a reader would be unlikely to find the source without it.) Citations for **other common sources** include other information—for example, the name of the vendor of a CD-ROM, or the location of the library where a particular manuscript can be found, or the medium of publication for a radio or television broadcast.

We will focus on these three major categories:

- Print sources (pp. 307–16)
- Web sources (pp. 317–20)
- Other common sources (pp. 321–23).

## Print Sources

### Author's Name

Note that the last name is given first, but otherwise the name is given as on the title page. Do not substitute initials for names written out on the title page. (Books by more than one author are treated later in this discussion, p. 309.)

If your list includes two or more works by an author, the author's name is not repeated for the second title but is represented by three hyphens followed by a period and two spaces. When you give two or more works by the same author, the sequence is determined by the alphabetic order of the titles, as in the following example, listing two books by Blassingame, where *Black* precedes *Slave*.

Bishop, Robert. *American Folk Sculpture*. New York: Dutton, 1974. Print.

Blassingame, John W. *Black New Orleans, 1860–1880*. Chicago: U of Chicago P, 1973. Print.

---. *The Slave Community: Plantation Life in the Antebellum South*. Rev. ed. New York: Oxford UP, 1979. Print.

Danto, Arthur. *Embodied Meanings*. New York: Farrar, 1994. Print.

We have already discussed the treatment of an anonymous work; in a few moments we will discuss books by more than one author, government documents, and works of corporate authorship.

### Title of Book

Take the title from the title page, not from the cover or the spine, but disregard any unusual typography—for instance, the use of only capital letters or the use of & for *and*. Italicize the title and subtitle. A peculiarity: If a title of a book itself includes the title of a book (for instance, a book about Mary Shelley's *Frankenstein* might include the title of her novel in its own title), the title-within-the-title is *not* italicized. Thus the title would be given as

*The Endurance of* Frankenstein

### Place of Publication, Publisher, Date, and Medium of Publication

For the place of publication, give the name of the city (you can usually find it either on the title page or on the copyright page, which is on the reverse of the title page). If several cities are listed, give only the first. If the city is not likely to be widely known, or if it may be confused with another city of the same name (for instance, Cambridge, Massachusetts, and Cambridge, England), add the abbreviated name of the state or country (Cambridge, MA, or Cambridge, Eng.).

The name of the publisher is shortened. Usually the first word is enough (Random House becomes Random; Little, Brown and Co. becomes Little), but if the first word is a first name, such as in Alfred A. Knopf, the surname (Knopf) is used instead. University presses are abbreviated thus: Yale UP, U of Chicago P, State U of New York P.

The date of publication of a book is given when known; if no date appears on the book, write "n.d." to indicate "no date" (without the quotation marks).

For all print sources, the medium of publication is "Print."

Following are sample entries, illustrating the points we have covered thus far:

> Douglas, Ann. *The Feminization of American Culture*. New York: Knopf, 1977. Print.
>
> Early, Gerald. *One Nation Under a Groove: Motown and American Culture*. Hopewell, NJ: Ecco, 1995. Print.
>
> Feitlowitz, Marguerite. *A Lexicon of Terror: Argentina and the Legacies of Torture*. New York: Oxford UP, 1998. Print.
>
> Frye, Northrop. *Fables of Identity: Studies in Poetic Mythology*. New York: Harcourt, 1963. Print.
>
> ---. *Fools of Time: Studies in Shakespearian Tragedy*. Toronto: U of Toronto P, 1967. Print.
>
> Smith, Patti. *Just Kids*. New York: Ecco, 2011. Print.

Notice that a period follows the author's name, and another period follows the title. If a subtitle is given, as it is for Feitlowitz's book, it is separated from the title by a colon and a space. A colon follows the place of publication, a comma follows the publisher, a period follows the date, and a period follows the medium of publication.

### A Book by More Than One Author

A book written by *two or three authors* is alphabetized under the last name of the first author named on the title page. The names of other authors are given after the first author's name (with last name first) in the normal order, *first name first*.

> Palfrey, John, and Urs Gasser. *Born Digital: Understanding the First Generation of Digital Natives*. NY: Basic Books, 2008. Print.

Notice that a comma is put after the first name of the first author, separating it from the names that follow.

If there are *more than three authors*, give the name of only the first, and then add "et al." (Latin for "and others"), without the quotation marks.

A WRITER'S HANDBOOK

Belenky, Mary Field, et al. *Women's Ways of
Knowing: The Development of the Self, Voice,
and Mind*. New York: Basic Books, 1986. Print.

## Government Documents

If the writer is not known, treat the government and the agency as the author. Most federal national documents are issued by the Government Printing Office in Washington (abbreviated to GPO).

U.S. Congress. Office of Technology Assessment.
*Computerized Manufacturing Automation
Employment, Education and the Workplace*.
Washington: GPO, 1984. Print.

## Works of Corporate Authorship

Begin the citation with the corporate author, even if the same body is also the publisher, as in the first example:

American Psychiatric Association. *Psychiatric
Glossary*. Washington: American Psychiatric
Association, 1984. Print.
Carnegie Council on Policy Studies in Higher
Education. *Giving Youth a Better Chance:
Options for Education, Work, and Service*.
San Francisco: Jossey, 1980. Print.

## Republished Work

After the title, give the date of original publication (it can usually be found on the copyright page of the reprint you are using) followed by a period, then the place, publisher, and date of the edition you are using, then the medium of publication. The example indicates that Rourke's book was originally published in 1931 and that the student is using the Doubleday reprint of 1953.

Rourke, Constance. *American Humor*. 1931. Garden
City, NY: Doubleday, 1953. Print.

## A Book in Several Volumes

Friedel, Frank. *Franklin D. Roosevelt*. 4 vols.
Boston: Little, 1973. Print.

If you have used more than one volume in your essay, you will (as we explained on p. 300) indicate an in-text reference to, say, page 250 of volume 3 thus: (3: 250).

If, however, you have used only one volume of the set—let's say volume 3—in your Works-Cited entry, you should write, after the period following the date, "Vol. 3," as in the next entry:

```
Friedel, Frank. Franklin D. Roosevelt. 4 vols.
    Boston: Little, 1973. Vol. 3. Print.
```

In this case, the parenthetic citation in the text will be to the page only, not to the volume and page, since a reader will understand that the page reference must be to this volume. But notice that in Works Cited, even though you say you used only volume 3, you also give the total number of volumes.

### One Book with a Separate Title in a Set of Volumes

Sometimes a titled set of volumes also has a separate title for each book in the set. If you are listing such a book, use the following form:

```
Churchill, Winston. The Age of Revolution. Vol. 3
    of A History of the English-Speaking Peoples.
    New York: Dodd, 1957. Print.
```

### A Book with an Author and an Editor

```
Churchill, Winston, and Franklin D. Roosevelt.
    The Complete Correspondence. 3 vols. Ed.
    Warren F. Kimball. Princeton, NJ: Princeton
    UP, 1985. Print.
Shakespeare, William. The Sonnets. Ed. William
    Burto. New York: NAL, 1965. Print.
```

If you are making use of the editor's introduction or other editorial material, rather than of the author's work, list the book under the name of the editor, rather than of the author, following the form given below for an introduction, foreword, or afterword.

### A Revised Edition of a Book

```
Hall, James. Dictionary of Subjects and Symbols in
    Art. 2nd ed. New York: Harper, 1979. Print.
```

### A Translated Book

> Allende, Isabel. *Island Beneath the Sea*. Trans.
> Margaret Sayens Peden. New York: Harper,
> 2010. Print.

But if you are discussing the translation itself, as opposed to the book, list the work under the translator's name:

> MacAdam, Alfred, trans. *Family Portrait with*
> *Fidel: A Memoir*. By Carlos Franqui. New York:
> Random, 1984. Print.

### An Introduction, Foreword, or Afterword

> Wolff, Cynthia Griffin. Introduction. *The House*
> *Of Mirth*. By Edith Wharton. New York:
> Penguin, 1985. vii–xxvi. Print.

Usually a book with an introduction or some such comparable material is listed under the name of the author of the book (here Wharton), rather than under the name of the writer of the introduction (here Wolff), but if you are referring to the apparatus rather than to the book itself, use the form just given. The words *Introduction, Preface, Foreword*, and *Afterword* are neither enclosed within quotation marks nor italicized in the Works Cited entry.

### A Book with an Editor but No Author

Anthologies of literature fit this description, but here we have in mind a book of essays written by various people but collected by an editor (or editors), whose name appears on the collection.

> Baldick, Chris, ed. *The Oxford Book of Gothic*
> *Tales*. New York: Oxford UP, 1993. Print.

### A Work in a Volume of Works by One Author

The following entry indicates that a short work by Susan Sontag—an essay called "The Aesthetics of Science"—appears in a book by Sontag entitled *Styles of Radical Will*. Notice that the inclusive page numbers of the short work are cited—not merely page numbers that you may happen to refer to, but the page numbers of the entire piece.

> Sontag, Susan. "The Aesthetics of Science." In
> *Styles of Radical Will*. New York: Farrar,
> 1969. 3–34. Print.

## A Work in a Collection of Works by Several Authors

There are several possibilities here. Let's assume, for a start, that you have made use of one work in an anthology. In Works Cited, begin with the author (last name first) and title of the work you are citing, not with the name of the anthologist or the title of the anthology. Following is an entry for Coleridge's poem "Kubla Khan," found on pages 501-03 in the second volume of a two-volume anthology edited by David Damrosch and several others.

> Coleridge, Samuel Taylor. "Kubla Khan." *The Longman Anthology of British Literature*. Ed. David Damrosch et al. 2 vols. New York: Longman, 1999. 2: 501-03. Print.

Now let's assume that during the course of your essay, you refer to several works rather than to only one work in this anthology. You can, of course, list each work in the form just given. Or you can have an entry in Works Cited for Damrosch's anthology, under Damrosch's name, and then in each entry for a work in the anthology you can eliminate some of the data by simply referring to Damrosch, thus:

> Coleridge, Samuel Taylor. "Kubla Khan." Damrosch 2: 501-03. Print.

Again, this requires that you also list Damrosch's volume thus:

> Damrosch, David, et al., eds. *The Longman Anthology of British Literature*. 2 vols. New York: Longman, 1999. Print.

The advantage of listing the anthology separately is that if you are using a dozen works from the anthology, you can shorten the dozen entries in Works Cited merely by adding one entry, that of the anthology itself. Notice, of course, that in the body of the essay you would still refer to Coleridge and to your other eleven authors, not to the editor of the anthology—but the entries in Works Cited will guide the reader to the book you have used.

### A Book Review

> Vendler, Helen. Rev. of *Essays on Style*. Ed. Roger Fowler. Essays in *Criticism* 16 (1966): 457-63. Print.

If the review has a title, give it between the period following the reviewer's name and "Rev."

If a review is anonymous, list it under the first word of the title, or under the second word if the first word is *A, An,* or *The.* If an anonymous review has no title, begin the entry with "Rev. of" and then give the title of the work reviewed; alphabetize the entry under the title of the work reviewed.

### An Article or Essay—Not a Reprint—in a Collection

A book may consist of a collection (edited by one or more persons) of new essays by several authors. Here is a reference to one essay in such a book. (The essay, by Smith, occupies pp. 178-94 in a collection edited by Lubiano.)

> Smith, David Lionel. "What Is Black Culture?"
> *The House That Race Built*. Ed. Wahneema
> Lubiano. New York: Vintage, 1998. 178-94.
> Print.

### An Article or Essay Reprinted in a Collection

The previous example (Smith's essay in Lubiano's collection) was for an essay written for a collection. But some collections reprint earlier material—for example, essays from journals, or chapters from books. The following example cites an essay that was originally printed in a book called *The Cinema of Alfred Hitchcock*. This essay has been reprinted in a later collection of essays on Hitchcock, edited by Arthur J. LaValley, and it was LaValley's collection that the student used.

> Bogdanovich, Peter. "Interviews with Alfred
> Hitchcock." *The Cinema of Alfred Hitchcock*.
> New York: Museum of Modern Art, 1963. 15-18.
> Rpt. in *Focus on Hitchcock*. Ed. Albert J.
> LaValley. Englewood Cliffs, NJ: Prentice,
> 1972. 28-31. Print.

The student has read Bogdanovich's essay or chapter, but not in Bogdanovich's book, where it occupied pages 15-18. The student actually read the essay on pages 28-31 in a collection of writings on Hitchcock, edited by LaValley. Details of the original publication—title, date, page numbers, and so forth—were found in LaValley's collection. Almost all editors will include this information, either on the copyright page or at the foot of the reprinted essay, but sometimes they do not give the original page numbers. In such a case, you need not give the original numbers in the entry.

Notice that the entry begins with the author and the title of the work you are citing (here, Bogdanovich's interviews), not with the name of the editor of the collection or the title of the collection. In the following example, the student used an essay by Arthur Sewell; the essay was originally on pages 53-56 in a book by Sewell entitled *Character and Society in Shakespeare*, but the student encountered the piece on pages 36-38 in a collection of essays, edited by Leonard Dean, on Shakespeare's *Julius Caesar*. Here is how the entry should look:

> Sewell, Arthur. "The Moral Dilemma in Tragedy:
> Brutus." *Character and Society in Shakespeare*.
> Oxford: Clarendon, 1951. 53-56. Rpt. in
> *Twentieth Century Interpretations of Julius
> Caesar*. Ed. Leonard F. Dean. Englewood Cliffs,
> NJ: Prentice, 1968. 36-38. Print.

### An Encyclopedia or Other Alphabetically Arranged Reference Work

The publisher, place of publication, volume number, and page number do *not* have to be given. For such works, list only the edition (if it is given) and the date.

For a *signed* article, begin with the author's last name. (If the article is signed with initials, check the volume for a list of abbreviations—it is usually near the front, but it may be at the rear—which will say what the initials stand for, and use the following form.)

> Messer, Thomas. "Picasso." *Encyclopedia Americana*.
> 1998 ed. Print.

For an *unsigned article*, begin with the title of the article.

> "Automation." *The Business Reference Book*. 1977 ed.
> "Picasso, Pablo (Ruiz y)." *Encyclopaedia
> Britannica: Macropaedia*. 1985 ed. Print.

### An Article in a Scholarly Journal

The title of the article is enclosed within quotation marks, and the title of the journal is italicized. Some journals are paginated consecutively by volume—the pagination of the second issue begins where the first issue leaves off; but other journals begin each issue with page 1. For all scholarly journals, include both the volume and the issue number. (Formerly, the issue number was *not* included in Works-Cited entries that were paginated by volume—but it is included now.)

*Article in a journal that is paginated by volume:*

> Skowronek, Stephen. "Why Small, Centrist Parties
> Motivate Policy Divergence by Major Parties."
> *American Political Science Review* 100.3
> (2006): 385-401. Print.

Skowronek's article occupies pages 385–401 of volume 100, issue 3, which was published in 2006. Note that the volume number is followed by a period and then by the issue number followed by a space, and then by the year, in parentheses, and then by a colon, a space, and the page range for the entire article. The word *Print* is the final element.

*Article in a journal that is paginated by issue:*

> Wasserman, Howard M. "If You Build It, They Will
> Speak: Public Stadiums, Public Forums, and
> Free Speech." *NINE: A Journal of Baseball
> History and Culture* 14.2 (2006): 5-26. Print.

### An Article in a Weekly, Biweekly, or Monthly Publication

The date and page numbers are given, but volume numbers and issue numbers are usually omitted for these publications. (Note that month names of more than four letters are abbreviated; "June" is "June," but "September" is "Sept.") The following example is for an article in a weekly publication:

> Malcolm, Janet. "Gertrude Stein's War." *New Yorker*
> 2 June 2003: 58-81. Print.

### An Article in a Newspaper

Because a newspaper usually consists of several sections, a section number or a capital letter may precede the page number. The following entry is to an article that begins on page 1 of section A; the plus sign indicates that it continues on a later (but not necessarily subsequent) page:

> Urbina, Ian. "Voter ID Battle Shifts to Proof
> of Citizenship." *New York Times* 12 May 2008:
> A1+. Print.

## Web Sources

Eight elements are common to *all* Works-Cited entries for Web sources:

1. Name of the author, director, narrator, performer, compiler, or producer of the work. For works with more than one author or a corporate author, or for anonymous works, follow the guidelines for print sources. (If no author is given, begin the entry with item 2, the title of the work.)
2. Title of the work. Italicize the title, unless it is part of a larger work. Titles that are part of a larger work should be enclosed in quotation marks.
3. Title of the overall Web site (in italics) if this is distinct from item 2.
4. Version or edition of the site, if there is more than one.
5. Publisher or sponsor of the site. This information can often be found at the bottom of the Web page. If this information is not available, use n.p. (for no publisher).
6. Publication date. If no date is given, use n.d.
7. Medium of publication. **For all online sources, the medium of publication is Web**.
8. Date of access, that is, the date on which *you* accessed the source (day, month, year).

*Example:*

> Cook, John. "Cult Friction." Radaronline.com.
> *Radar Magazine*, Apr. 2008. Web. 2 May 2011.

As we have noted, a URL is included only if your readers are unlikely to be able to locate your source without it. Most often, it will not be included. But when you must include the URL, use the following format:

- Place a period and a space after the date of access; insert the URL as the last item of the entry.
- Enclose the URL in angle brackets, followed by a period.
- Give the complete URL, including the access-mode identifier (*http, ftp,* etc.). For accuracy, use your browser's copy-and-paste function to move the URL directly from the address bar to your text.
- Break a URL only *after* a slash.
- Do not hyphenate a URL or allow your word processor to insert a hyphen.

> "Service Learning and Volunteer Opportunities."
> *Ed.gov*. US Dept. of Education, n.d. Web. 12
> May 2011 <http://www.ed.gov/students/involve/
> service/edpicks.jhtml?src=ln>.

Those are the general rules. Following are specific examples of sources found through Web sites, sources found through databases and scholarly projects, and sources also available in another medium.

### Sources Found Through Web Sites
### *Entire Online Site*

> McGann, Jerome J., ed. *The Rossetti Archive*. U
> of Virginia, n.d. Web. 2 May 2011.

### *Part of a Site*

> "Apple: iPhone Sold Out." *CNN.com*. Cable News
> Network, 12 May 2008. Web. 12 May 2011.
> Juffer, Jane. "Sandra Cisneros: Biographical
> Note." *Modern American Poetry*. Dept. of
> English, U of Illinois, Urbana-Champaign,
> 2002. Web. 12 May 2011.

### *Online Magazine Article*

> "Microsoft Throws in the Towel." *The Economist*.
> The Economist, 4 May 2008. Web. 12 May 2011.

### *Online Newspaper Article*

> Gelfand, Lou. "Episode on Campaign Trail
> Illustrates the Fine Line Journalists Must
> Observe." *Star Tribune*. Star Tribune, 27 Jan.
> 2008. Web. 3 May 2011.

### *Online Reference Article*

> "Film Noir." *Encyclopaedia Britannica Online*.
> Encyclopaedia Britannica, 2008. Web.
> 12 May 2011.

### *Online Scholarly Journal Article*

For scholarly journal articles that exist only online in independent Web sites—as opposed to articles accessed from a database—use the format for an article from a print journal. Include *Web* as the medium of publication, followed by the date of access. If page numbers are not included, use *n. pag.*

> Sandifer, Philip. "When Real Things Happen to
> Imaginary Tigers." *ImageText* 3.3 (2007):
> n. pag. Web. 5 May 2011.

## Wiki

> "Pottery of Ancient Greece." *Wikipedia*. Wikimedia
> Foundation, 2008. Web. 6 Oct. 2011.

## Blog

> Creamer, Robert. "Top Ten Reasons Obama Defeated
> Clinton for the Democratic Nomination."
> *Huffington Post*. HuffingtonPost.com, 12 May
> 2008. Web. 12 May 2011.

## Podcast

> "Africa Today." *BBC World Service*. BBC, 2 Apr.
> 2009. Web. 5 May 2011.

## Online Audio or Video

> "Hip Hop Dancer." *Made*. Exec. Prod. Dave
> Sirulnick. *MTV Overdrive*. MTV Networks,
> 19 Feb. 2008. Web. 12 Feb. 2011.
> Connecticut Forum. "Jennifer Weiner and Joyce
> Carol Oates." *YouTube*. YouTube, 30 Mar. 2007.
> Web. 12 May 2011.

## Sources Found Through a Database or Scholarly Project

### Book Accessed from a Scholarly Project

> Rossetti, Dante Gabriel. *Ballads and Sonnets*.
> London: Chiswick, 1881. *The Rossetti Archive*.
> Web. 3 May 2011.

### Scholarly Journal Accessed from a Database

For scholarly journal articles accessed through a database, use the format for an article from a print journal. Include Web as the medium of publication, followed by the date of access. If page numbers are not included, use n. pag.

Include the title of the database or Web site from which the content was retrieved, in italics. Do not include the database URL or (for a library-based subscription) information about the library system.

Dejardins, Mary. "The Incredible Shrinking Star: Todd Haynes and the Case History of Karen Carpenter." *Camera Obscura* 19.3 (2004): 22-25. *Project Muse.* Web. 3 May 2011.

### Magazine Article Accessed from a Database

Ward, Jacob, Doug Cantor, and Bjorn Carey. "The Hard Science of Making Videogames." *Popular Science.* Oct. 2007: 68-76. *Academic Search Premier.* Web. 6 June 2011.

### Government Document Accessed from a Database

United States. Extension Series. *4-H and the War.* N.d. *Historic Government Publications from World War II.* Web. 7 May 2011.

## Electronic Sources Also Available in Another Medium

When you cite an online source that is also available in another medium—such as a painting that you view online—you may choose to include publication information for that other medium if you decide that your readers would find that information useful.

Use the citation format for the other medium, but use *Web* as the medium of publication. End the entry with the following information:

1. The title of the database or Web site (in italics) from which you retrieved the content;
2. the medium of publication (Web); and
3. the date of access (day, month, and year).

### Work of Art Accessed Online

Hepworth, Barbara. *Square Forms with Circles.* 1963. Storm King Art Center. *The Collection: Highlights of the Collection.* Web. 5 May 2011.

### Film Accessed Online

*Theodore Roosevelt, Friend of the Birds.* Dir. Caroline Gentry. Roosevelt Memorial Assn., 1928. Broadcasting and Recorded Sound Div., Lib of Cong. *The Evolution of the Conservation Movement.* Web. 5 May 2011.

## Other Common Sources

### An Electronic Book

A Kindle, Nook, or other electronic version of a book is referenced in the same way as the print version, but instead of "print" at the end of the entry, the name of the medium is given.

> Fuller, Alexandra. *Cocktail Hour under the Tree of Forgetfulness*. New York: Penguin, 2011. Kindle edition.

### A Video Recording or Film

Begin with the director's name (last name first), followed by "dir." Next give the title of the film, italicized, then a period, a space, the name of the distributor, the date of release, and a period. List the medium last.

> Hardwicke, Catherine, dir. *Twilight*. Summit Entertainment, 2008. DVD.

### A CD or Other Sound Recording

List the medium last, after the manufacturer's name and date of release.

> Springsteen, Bruce. *Working on a Dream*. Columbia, 2009. CD.

### A Television or Radio Program

> Davies, Andrew, adapt. "Emma." By Jane Austen. Perf. Kate Beckinsale and Mark Strong. *The Complete Jane Austen. Masterpiece*. PBS. WGBH, Boston, 23 Mar. 2008. Television.
> "iCook." *iCarly*. Nickelodeon, 19 Sept. 2009. Television.

### An Interview

If the source is a published or recorded interview, include the medium of publication (Radio, Television, Web, etc.), if the interview was in fact published, at the end of the entry.

> Gessner, David. Interview by Mindy Todd. *The Point*. NPR. WCAI, The Cape and the Islands, 12 Apr. 2007. Radio.

If the source is an interview you conducted yourself, give the name of the person interviewed, the kind of interview (Personal interview, Telephone interview), and the date the interview was conducted.

> Curley, Caroline. Personal interview. 1 Mar. 2005.

### An E-mail Message

Give the name of the author of the message, and use the subject line as the title (in quotation marks). The recipient of the message must be named; if the recipient is you, use "Message to the author." Give the date, and then indicate that e-mail is the medium of delivery.

> Wood, Ruth. "Re: Literature for Composition."
>       Message to Margaret Collins. 23 Aug. 2011.
>       E-mail.

### An Oral Presentation (A Lecture, Address, or Speech)

In addition to the date of the presentation and the name of the speaker, the citation should include the title of the presentation (if there is one) and the place it was given. If there is no title, use a descriptive word or phrase such as "Class lecture," but do not use quotation marks. If the lecture was sponsored by a particular organization or group, give that information before the date.

> Cahill, Patricia A. Emory Univ. 20 Sept. 2011.
>       Class lecture.
> McNamara, Eileen. "Truth and Ethics in Writing."
>       The Writers Writing for a Living Wellesley
>       College Writing Program, Wellesley, MA. 10
>       Feb. 1999. Address.

### Visual Art

Include the date of composition after the title, or n.d. if the date is unknown. Include the location of a private collection if one location is available; use n.p. if not. When the source is the original work of art itself, include the medium of composition after the date of composition.

> Murakami, Takashi. *Tan Tan Bo*. 2001. Acrylic on
>       canvas mounted on board. Collection of John
>       A. Smith and Victoria Hughes, n.p.

When the source is a reproduction (a print or an online reproduction), include the medium of publication (Print or Web) as well as the date of access.

```
Rodin, Auguste. Monument to Balzac. 1898. Museum
     of Mod. Art, New York. MOMA.org. Web.
     20 Feb. 2011.
```

### Digital File

This new category includes computer files such as PDFs, Word documents, JPEGs, MP3s, and so forth that are not retrieved from a Web site or online database. To cite this kind of source, first determine what kind of work you are citing (book, photograph, sound recording, etc.) and follow the guidelines for that kind of work. Include "file" preceded by the specific kind of file you are citing as the medium of publication. If you can't identify the kind of file, use "Digital file" as the medium of publication.

```
Castellucci, William. "The Elimination of the
     Soldier from the Battlefield." 2008.
     Microsoft Word file.
```

**Note:** On pages 207–21 we reprint a research essay written by a student using the MLA format.

Although we have covered the most common sources, it is entirely possible that you will come across a source that does not fit any of the categories that we have discussed. For several hundred pages of explanation of these matters, covering the proper way to cite nearly all imaginable sources, see the *MLA Handbook for Writers of Research Papers,* 7th ed. (NY: MLA, 2009).

# APA Format

The MLA style is used chiefly by writers in the humanities. Writers in the social sciences and in business, education, and psychology commonly use a style developed by the American Psychological Association. In the following pages we give the chief principles of the APA style, but for full details the reader should consult the sixth edition of the *Publication Manual of the American Psychological Association* (2010).

A paper using the format prescribed by the American Psychological Association will contain brief parenthetical citations within the text and will end with a page headed "References," which lists all of the author's sources. This list of sources begins on a separate page, continuing the pagination of the last page of the essay itself. Thus, if the text of the essay ends on page 8, the first page of references is page 9.

Here are some general guidelines for formatting both the citations within the text and the list of references at the end of the essay. Some sample references follow the general guidelines.

## Citations Within the Text

The APA style emphasizes the date of publication; the date appears not only in the list of references at the end of the paper but also within the paper itself, when you give a brief parenthetic citation of a source that you have quoted or summarized or in any other way used. Here is an example:

```
Statistics for church attendance are highly
unreliable (Catherton, 1991, p. 17).
```

Note that unlike the MLA, the APA style uses commas to separate elements inside the parenthetic citation and that a "p." precedes the page number. The parenthetic citation may appear at the end of the sentence, or after the clause that contains the references, or after the author's name—whichever placement makes things clearest for the reader. In the example below, the date of publication appears immediately after the author's name; the page reference is given at the end of the sentence:

```
According to Catherton (1991), statistics for
church attendance are highly unreliable (p. 17).
```

The title of Catherton's book or article will be given in the list entitled References. By turning to the list, the reader will learn in what publication Catherton made this point.

### A Summary of an Entire Work
```
Catherton (1991) concluded the opposite.
```
or
```
Similar views are easily found (Catherton, 1991;
Brinnin and Abse, 1992).
```

### A Reference to a Page or Pages
```
Catherton (1991, p. 107) argues that "church
attendance is increasing but religious faith is
decreasing."
```

## A Reference to an Author Represented by More Than One Work Published in a Given Year in the References

As we explain in discussing the form of the material in references, if you list two or more works that an author published in the same year, the works are listed in alphabetic order, by the first letter of the title. The first work is labeled *a*, the second *b*, and so on. Here is a reference to the second work that Catherton published in 1997:

> Boston is "a typical large Northern city" so far as church attendance goes (Catherton, 1997b).

## *The List of References*

### Form on the Page

1. Begin each entry flush with the left margin, but if an entry runs to more than one line, indent five spaces for each succeeding line of the entry.
2. Double-space each entry, and double-space between entries.

### Alphabetic Order

1. Arrange the list **alphabetically by author**.
2. Give the **author's last name first**, then the initial only of the first and of the middle name (if any).
3. **If there is more than one author**, name all of the authors, again inverting the name (last name first) and giving only initials for first and middle names. (But do not invert the editor's name when the entry begins with the name of an author who has written an article in an edited book. See the example on p. 314, illustrating a work in a collection of essays.) When there are two or more authors, use an ampersand (&) before the name of the last author. When there are more than six authors—and there often are for papers published in the social sciences—the seventh and all additional authors are indicated with "et al." Here is an example of an article with three authors in the seventh volume of a journal called *Journal of Experimental Social Psychology:*

> Berscheid, E., Hatfield, E., & Bohrnstett, G. (1971).
> Physical attractiveness and dating choice: A
> test of the matching hypothesis. *Journal of
> Experimental Social Psychology, 7,* 173–189.

4. **If there is more than one work by an author**, list the works in the order of publication, the earliest first. If two or more works by an author were published in the same year, give them in alphabetic order

by the first letter of the title, disregarding *A, An,* or *The,* and their foreign equivalents. Designate the first work as *a,* the second as *b,* and so on. Repeat the author's name at the start of each entry.

If the author of a work or works is also the coauthor of other works listed, list the single-author entries first, arranged by date. Following these, list the multiple-author entries, in a sequence determined alphabetically by the second author's name. Thus, in the example below, notice that the works Bem wrote unassisted are listed first, arranged by date, and when two works appear in the same year they are arranged alphabetically by title. These single-author works are followed by the multiple-author works, with the work written with Lenney preceding the work written with Martyna and Watson.

Bem, S. L. (1974). The measurement of psychological androgyny. *Journal of Consulting and Clinical Psychology, 42,* 155–162.

Bem, S. L. (1981a). The BSRI and gender schema theory: A reply to Spence and Helmreich. *Psychological Review, 88,* 369–371.

Bem, S. L. (1981b). Gender schema theory: A cognitive account of sex typing. *Psychological Review, 88,* 354–364.

Bem, S. L., & Lenney, E. (1976). Sex-typing and the avoidance of cross-sex behavior. *Journal of Personality and Social Psychology, 33,* 48–54.

Bem, S. L., Martyna, W., & Watson, C. (1976). Sex-typing and androgyny: Further exploration of the expressive domain. *Journal of Personality and Social Psychology, 34,* 1016–1023.

## Form of Title

1. In references to books, capitalize only the first letter of the first word of the title (and of the subtitle, if any) and capitalize proper nouns. Italicize the complete title and type a period after it.

2. In references to articles in periodicals or in edited books, capitalize only the first letter of the first word of the article's title (and subtitle, if any) and all proper nouns. Do not put the title within quotation marks. Type a period after the title of the article. For the title of the journal, and the volume and page numbers, see the next instruction.

3. In references to periodicals, capitalize all important words, as you would usually do. (Note that the rule for the titles of periodicals differs

from the rule for books and articles.) Give the volume number in Arabic numerals, and italicize it. Do *not* use *vol.* before the number, and do not use *p.* or *pp.* before the page numbers.

## Sample References

### A Book by One Author

Lancaster, R. M. (2003). *The trouble with nature: Sex in science and popular culture*. Berkeley: University of California Press.

### A Book by More Than One Author

Spence, J. T., & Helmreich, R. L. (1978). *Masculinity and femininity*. Austin: University of Texas Press.

### A Collection of Essays

Bhabha, H. K. (Ed.). (1990). *Nation and narration*. London: Routledge.

### A Work in a Collection of Essays

Rogers, B. (1985). The Atlantic alliance. In W. P. Bundy (Ed.). *The Nuclear controversy* (41–52). New York: New American Library.

### Government Documents

If the writer is not known, treat the government and the agency as the author. Most federal documents are issued by the Government Printing Office in Washington.

U.S. Congress. Office of Technology Assessment (1984). Computerized manufacturing automation: Employment, education, and the workplace. Washington, DC: U.S. Government Printing Office.

### A Journal Article

Articles published in journals that begin each issue with page 1 are treated differently from journals with continuous pagination. Entries for journals with continuous pagination require issue and volume numbers. Those that begin each issue with page 1 need only volume numbers.

Lyons, H. (2008). The secret of the totem:
    Religion and society from McLennan to Freud.
    *Journal of the History of Sexuality, 17*(3),
    483-186.

### An Article from a Monthly or Weekly Magazine

Chelminsky, R. (2003, April). *The curse of Count
    Dracula.* Smithsonian, 110.

### An Article in a Newspaper

Perry, T. (1993, 16 February). Election to give
    Latinos new political clout in San Diego.
    *Los Angeles Times*, sec. A, p. 3.

If no author is given, simply begin with the article title, followed by
the date in parentheses. Note that in the case of a newspaper article,
"p." or "pp." precedes the page number or numbers.

### A Book Review

Bayme, S. (1993). Tradition or modernity? Review
    of Neil Gillman, *Sacred fragments: Recovering
    theology for the modern Jew. Judaism, 42,*
    106-113.

Bayme is the reviewer, not the author of the book. The book under
review is called *Sacred fragments: Recovering theology for the modern Jew*,
but the review, published in volume 42 of a journal called *Judaism*, had
its own title, "Tradition or modernity?"

### Electronic Sources

References to electronic sources generally follow the format for printed
sources and include the following information:

- Author
- Year of publication (in parentheses)
- Title (and edition, if applicable)

Additional information is given next. The principle is to include only
the information a reader will need to retrieve your source—the principle,
in other words, is *less not more.* The elements may include:

- Date retrieved—but only if it is possible that the source will be revised or changed; the date may be omitted for electronic versions

of books or articles—material, in other words, that is fixed. If the source is a wiki—Wikipedia, for example—then the retrieval date is essential.

- Name and/or the address of the source. Use the DOI (digital object identifier) if it is available; if not, use the URL.
- The name of the database through which the source was retrieved—but only if a reader is unlikely to find the source (a rare book, perhaps) without it.
- The menu or home page URL for dictionaries and other reference works (not the URL for the individual entry).

The examples below follow guidelines set forth in the APA *Style Manual* (2010).

1. **Journal article:**
de Bruyn, P. J., Tosh, C. A., & Bester, M. N.
     (2008). Sexual harassment of a king pen-
     guin by an Antarctic fur seal. *Journal of
     Ethology, 26* (2), 295-297. doi: 10.1007/
     s10164-007-0073-9

2. **Fact sheet:**
National Cancer Institute (2007). Secondhand
     smoke, questions and answers. [Fact sheet].
     Retrieved from http://www.cancer.gov/
     cancertopics/factsheet/Tobacco/ETS

3. **Encyclopedia article:**
Muckraker. (n.d.) In *Encyclopaedia Britannica
     Online*. Retrieved from http://www.britannica
     .com

4. **Newspaper article:**
Leary, W. E. (2003, November 3) Study finds that
     nitrites in the body greatly aid blood flow.
     *The New York Times*. Retrieved from http://
     www.nytimes.com

5. **Book:**
Riis, J. (1890). *How the other half lives*.
     Available from http://books.google.com/books/
     harvard?id=zhcv_oA5dwgC&printsec=frontcover&d
     q=how+the+other+half+lives#PPP1,M1

6. **Wiki:**
      Muckraker. (n.d.) Retrieved February 24, 2011,
          from http://en.wikipedia.org/wiki/Muckraker

# A Note on Other Systems of Documentation

The MLA style is commonly used in the humanities, and the APA style is commonly used in the social sciences. The documentation system detailed in *The Chicago Manual of Style*, 16th edition (Chicago: University of Chicago Press, 2010) is used by some social scientists and by many historians. But many other disciplines use their own styles. The following handbooks discuss the systems used in some other disciplines.

### Biology and Other Sciences

Style Manual Committee, Council of Science Editors. *The CSE Manual for Authors, Editors, and Publishers*. 7th ed. New York: Cambridge University Press, 2006.

### Chemistry

American Chemical Society. *ACS Style Guide: A Manual for Authors and Editors*. 3rd ed. Washington, DC: American Chemical Society, 2006.

### Journalism

Associated Press. *The Associated Press Stylebook and Briefing on Media Law*. New York: Basic Books, 2011.

### Law

*The Bluebook: A Uniform System of Citation*. 19th ed. Cambridge, MA: Harvard Law Review Association, 2010.

### Medicine

American Medical Association. *Manual of Style*. 10th ed. Acton, MA: Publishing Sciences Group, 2007.

### Physics

American Institute of Physics. *Style Manual for Guidance in the Preparation of Papers*. 4th ed. New York: American Institute of Physics, 1990–97.

# CHAPTER 14

# Preparing the Manuscript

I love being a writer. What I can't stand is the paperwork.

—Peter De Vries

## Basic Manuscript Form

When you submit—in print, or electronically—a piece of writing to your instructor or to anyone else, make it look good. You want to convey the impression that you care about what you've written, that you've invested yourself and your time in it, that the details matter to you.

Much of what follows is ordinary academic procedure. Unless your instructor specifies something different, you can adopt these principles as a guide.

1. **Print your essay on 8½-by-11-inch paper of good weight**. Use fresh, plain white paper; don't use the reverse sides of an old draft or lab report; avoid fancy or colored paper.

2. **Make sure that the printer has enough ink and that the print is dark and clear**. One sure way to irritate your instructor is to turn in an essay with nearly invisible print.

3. **Do not use a fancy font**. Unless your instructor specifies something else, stick to Times or Courier. And use a reasonable point size: Generally a 12-point font will do.

4. **Print your essay on one side of the paper only**. If for some reason you have occasion to submit a handwritten copy, use lined paper and write on every other line in black or dark blue ink.

5. **Set the line spacing at "double."** The essay (even the heading) should be double-spaced—not single-spaced, not triple-spaced.

6. **In the upper-left corner, one inch from the top, put your name, your instructor's name, the course number, and the date**. Put your last name before the page number (in the upper-right corner) of each subsequent page, so the instructor can easily reassemble your essay if somehow a page gets detached and mixed with other papers.

7. **Titles**. Use this form for your title: Press the *enter* (or *return*) key *once* after the date and then center the title of your essay. We give instructions for punctuating titles in Chapter 11, but we'll reiterate the most important points here: Capitalize the first letter of the first and last words of your title, the first word after a semicolon or colon if you use either one, and the first letter of all the other words except articles, conjunctions, and prepositions, thus:

Two Kinds of Symbols in *To Kill a Mockingbird*

Notice that your own title is neither italicized nor enclosed in quotation marks. (If, as here, your title includes material that would normally be italicized or in quotation marks, that material continues to be so written.) If the title runs more than one line, double-space between the lines.

8. **Begin the essay just below the title**. (Again, you'll press the *enter* key or return only once.) If your instructor prefers a title page, begin the essay on the next page and number it 1. The title page is not numbered.

9. **Margins**. Except for page numbers, which should appear one-half inch from the top of the page, leave a one-inch margin at top, bottom, and sides of text.

10. **Number the pages consecutively**, using Arabic numerals in the upper-right corner, half an inch from the top. Do not put a period or a hyphen after the numeral, and do not precede the numeral with "page" or "p." (Again, if you give the title on a separate sheet, the page that follows it is page 1. Do not number the title page.)

11. **Paragraphs**. Indent the first word of each paragraph five spaces or one-half inch from the left margin.

12. **Proofreading**. Check for typographical errors, and check spelling. Use your word processor's spell-check program—but don't rely on it exclusively. This program will flag words that are not in its dictionary and offer suggestions for correcting mistakes. (A misspelled word is, of course, not in the dictionary and thus flagged.) But a word flagged is not necessarily misspelled; it may simply not be in the program's dictionary. Proper names, for example, regularly get flagged. Keep in mind also that most programs cannot distinguish between homophones (to, too, two; there, their; alter, altar), nor can they tell you that you should have written "accept" instead of "except."

13. **Print a copy of your essay for yourself and keep it until the original has been returned**. It is a good idea to keep notes and drafts too. They may prove helpful if you are asked to revise a page, substantiate a point, or supply a source you omitted.

14. **Fasten the pages of your paper with a paper clip in the upper-left corner**. Stiff binders are unnecessary; indeed, they are a nuisance to the instructor, adding bulk and making it awkward to write annotations.

*1"*

Your Name

*Double-space*
Your Instructor's Name — *Font is Courier*

Writing 127

April 1, 2009
*Capitalize main words in title*

Formatting Your Essays: The Right
*Center title*
Way to Do It

   Print your essay on 8 1/2-by—11-inch
paper of good weight, and make sure that the
printer has enough ink and that the print is
dark and clear. Do not use a fancy font. Unless
your instructor specifies something else, stick
to Times or Courier. And use a reasonable point
size: Generally a 12-point font will do. The
essay (even the heading) should be double-
spaced--not single-spaced, not triple-spaced--
and it should be printed on one side of the
paper only.

*5 spaces, or tab*
   In the upper-left corner, one inch from
the top, put your name, your instructor's name,
the course number, and the date, all on separate
lines. Put your last name before the page number
(in the upper-right corner) of each subsequent
*◄— 1" —►* page, so the instructor can easily reassemble
your essay if somehow a page gets detached and
mixed with other papers. Press the Enter key
*once* after the date and then center the title
of your essay. Capitalize the first letter of
the first and last words of your title, the
first word after a semicolon or colon if you
use either one, and the first letter of all the

*1"*

other words except articles, conjunctions,and preposition. Notice that your own title is neither italicized nor enclosed in quotation marks. If the title runs more than one line, double-space between the lines. Begin the essay just below the title. (Again, you'll press Enter only once.) If your instructor prefers a title page, begin the essay on the next page and number it 1.

Except for page numbers, which should appear one-half inch from the top of the page, leave a one-inch margin at top, bottom, and sides of text. Number the pages consecutively, using Arabic numerals in the upper-right corner, half an inch from the top. Do not put a period or a hyphen after the numeral, and do not precede the numeral with "page" or "p."

Indent the first word of each paragraph five spaces from the left margin.

Fasten the pages of your paper with a paper clip in the upper-left corner. Stiff binders are unnecessary; indeed, they are a nuisance because they add bulk and make essays difficult to annotate. Spell-check your essay and proofread it carefully; make a copy for yourself, and then turn the essay in.

# credits

## Text Credits

**p. 110:** Pinker, Steven. "Mind over Mass Media" from *The New York Times*, Op-Ed Section, June 11, 2010. Copyright © 2010 The New York Times. All rights reserved. Used by permission and protected by the Copyright Laws of the United States. The printing, copying, redistribution, or retransmission of the material without express written permission is prohibited.

**p. 130:** Lowe, Carmen. "Quiz Yourself: How Much Do You Know About Citing Sources?" Reprinted by permission of Carmen Lowe, Tufts University Academic Resource Center.

**p. 144:** Hayden, Dolores. "Advertisements, Pornography, and Public Space," from *Redesigning the American Dream: The Future of Housing, Work, and Family Life*. Copyright © 1984 by Dolores Hayden. Used by permission of W.W. Norton & Company, Inc.

**p. 159:** Mandelbaum, Anne Hebald. "It's the Portly Penguin That Gets the Girl, French Biologist Claims," *Harvard Gazette*, January 30, 1976. Reprinted by permission.

**p. 182:** Stubbs, Marcia. "Laptops in the Classroom? No Problem," Stubbs, Marcia; Barnet, Sylvan. *The Little Brown Reader*, 12th Edition © 2012. Reprinted by permission of Pearson Education, Inc., Upper Saddle River, N.J.

**p. 182:** Rotella, Carlo. "Tuition Lost on the Techno Dependent." Published in the *Boston Globe* in 2010. Reprinted by permission of Carlo Rotella.

## Image Credits

**p. 4:** *Migrant Mother*, Nipomo, California 1936, by Dorothea Lange. Gelatin silver print. Corbis.

**p. 44:** Cheryl Lee family photo. From *The Story Behind the Gestures: A Family Photograph*. Reprinted by permission of the author, Cheryl Lee Rim.

**p. 47:** *Mona Lisa, La Gioconda*. Leonardo da Vinci (1452–1519). Louvre, Paris, France. Alinari/Art Resource.

**p. 66:** © The New Yorker Collection 1971. Al Rossi from cartoonbank.com. All Rights Reserved.

**p. 76:** www.CartoonStock.com

**p. 82:** © The New Yorker Collection 1972. J. B. Handelsman from cartoonbank.com. All Rights Reserved.

**p. 105:** © Bettmann/Corbis

**p. 117:** www.CartoonStock.com

**p. 136:** Albertina Museum, Vienna, Austria

**p. 139:** Advertising Archives

**p. 153, top left:** Photograph ©(1/12) Museum of Fine Arts, Boston

**p. 153, top right:** Photograph ©(1/12) Museum of Fine Arts, Boston

**p. 176:** © The New Yorker Collection, 1983. Robert Mankoff from cartoonbank.com. All Rights Reserved.

**p. 197:** © The New Yorker Collection 1993. Peter Steiner from cartoonbank.com. All Rights Reserved.

**p. 264:** www.CartoonStock.com

**p. 270:** DILBERT © Scott Adams/Dist. By United Feature Syndicate, Inc.

**p. 282:** www.CartoonStock.com

# index

# Student Resource

Pearson is proud to offer your students access to the new MyCompLab website, a state-of-the-art resource for use in first-year writing courses, either as a media supplement or as a course management system. MyCompLab offers students a composing space, where assignments can be created and graded, and a wealth of resources for improving writing. The result is a revolutionary application that offers a seamless, flexible teaching and learning environment built specifically for writers. MyCompLab was created after years of extensive research and in partnership with composition faculty and students across the country. The new MyCompLab provides help for writers in the context of their writing, with instructor and peer commenting functionality; multimedia tutorials and exercises for writing, grammar, and research; an e-portfolio; an assignment-builder; a bibliography tool; tutoring services; and a gradebook and course management organization created specifically for writing classes. Visit www.mycomplab .com for more information.